THE JOHNS HOPKINS UNIVERSITY STUDIES IN HISTORICAL AND POLITICAL SCIENCE

Under the Direction of the Departments of History,
Political Economy, and Political Science

SERIES LXXVIII   NUMBER 1
(1960)

THE NOBILITY OF TOULOUSE IN THE EIGHTEENTH CENTURY:

A SOCIAL AND ECONOMIC STUDY

THE NOBILITY OF TOULOUSE IN THE EIGHTEENTH CENTURY:

A Social and Economic Study

By

ROBERT FORSTER

1971

OCTAGON BOOKS

New York

Reprinted 1971
by special arrangement with The Johns Hopkins Press

OCTAGON BOOKS
A Division of Farrar, Straus & Giroux, Inc.
19 Union Square West
New York, N. Y. 10003

Library of Congress Catalog Card Number: 79-159186

ISBN 0-374-92817-7

Printed in U.S.A. by
NOBLE OFFSET PRINTERS, INC.
NEW YORK 3, N. Y.

TO ELBORG

PREFACE

Despite the provocative suggestions of Marc Bloch on the
"seigniorial reaction" in 1931 (*Les caractères originaux de
l'histoire rurale française*, Paris, 1952, pp. 131-155) and his
subsequent appeal in the *Annales* for archival research on this
problem, French historiography has not produced those regional
studies that would reveal the exact nature of the nobleman's
role in the rural community during the Ancien Régime. The
monumental studies of Georges Lefebvre on the *Département
du Nord*, of Henri Sée on Brittany, and of Marcel Marion on
the Bordelais have focused almost entirely on the social conse-
quences of the seigniorial regime without giving sufficient
attention to the internal operation of the seigniorial domain as
an economic unit. The more general works of Jean Loutchisky,
Henri Carré, and Philippe Sagnac have at some points touched
the activities of the *gentilhomme-campagnard* but without
sufficient emphasis and elaboration. Two little known studies,
Pierre de Vaissière's *Les gentilshommes campagnards de l'ancienne France du 16ᵐᵉ au 18ᵐᵉ siècle* (Paris, 1904) and Paul
de Rousier's *Une famille de hoberaux pendant six siècles* (Paris,
1933), though sympathetic toward the rural nobleman, have
nevertheless perpetuated the common notion that the country-
gentleman was an impoverished rustic, pining for Parisian *salon*
society, and hopelessly condemned to a declining revenue and a
crumbling château. The literary caricatures of Molière, La
Bruyère, and, above all, Chateaubriand, have contributed nothing to dispel this false picture. The recent work of C. E.
Labrousse on price history and the new emphasis placed on
demographic factors in eighteenth century France by Marcel
Reinhard and Jacques Godechot have again, after a generation,
exposed the need of investigating the rural nobleman's economic
position before the Revolution. In the 1954 issue of the
Annales, Paul Leuilliot reiterated the demand of Bloch for
precise regional studies, not of the nobleman's political and
judicial function, but of noble fortunes.

This is a study of the gentlemen of Toulouse in the eighteenth
century. Such a regional study cannot pretend to draw conclusions for the French provincial nobility as a whole. Only

after a large number of such geographically limited studies have been made will a reasonably accurate picture of the French nobility emerge. The complex notion of "class" and the peculiarities of each region in the France of the Ancien Regime would make a more general approach so tenuous as to be almost valueless by the accepted tenets of historical research. Even a regional study of this nature presents serious obstacles to bold generalizations.

On the other hand, a study of the "bread and butter" activities of this limited social group should reveal the scope and diversity of aristocratic social and economic life in the provincial community. It should describe not only economic interests and investments, but also the manner in which they were administered. Some activities follow the classic pattern of "seigniorial reaction" and thus spell out in detail the questions so well posed by Marc Bloch. Others suggest that the Toulousan gentlemen were conscientious landlords. Still others seem unimportant from the point of view of revenue, but significant as completing the picture of aristocratic provincial life. The Toulousan noble was essentially a *gentilhomme-campagnard* in regard to his source of revenue, his outlook, and his mode of living. The following chapters should make clear the full meaning of this expression.

This study was made possible by a French Government Fellowship at the University of Toulouse and a Gustav Bissing Fellowship from The Johns Hopkins University. I am very grateful to Professor Jacques Godechot, Professor Philippe Wolff and M. Jean Sentou of the University of Toulouse, and to the staff of the Departmental Archives for the information and help they so generously gave me during my stay at Toulouse. Above all, I am deeply indebted to Dr. David Spring of The Johns Hopkins University who contributed patiently and untiringly of his time in making this study readable. I am also indebted to Dr. Frederic C. Lane, Dr. Sidney Painter, and the members of The Johns Hopkins History Seminar for their suggestions and corrections on various parts of the manuscript. Finally, I wish to extend a special thanks to Professor George P. Cuttino of Emory University whose constant encouragement as a scholar and as a friend made this project possible.

Lincoln, Nebraska   R. F.
December, 1958.

TABLE OF CONTENTS

TABLES

ILLUSTRATIONS

13

THE NOBILITY OF TOULOUSE IN THE EIGHTEENTH CENTURY:

A Social and Economic Study

ABBREVIATIONS

A. D.   —Archives Départementales de la Haute-
         Garonne, France.

A. Not. —Archives Notariales de la Haute-
         Garonne, France.

A. M.   —Archives Municipales, Toulouse, France.

Gardouch—Fonds de Gardouch, Archives Départe-
         mentales de la Haute-Garonne, France.

CHAPTER I

THE DIOCESE OF TOULOUSE IN 1750:
TOWN AND COUNTRY

In 1787, Arthur Young, the famous English agronomist, looked southward from the city ramparts of Montauban toward the Toulousan plain. His journal reads, " This noble valley, or rather this plain, is one of the richest in Europe and stretches on one hand to the sea and on the other to the Pyrenees." [1] More precisely, the valley extended southward along the Garonne River from Montauban to Toulouse and then southeastward along the *Canal du Midi* almost to Carcassonne. Second only to the Beauce and Flanders in richness of soil, the Toulousan plain has always been the granary of the *Midi*. In the mid-eighteenth century the produce of this area provided the local population its principal economic activity and for some of their number the source of a considerable prosperity.

From an administrative point of view, this region corresponded with the civil diocese of Toulouse. The diocese had 720 square miles and a population in 1750 of approximately 120,000 inhabitants.[2] Except for the city of Toulouse, it was completely rural. Its villages counted only a few hundred people and its largest market towns numbered no more than a thousand. The diocese formed an oval design 35 miles long and 20 miles wide, the main axis of which followed the Garonne River and the *Canal du Midi* from Castelnau d'Estretefonds to Villefranche-Lauragais. It was one of twenty-four dioceses that composed the old province of Languedoc and was administered by a royal subdelegate responsible to the Intendant at Montpellier. Side by side with the royal administration was the older provincial administration represented by the diocesan assembly, an assembly of the three Estates that functioned as

[1] Arthur Young, *Voyages en France, 1787, 1788, 1789* (Paris, 1931), I, p. 105.
[2] Léon Dutil, *L'état économique du Languedoc à la fin de l'Ancien Régime (1750-1789)* (Paris, 1911), p. 780.

a local branch of the Provincial Estates at Montpellier. Finally, the judicial system at the diocesan level consisted of a royal presidial court linked by appeal to the Parlement at Toulouse.[3]

At the center of this plain at the junction of the Garonne River and the *Canal du Midi* lies the city of Toulouse, a conglomeration of red-brick baking in the sun of the *Midi*. Called the *Ville Rose* because of the ubiquitous construction of red brick and tile found so abundantly in the neighboring country-side, the provincial capital boasted a population of about 40,000 inhabitants at the mid-century. Approaching the city from the West Gate by eighteenth century carriage, one traversed the poor quarter of Saint Cyprien and crossed the Garonne by the Pont Neuf, splendid monument of the seventeenth century architect, Nicolas Bachelier. By this main artery one entered the oldest section of the city, passing near the churches of the Daurade and Dalbade, the sumptuous Hôtel d'Assézat, the teeming grain market off the rue des Changes, and the town-houses of the Parlementary nobility facing on narrow, winding streets leading to a classic brick structure that was the Parlement of Toulouse.[4]

Since the Intendant of Languedoc and the Provincial Estates were installed at Montpellier instead of Toulouse, the Parlement assumed a special luster. Founded in 1444 by Charles VII, the Parlement of Toulouse was the kingdom's second sovereign court with appellate jurisdiction over the provinces of Languedoc, Foix, half of Gascogne, Rouergue, and Quercy south of the Dordogne River. From 28 officers under Charles VII the Parlement had grown to 112 noble officers by the end of the eighteenth century. The families of these proud presidents, councilors, and attorneys numbered perhaps six hundred individuals. The annual convocation of the Parlement was a holiday for the city populace, providing processions, fire-works, and, above all, attendance at the ceremonial entry of the lawyers and judges into the Place du Salin. Here one might catch a glimpse of the ermine-collared red robes and

[3] F. Astre, *De l'administration publique en Languedoc avant 1789* (Toulouse, 1874).

[4] A. Praviel, *Monsieur du Barrie et sa famille* (Paris, 1932), pp. 64-65; Apart from the grain-market, two centuries have not changed this quarter of the city. The old grain-market is now the Place Esquirol.

mortar-boards of the presidents and councilors followed by the black clad advocates, their sacks of law suits suspended from their belts by strong cords. Nobles of the high robe, these proud

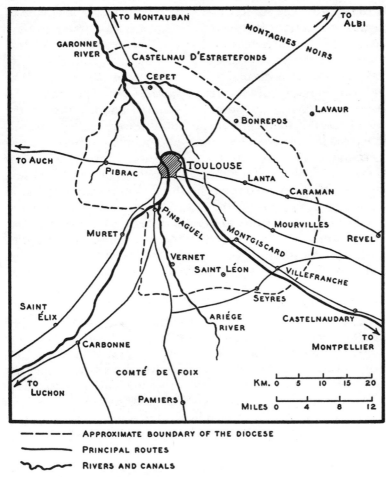

The Diocese of Toulouse in the Eighteenth Century

gentlemen composed at least half of the Toulousan nobility and their illustrious blazons marked, not only the town-houses of the Dalbade quarter, but also innumerable châteaux in the surrounding countryside.[5]

[5] M. Dubédat, *Histoire du Parlement de Toulouse* (Paris, 1885); H. Ramet, *Le Capitole et le Parlement de Toulouse* (Toulouse, 1926), p. 125 ff.

From the Parlement one might turn onto the rue Nazareth to enter the St. Etienne Quarter—the Faubourg St. Germain of Toulouse. This was the eighteenth-century aristocratic quarter *par excellence*, housing the oldest families of the nobility of the sword. The sober, classic lines of the newer town-houses created an austere, conservative atmosphere that contrasted sharply with the Renaissance baroque façades of the Dalbade quarter. Characteristic was the three-story dwelling with an interior court and a circular stairway enclosed in a tower. The larger town-houses did not face the street but were reached by majestic carriage-gates opening on large courts. Behind the town-houses of the richest noble families were walled gardens, often shaded by umbrella pines and accessible from narrow back alleys. Here on the rue Velane, St. Jacques, Ninau, or Mage, the families Avessens, Escouloubre, Dupuy-Montbrun, Espie, or MacCarthy enjoyed the three month winter season at Toulouse. Here, during the cold months, the good families could gather a social elite in their high ceilinged *salons* or translate a Latin sonnet in their well-stocked libraries. On the fringe of the quarter, the city government had recently built an oval park (the *Jardin Royal*) from which radiated five broad, tree-lined avenues which served as fashionable promenades for the cream of Toulousan high society.[6]

From St. Etienne Cathedral which marks the center of this sedate aristocratic section of the city, tortuous cobblestone streets led to the rue des Pommes and the bustling and odorous center of the city. Entering the Place Royale one faced the new *Capitoulat*, the municipal palace recently enlarged to house both the theater and the municipal government. From here the Capitouls, the eight ennobled city magistrates, governed the city and held their social receptions in the splendid *Salle des Illustres*.

The *Capitouls* were aided in the city administration by the Political Council, reorganized in 1778 to include 14 nobles (of four quarterings), 14 former *Capitouls*, and 14 notables. Among the notables were always included the First President of the Parlement, the Attorney-General, the Advocate-General,

---

[6] Paul Mesple, *Vieux hôtels de Toulouse* (Toulouse, 1948), pp. 83-103, 155-174. Like the Dalbade quarter, the St. Etienne quarter has lost little of its eighteenth century atmosphere.

four Councilors, and other dignitaries of the influential robe. The local administration was further staffed with 68 officers of the Seneschal Court, 5 officers of the Forestry Court, 33 officers of the Treasury, 13 officers for the administration of the indirect taxes and the royal domain, 5 officers of the tax-farms, 11 officers for the coinage, and a dozen officers and scribes in the commission of "Waters and Forests," plus 120 so-called "minor functionaries." Even contemporaries had the impression that half of Toulouse was composed of civil servants.[7]

Not far from the Place Royale at the end of the rue des Lois was the University of Toulouse, founded in 1229 and proud of its illustrious Renaissance scholars, among whom were Rabelais, Montaigne, l'Hôpital, and Cujas. In 1754 there were 23 professors and 1000 students, of whom 380 were in the Faculty of Law, 475 in the Faculty of Theology, and 75 in the Faculty of Medicine. Even more esteemed at this time were the secondary schools, including the Collège de l'Esquile (967 students), the Collège des Jesuites (1200 student), and the new Collège Royal (1500 students). The classrooms of the university and collèges were filled with the sons of Parlementarians, royal officials, nobles of the sword, and of the few rich merchants of the city—in short, the gilded youth of Toulouse.

The intellectual life of the city was completed by a number of academies. The Académie des Jeux Floraux, founded in 1323 for the study of occitane poetry, was justifiably proud of being the oldest academy in Europe. The Académie des Sciences, Inscriptions et Belles Lettres, founded in 1729, was a typical product of the Enlightenment. In the course of the century it patronized and built the new Observatory (1775) and the Botanical Gardens. Most recent was the Académie des Peintures, Sculptures et Architecture (1750) which sponsored an annual showing and a school of beaux-arts. Finally, the Académie de Musique, patronized by the Marquis de Caraman, was reorganized in 1729 and met regularly from 1747 to 1788. These academies carried on a tradition as old as Raymond of Toulouse and the Troubadours. In the eighteenth century they

[7] E. Lemouzèle, Essai sur l'administration de la ville de Toulouse, 1783-1790 (Paris, 1910), pp. 4 ff.

were patronized almost exclusively by the nobility and the Church.[8]

The Basilicas of St. Sernin, the Daurade, and the Jacobins were magnificent architectural symbols of a vigorous and ortho-dox religious life. A Catholic stronghold during the Wars of Religion, Toulouse became a haven for numerous refugee orders during the sixteenth century. Between 1590 and 1709 Toulouse added seven new male orders, 14 female orders, and seven seminaries. By the end of the seventeenth century, con-vents occupied literally half the city and outnumbered those of any other city in the Kingdom, Paris included. By 1789 the list of religious institutions at Toulouse was impressive indeed. Beside being the seat of an archbishopric and of the " Sovereign Chamber of the Clergy " for 28 dioceses, Toulouse had two chapters, one abbey, 23 male convents, 28 female convents, one Grand Priory of Malta, 10 parishes, 30 sanctu-aries, and 9 brotherhoods. Like the colleges and the academies, these religious orders were dowered by rich noble families, many members of which occupied their somber halls.[9]

This brief survey is sufficient to outline the characteristic features of Toulouse in the mid-eighteenth century. Here in relief is the city's Parlement, the town-houses of its *noblesse d'épée*, its *Capitoulat*, its university, its academies, and its con-vents. Above all, Toulouse was aristocratic. Its newer nobilities, produced by its judicial and administrative institutions, added a robe and a municipal *noblesse* to an older military one. Despite their diverse origins, these nobilities formed a single social group setting a uniform tone to the city's judicial and political direction, sustaining its economy, and patronizing its intellectual and religious life.

The influence of this artistocracy becomes more apparent when one realizes the corresponding feebleness of the Toulousan bourgeoise. Despite the efforts of Colbert, the vigorous com-mercial life that characterized the Renaissance age of woad kings could not be recreated. Wheat had replaced the dye-plant as the principal economic resource of the region in the

[8] J. Coppolani, *Toulouse, Etude de géographie urbaine* (Toulouse, 1954), pp. 77-79; P. Barrière, " Les Académies et la vie intellectuelle dans la société méridionale au XVIIIe siècle," *Annales du Midi*, LXII (1950), pp. 341-350.
[9] Coppolani, *op. cit.*, pp. 80-81.

eighteenth century, and wheat was a gentleman's commodity at Toulouse. Curiously, although blessed with an advantageous geographic position and a relatively good road and canal system, Toulouse developed neither an important local textile industry nor an active middleman trade. Perhaps the very agricultural wealth of the surrounding area discouraged any alternate economic activity that would produce a truly commercial middle class.[10]

Cloth-making was carried on in some thirty small factories and produced only a handful of prosperous cloth merchants. The balance of the merchant class was engaged largely in the grain trade, buying up the grain collected in small quantities by the army of grain brokers who circulated with their mules in the countryside at harvest time. Even this activity was lessened by the increasing tendency of the grain-grower to market his produce directly.[11] The professional groups, especially the lawyers, produced in prodigious numbers by the Faculty of Law, aspired to fill the lower ranks of the city administration and judiciary, working and waiting for the day they could enter either the *Capitoulat* or the Parlement and become ennobled. Of the petty bourgeoisie and artisan class, many depended upon the market for linens and hats, perfumes and jewelry, carriages and saddles, wines of Gaillac and Bordeaux, and other luxury items purchased almost exclusively by the local nobility.[12] The millers and bakers benefited from a much wider market, but they too depended on the gentleman-farmer for their grain supply and on the *Capitouls* who made the grain regulations for the Toulouse market.[13] In short, the merchants, the lawyers, and the artisan class hardly constituted an effective counterweight to the prestige, wealth, and influence of the city's noble class.

[10] *Archives Départementales, Série C, liasse* 106. Hereafter cited as A. D. C-106. The Syndic of the Diocese of Toulouse wrote to the Provincial Estates in April 17, 1762, " Land is almost the only source of revenue in this diocese. Commerce is dependent upon agriculture."

[11] Dutil, *op. cit.*, p. 335; G. Jorré, " Le commerce des grains et la minoterie à Toulouse," *Revue géographique des Pyrénees et du Sud-Ouest*, 1933, p. 30 f.

[12] J. Sentou, " Faillites et commerce à. Toulouse en 1789," *Annales historiques de la Révolution française* (July-Sept., 1953), pp. 1-40; " Impôts et citoyens actifs à Toulouse au début de la Révolution," *Annales du Midi*, LXI (1948), pp. 159-179.

[13] L. Viala, *La question des grains et leur commerce à Toulouse au 18me siècle (1715-1789)* (Toulouse, 1909).

Not since the Middle Ages had the Toulousan aristocracy been so secure against bourgeois competition as in the eighteenth century. The vigorous merchant class of the fifteenth and sixteenth centuries had been gradually absorbed into the nobility in the course of the seventeenth century.[14] By the eighteenth century there was hardly an important bourgeois who did not marshall all of his talents to attain this nobility. For the secret to the success of the Toulousan aristocracy was not in its exclusiveness but rather in its capacity to absorb bourgeois wealth via the purchase of noble land and ennobling office.

The history of the Assézat family is illustrative of this process of absorption into the noble class. Woad merchants in the sixteenth century, the Assézat had purchased lands first at Venergue-Vernet and later at Lanta-Préserville in the diocese. Becoming *Capitouls* and Catholics at the end of the Wars of Religion, they built the most magnificent town-house in Toulouse and capped their Renaissance Italian mansion with the highest tower in the city, conspicuous symbol of their new *noblesse*. By the seventeenth century the family was furnishing a steady stream of councilors to the Parlement, leaving far behind vulgar speculations in woad for the gentlemanly existence of distinguished lawyers and estate owners.[15]

Simon de Bertier, fifteenth century woad merchant, bought the barony of Pinsaguel in 1495 and inaugurated a line of barons of Pinsaguel.[16] His brother Guillaume, ennobled by the *Capitoulat* in 1483, founded a cadet branch of barons of Montrabe. The two branches of the Bertier family produced five bishops and three Presidents of Parlement in the seventeenth century, most of whose severe portraits still decorate the château at Pinsaguel. At the beginning of the eighteenth century the family boasted fewer illustrious churchmen and parlementarians and more conscientious gentlemen-farmers who revealed their prosperity by reconstructing the family château in 1750. So well had the Bertier entrenched themselves behind

---

[14] Mme. M. Thoumas-Schapira, " La bourgeoisie toulousaine à la fin du XVIIᵉ siècle," *Annales du Midi*, LXVII (1955), pp. 313-329.

[15] J. Villain, *La France moderne généalogique* (*Haute-Garonne et Ariège*) (Montpellier, 1911), p. 1583; A. D. C-1330 (Vernet), C-1326 (Préserville).

[16] P. Wolff, " Les Ysalguier de Toulouse," *Mélanges d'histoire sociale* (1941-42), pp. 51, 57.

the blazons and titles of nobility that their descendants still half-believe that they are descendants of the Franks.[17]

The Riquet family, disgraced by entrance into commerce in the early seventeenth century, was rescued by the enterprising Pierre-Paul Riquet who financed, designed, and built the famous *Canal du Midi* and in one generation pulled the family from obscurity to fame and fortune. Granted by the King a seigniorial monopoly of the canal plus two rich seigniories at Caraman and Bonrepos, Riquet entered the Parlement with ease, and even reconstructed the family tree, claiming descent from thirteenth century Italian nobility. By the end of the eighteenth century a Riquet de Bonrepos was attorney-general at the Parlement and a Riquet de Caraman was commander-in-chief of the royal armies in Provence. Emmanuel Cambon-Riquet, First President of the Parlement was perhaps the richest and most prominent nobleman at the provincial capital on the eve of the Revolution.[18]

"*Monnoie fait tout*" ran the Toulousan street saying, and nobility was worth both a mass and a commercial fortune, judging by the number of eighteenth century noblemen whose ancestors were bourgeois merchants. Sometimes the transition was very rapid. The bourgeois merchant, Mathurin Rolland, bought up the seigniory of Saint-Rome between 1714 and 1728, made his son a *Capitoul* in 1755, and placed his grandson in the Condé-Dragoons with full title of "*Chevalier Hippolyte de Rolland, Seigneur de Saint-Rome et autres places*." Thus, the Rolland passed from merchants to military nobility in three generations.[19] The family Jacob, tax-farmers, attained the *Capitoulat* at the end of the seventeenth century, bought the seigniory of Saint Elix in 1702, changed their name to Ledesme by marriage in the next generation, and became barons of Saint Elix after 1760. Their Renaissance château together with its excellent library was partially destroyed during the Revolution, final proof of their arrival in the third generation.[20] The rise

---

[17] Villain, *op. cit.* (de Bertier).

[18] *Ibid.*, pp. 601; 1068; A. D. E-642 "Livre de Raison de Riquet-Cambon, 1778-80."

[19] J. R. de Fortanier, *Les droits seigneuriaux dans la sénéchausée de Lauragais* (1553-1789) (Toulouse, 1932), p. 338.

[20] L. Dutil, *La Haute-Garonne et sa région* (Toulouse, 1928), II, p. 138; A. D. E-1760, 1762, 1777-81, 1810. "St-Elix-le-Chateau" family papers.

of the merchant family Picot, bourgeois of Aude, was meteoric. Ennobled by the *Capitoulat* in 1738, Noble Philippe Picot bought the seigniory of Lapeyrouse in 1750. His son, Philippe Isidore Picot, Baron de Lapeyrouse amassed a formidable collection of honors. He became advocate-general at the Parlement, a celebrated naturalist, member of the Academy of Science at Toulouse, Paris, and Stockholm, member of the local assembly of *noblesse* in 1789, mayor of Toulouse (1800-1806), and Baron of the Empire in 1808.[21]

To be sure, certain barriers to complete acceptance of these parvenus into the ranks of the ancient blood nobility remained. Admission into the Provincial Estates still required four generations of nobility on the male side, and the titles of duke, marquis, and count were reserved for families who could prove such lineage. But for all practical purposes, the purchase of " noble land," albeit with the payment of the *franc-fief* (a year's revenue every twenty years to the King), prepared the way for the purchase of an ennobling office and legitimate *noblesse*. Title and rank once attained, the family completely abandoned commercial life and succeeding generations lived " *noblement* " from their revenues. Occasional social snubs and petty disputes over precedence did not hamper the fundamental solidarity of the class.[22] The interdependence of administration, judiciary, and seigniory was too compelling.

This was strengthened by certain changes that had taken place in the habits and mores of even the oldest noble families. With neither the need nor the desire to enter into purely commercial activity, the Toulousan nobility nevertheless progressively adopted certain business attitudes in the administration of its resources. Whether the entrance of a new nobility into the ranks of the old feudal blood nobility during the sixteenth and seventeenth centuries infused different mores into the class as a whole, or whether the eighteenth century economic environment was particularly encouraging to the values of family discipline and strict estate management, need not concern us here. It seems certain, however, that the Toulousan nobles

---

[21] *Ibid.*, II, 319; Villain, *op. cit.*, 313.
[22] A. D. C-2410, 2414 (on proofs of *noblesse* for the Estates); C-40 (confirmation of the *noblesse* of Capitouls); C-69 (enforcement of the *franc-fief*); Dubédat, *op. cit.* (robe vs. sword), I, pp. 661-675.

found ever greater solidarity in their interests and their habits as the century progressed. Their revenues, particularly their agricultural revenues, were favored by a rapidly expanding market and were not to be squandered by a reversion to traditional class habits of *largesse* and conspicuous waste. Good management and austere living were virtues worthy of practice —less chivalrous than the virtues of medieval noble ancestors perhaps, but equally distinguished in a provincial environment and much more profitable.

How advantageous it was to fortify these newer virtues with a local judiciary and administration staffed largely by one's own kind and kin! How convenient that the Parlement of Toulouse, the Provincial Estates, and the *Capitoulat* provided a solid front on such problems as the grain trade, seigniorial rights, and the thousands of contract and property cases that arise in the everyday life of an agrarian provincial community! Arthur Young could not make an exception of the Parlement of Toulouse when he wrote:

The conduct of the parliaments was profligate and atrocious. Upon almost every case that came before them, interest was made openly with the judges . . . for all that mass of property which comes in every country to be litigated in the courts of justice, there was not even the shadow of security, unless the parties were totally and equally unknown and totally and equally honest; in every other case, he who had the best interest with the judges was sure to be the winner.[23]

How convenient too, that the bulk of the literate population outside of the nobility—the lawyers in particular—earned so much of their livelihood as experts on seigniorial rights, as special attorneys for land surveys and transfers, as estate stewards, and as notaries for all possible forms of proprietary contracts! The fact that notarial fees were proportioned to the value of contracts negotiated, provided a special incentive to the lawyers to work for wealthy noble clients. Attached to the Parlement alone and excluding the nobles of the high robe, were 204 advocates, 101 attorneys, 37 bailiffs, and 24 notaries plus a veritable army of litigants and *gens de loi* in the inferior jurisdictions.[24]

[23] A. Young, *On the Revolution in France*, Miss Edwards ed., pp. 320-321, quoted in P. Sagnac, *La formation de la société française moderne* (Paris, 1946), II, p. 221 n.

[24] Coppolani, *op. cit.*, p. 82.

Even the Royal Subdelegate was called upon to act as a lawyer for the nobility. In 1759, the Intendant wrote to the Subdelegate of Toulouse:

I received, sir, a letter from M. le Comte d'Entraigne, my son-in-law, stating that he has chosen you as advocate at the Parlement and charging me to pay for his attorney.[25]

The Subdelegate answered that he would do all possible for the count and that he had already spent 150 livres on his behalf.[26] On another occasion, the Intendant wrote:

I am linked by friendship, sir, with M. le Comte de Solages d'Armagnac, Marquis de St. Sernin who has a lawsuit at the Parlement of Toulouse. . . . I shall be very obliged to you if you offer him all the services you can, and ask him to give you a list of his judges in order to sollicit them in my name.[27]

The Vicomte de Saint Priest had been a noble of modest fortune when he assumed the office of Intendant in 1756. By 1785, however, he had no less than six seigniories, his eldest son had become *Intendant-adjoint* in 1764, and his younger son had been nominated " colonel in second " in the order of *chevaliers* by the Estates of Languedoc in 1784.[28] In brief, the Intendant had considerably improved his economic and social position and was not adverse to using the prestige of his office on behalf of his noble friends and relatives.

Finally, it will be recalled that the professional class as a whole and the Subdelegate in particular aspired to the honored status of *noblesse.* When the need arose, the nobility was quite capable of exploiting this situation. In a letter to the Subdelegate explaining the " difficulties and inconvenieces " of executing a royal order to cart wood to Toulouse, M. de Polastron-Lahillere de Grepiac wrote:

M. d'Assézat has written me that you have the kindness of being our arbiter against Sr. Gabile. . . . I am charmed that this occasion will give me the opportunity of meeting you and assuring you of the respect with which I have the honor. . . .[29]

[25] A. D. C-56. Intendant to Subdelegate, June 19, 1759.
[26] *Ibid.* Subdelegate to Intendant, June 23, 1759.
[27] *Ibid.*, Intendant to Subdelegate, August 7, 1756.
[28] Dom Claude Devic, et Dom Jean Joseph Vaissete, *Histoire générale du Languedoc* (Toulouse, 1872-1914), XIII, pp. 1106, 1336.
[29] A. D. C-320 M. de Polastron-Lahillère to Subdelegate, June 23, 1754.

In 1758, Noble Jean Louis de Lamothe, after a long discourse on his 173 years of nobility and his need for tax relief, wrote to the Subdelegate:

I have learned with true pleasure that we will have you as head of the consistory next year. If everyone thinks as I do about you, the satisfaction will be general . . . you will not be over-burdened with the work of your office for our Palace [Parlement] to feel it.[30]

Clearly, the Subdelegate was moving up the scale of offices and both Polastron and Lamothe were discretely reminding him that it was unwise to make enemies among those who could help him.

Noble prestige and influence did not end at the city gates. The judicial and political powers of the class were even less contested in the rural community. The right of seigniorial justice was a key institution in the maintenance of the noble's interests in general and of the seigniorial system in particular. It was a handy instrument to force delinquent tenants to pay their rent arrears and seigniorial dues. In many cases penalties were invoked for failure to pay and the lands of the peasant attached to the noble domain.[31] In the community of St. Felix-Caraman, the noble seigneur " in full justice " had a local peasant condemned to death for burning straw, cutting fruit trees, and stealing vines and wheat. The seigneur was awarded a fine in the form of confiscation of half the peasant's lands.[32] In 1761 at Pinsaguel the Marquis de Bertier ordered one Sieur Picard to pay his rent or be put in the seigniorial prison.[33]

Although seigniorial justice handled minor infractions of the criminal law in the village community with relative dispatch, in all property cases the seigneur was in effect prosecutor, judge and executioner, and his interests would be protected. Theoretically, the peasant had the right to appeal to the royal presidial court at Toulouse. But a law case cost money and, in a contest against the seigneur, a battle of influence was engaged that put the average illiterate peasant at a decided disadvantage. Clearly, the seigneur who might himself be a

[30] A. D. C-114 Noble de Lamothe to Subdelegate, December 2, 1758.
[31] Fortanier, op. cit., 42 f.
[32] Morère, M. l'abbé G. B., Histoire de St. Felix-Caraman (Toulouse, 1899), pp. 220-221.
[33] A. D., 6-J, 26.

judge at Toulouse, was in the best position to negotiate the legal jungle of appeals, objections, and questions of competence that characterized the judiciary.[34] Moreover, even if a case did reach the presidial court, it could be again appealed to the Parlement of Toulouse. Once in the hands of the *noblesse de robe*, a local seigneur had little to fear. Barring cases of high treason or "royal cases" that gained wide publicity outside the village community, seigniorial justice was an institution still very much in vigor at the end of the Ancien Regime.

At the end of the seventeenth century Louis XIV had temporarily threatened seigniorial control over the village community by creating the offices of mayor and lieutenant-mayor, appointed by the Subdelegate. The needs of the royal treasury proved decisive, however, and the local seigneurs bought up the new offices and even filled them in person. Thus, the noble family d'Avessens were mayors of Montesquieu without interruption from 1696 to 1766, the Gavarret at Saint Léon for about the same span of time, the Villèle at Mourvilles, and the Puybusque at Verfeil.[35] In 1774 the Provincial Estates neutralized what few offices remained in non-noble hands by purchasing them all *en bloc*.[36]

The village community was nominally governed by four town elders called "consuls" who were nominated by all the members of the community that practiced trades (*métiers*) assembled in the parish church. A list of eight was then presented to the seigneur who chose four and later read the sermon of inauguration to them at the château.[37] Theoretically, these consuls could gain the ear of the Subdelegate without first consulting the seigneur. But in practice this was both difficult and unwise. It was difficult because the vast majority of consuls were illiterate and therefore dependent on the two literate individuals

---

[34] One of the rare *cahiers* of the Toulouse area states, "The rich ruin the poor by taking them from court to court." The *cahier* characterized the seigniorial judges as "mercenaries created by the seigneur at will." Cf. A. D. C-2161, "Cahier de Lauriac, April 13, 1789."

[35] A. Cazals, *Histoire de la ville et communauté de Montesquieu-sur-canal* (Toulouse, 1883), pp. 187-195; Abbé H. Aragon, *La Seigneurie de St.-Léon et Caussidières (1030-1793)* (Toulouse, 1895), p. 38; A. D. C-962.

[36] Théron de Montaugé, *L'agriculture et les classes rurales dans le pays toulousain depuis le milieu du 18me siècle* (Paris, 1869), p. 140 f.

[37] Fortanier, *op. cit.*, pp. 87, 360-361.

of each village, the seigneur and the parish priest.[38] It was unwise because the seigneur had more influence over the office-seeking Subdelegate than the consuls had, and since the consuls were often the seigneur's millers and blacksmiths, they risked reprisals in the form of higher rents. Furthermore, the peasant class from which the consuls were usually drawn, was demarcated from the bourgeoisie and upper classes, not only by its rustic, immobile existence, but also by a *patois* that was a melange of Celtic, Latin, and *Occitan*.[39] Obviously, a peasantry that could not even speak French was at a serious disadvantage in dealing with the royal administration.

Secure against outside competition, the nobility of Toulouse was supported by an administrative and judicial system that extended from the Parlement and *Capitoulat* in Toulouse to the seigniorial judge and village consul in the smallest community of the diocese. Thus shielded, the nobility was prepared to husband and expand its economic resources. Of what did these consist?

II

Crossing the *Canal du Midi* by the Saint Michel Gate, one entered the richest part of the Toulousan plain known as the Lauragais. All along the royal route from Toulouse for thirty miles southeastward to Castelnaudary, this well-watered valley of deep and well-balanced soils produced the grain destined for the markets at Villefranche, Montgiscard, Lanta, and Toulouse, plus a portion earmarked for transhipment via the canal to Agde and export outside of the province. Here, among others, were the country-estates of Becarie de Pavie at Fourquevaux, of Grammont at Lanta, of Villèle at Mourvilles-Basses, of Escouloubre at Vieillevigne, of Hautpoul at Seyres, and of Gavarret at Saint Léon—all domains of the old nobility.[40]

Characteristic of this region was the seigniorial domain of the Marquis d'Escouloubre at Vieillevigne, eighteen miles southeast of Toulouse. A village of a hundred inhabitants, Vieillevigne's principal street mounted a small hill upon which the

[38] A. D. C-109. These reports on the forage constantly allude to the illiteracy of the consuls.

[39] Aragon, *op. cit.*, p. 38.

[40] Montaugé, *op. cit.* Introduction. Above all, see the noble declarations for the ving*tième* tax in 1750, A. D. C-1312-1330.

parish church faced a modest common. A few houses beyond, the village ended where the mill stood at the edge of some 20 acres of the Marquis's wood. In the opposite direction at the foot of the hill was the village oven and the *tuilerie* furnishing the basic necessities of communal existence, bread and tile. In still another direction on the crest of a neighboring hill and half hidden by a cluster of umbrella pines and semi-tropical vegetation was the seigniorial château. A thirteenth century structure, it still retained the outward appearance of a fortress with its high, small windows, its thick walls, and its four conical towers. On closer inspection, however, the palm-studded terrace and the circular well-tended garden of tropical plants blunted the harsher lines of plastered brick to suggest a country-house rather than a feudal stronghold. Aside from the short avenue of low hanging pines that led from the stables to the steps of the terrace and the small garden, there was nothing that could be called a formal park. Almost to the walls of the château, carefully kept rows of fruit trees lined the hillside. At the foot of this rise, not far from the stables, were equally well tended rows of vineyards supplying the château household with its annual stock of *vin du pays*.[41]

From the high ground on the other side of the château, one gained an excellent view of the valley of the Lauragais and, in the immediate foreground, the domain lands of the Marquis d'Escouloubre. Several clumps of trees shaded groups of long, low buildings that marked the centers of three farms (*métairies*). These rough-clay, windowless buildings housed farm-animals, a few primitive tools, some grain and forage, as well as the peasant families who worked the adjoining lands for the Marquis. Each farm consisted of between 25 and 50 arpents (35 and 70 acres) of grain land with dependent meadow and woodland, and worked by one or two pairs of oxen. About 45% of the cultivated land was in wheat, another 15% in maize and beans (*fèves*), and the remaining 40% in fallow.[42]

The peasant families who worked these farms were known

[41] A. D. E-1752, "Plan de Vieillevigne, 18ᵐᵉ siècle." Today, the mill, the oven, and the *tuilerie* have been abandoned. Otherwise Vieillevigne is unchanged. The owner of the château in 1955 was a professor at the University of Geneva.
[42] A. D. C-1329 (Vieillevigne).

as *maîtres-valets*. Each family was supplied by the Marquis with livestock, tools, a cottage, garden, salt, olive oil, and an annual wage of 8 setiers (21.12 bushels) of grain (half wheat and half maize) and 12 livres coin. Although the *maître-valet* had a certain prestige among the peasants, his family having worked the Marquis's land for generations, he was in fact a wage-laborer. The entire grain harvest, after deduction for seed and harvest costs, went to the Marquis's storage bins. These farms were supervised personally by Marquis d'Escouloubre with the aid of Monsieur Théron, his steward, who acted as accountant for the entire estate.[43]

Separate from these three contiguous farms and barely discernible in the neighboring community of Saint-Rome was another of the Marquis's farms, also worked by *maîtres-valets*. Further away in the neighboring communities of Gardouch and Montesquieu-Lauraguais were still three more farms belonging to the same domain. These were worked by *métayers* or *bordiers*. The *métayer* was a sharecropper who received in principle half of the production derived from the plow after deductions for seed and harvest costs. The sharecropper supplied at his own expense all the necessary tools and held on lease all farm animals. Sharecropping contracts were verbal on the Marquis's farms, common practice in the Lauragais at this date.[44]

Altogether, then, there were seven farms totalling 440 arpents (616 acres) in the vicinity of Vieillevigne administered directly by the Marquis d'Escouloubre in 1750. This was the Marquis's *domaine proche* or estate proper. These seven farms yielded about 1100 setiers (2900 bushels) of wheat and maize after deduction for seed and payment of the harvest hands. After paying the portions of the sharecroppers and the wages of the *maîtres-valets*, the Marquis had about 400 setiers (1056 bushels) of wheat and 240 setiers (633.6 bushels) of maize to market on his own account. At the current market price in 1750 of 10 livres per setier of wheat and 5 livres per setier of maize, the domain cereals brought a revenue of 5,200 livres. The dependent woodland, meadow, and vines produced about

[43] *Ibid.*; Picot de Lapeyrouse, *The Agriculture of a District in the South of France* (London, 1819), pp. 16-18.
[44] *Ibid.*; A. D. C-1329 (Saint Rome), C-1319 (Gardouch), C-1323 (Montesquieu).

1000 livres, bringing the revenue of the estate (before taxes) to over 6000 livres.[45]

In Languedoc the *taille* was *réelle*, that is, based on land, so that nobles who owned " common land " (*terre roturière*) paid this tax as any other property owner. Since most of the Marquis's land was " noble," he paid a *taille* of only 240 livres on his " common lands." After negotiation with the local administration, his *vingtième*, the new 20th tax on income, was fixed at 209 livres. His *capitation* was 136 livres. Thus, the Marquis's total tax bill was 585 livres or about 8% of domain revenue in 1750.[46]

Estate repair costs were so small that the Marquis did not even enter them as a deduction on his tax declaration. The buildings on the farms were extremely rudimentary and the Marquis's brick oven provided what little construction material was needed. Drainage and trenching was the responsibility of the peasant occupants. For special projects such as the redirection of waterways, Hers and Tezauque, the Marquis drew on funds raised by the Provincial Estates for public works.[47]

In addition to the resources of his estate proper, the Marquis, as seigneur of the community of Vieillevigne, commanded the revenues of certain seigniorial rights owed by the occupants of the *mouvances*, semi-independent properties located within the Marquis's seigniorial jurisdiction. The principal right was the *cens*, a perpetual ground-rent paid in kind by all of the property holders of Vieillevigne and totalling 30 setiers (79.2 bushels) of wheat. Second in revenue importance were the *banalités* (seigniorial monopolies) of mill and forge which were leased for 22 setiers (58.08 bushels) of wheat annually. At 10 livres per setier, the average market price for wheat in the decade, 1750-1760, these two rights were worth about 520 livres or about 7% of the gross estate revenue.[48]

There were a number of other seigniorial and honorific rights of insignificant value in yearly revenue, but, as will be shown in the following chapter, of considerable legal value to the Marquis. They included the right of option (*retrait féodal*) of the seigneur to purchase any lands recently sold or exchanged

[45] Cf. Appendix A for the method employed to arrive at these revenues.
[46] A. D. C-1329, C-1323, C-1319, C-822 " Rôle de Capitation."
[47] Montaugé, *op. cit.*, pp. 57 ff.
[48] A. D. C-1329.

within the seigniory; the right of *lods et ventes*, a claim to one-twelfth of the selling price of any land sold where the right of option was not exercised; the right of *acapte*, a claim to double *cens* when a *mouvance* passed from father to son; the *agrier* or *champart*, a claim of ⅕ to ⅑ of the harvest on 45 arpents (63 acres) of land in the community; and the *courroc* or *corvée*, one day labor service per year on the seigneur's domain and two *pugnères* (1.38 bushels) of oats from each inhabitant who owned a pair of oxen. Regarding the last two of these rights, the *champart* was extremely rare in the Lauragais and *corvée* was almost everywhere contested and seldom performed. The Marquis also had the honorific rights of the hunt, front bench in the parish church, first place in religious processions, and other such rights. Beside certain specific legal uses, all of these seigniorial rights served to perpetuate the legalistic notion that the *mouvances* were not freeholds in the English sense but lands potentially destined for reunion with the noble domain.[49]

Was the estate of the Marquis d'Escouloubre typical of the Lauragais with respect to area, administration, revenues, and expenses? Turning first to the question of area, let us examine the division of land among the social classes in the diocese. According to the tax rolls of 1750 for 78 of 214 communities, the proportions appear as follows: [50]

TABLE I

DISTRIBUTION OF LAND BY SOCIAL GROUPS

Social Group	Number of Properties	Extent	
		Hectares	% of Total
Clergy	132	3,629	6.5
Nobility	455	24,672	44.4
Bourgeoisie	820	14,136	25.2
Peasantry, artisans	5,355	12,535	22.5
Commons (*Communaux*)	—	683	1.2
	6,742	55,546 (138,865 acres)	99.8

[49] Fortanier, *op. cit.*, p. 360-361; A. D. C-1329.

[50] H. Martin, *Documents relatifs à la vente des biens nationaux, district de Toulouse* (Toulouse, 1916-24), pp. 516-517.

Thus, in 1750, the nobility, representing about 1% of the population of the diocese, owned 44% of the land. Dividing the land held by the number of properties one arrives at 54 hectares (135 acres) for the nobility, 17.1 hectares (42.8 acres) for the bourgeoisie, and 2.3 hectares (5.8 acres) for the peasantry. However, one must not conclude from this that the average noble family held 135 acres of land. In reality, the nobles often held many properties scattered throughout the diocese and even in neighboring dioceses.

The *vingtième* tax rolls for 1750 list 226 noble families in the diocese. The average landholding was 192.4 arpents or 267.4 acres. The following table indicates how the land was distributed among these 226 families.

TABLE II

DISTRIBUTION OF NOBLE LANDHOLDINGS IN THE DIOCESE OF TOULOUSE IN 1750

Area of Land (in arpents of 1.39 acres)	Number of Families
1000 arpents or more	1 (1166 arpents)
700 to 999	6
500 to 699	10
300 to 499	32
200 to 299	33
100 to 199	63
50 to 99	29
1 to 49	52
	226

Separating the older nobility of robe and sword from the newer nobility, principally of municipal origin (*noblesse de cloche*), the average holding of the first group (95 families) is 305.2 arpents or 424.2 acres while that of the second group (131 families) is only 110.6 arpents or 153.7 acres. At the threshold of its climb to wealth and prestige within the noble class, the newer nobility (*anciens capitouls, " nobles," écuyers*) represents the vast majority (69 out of 81) of those families owning less than 100 arpents. These newer *anoblis* lower the overall average noble holding to 192.4 arpents.[51]

[51] A. D. C-1331-1346. Cf. Appendix A for an explanation of the tax rolls used to arrive at these areas. The 226 noble families on these rolls in 1750

The typical diocesan community consisted of one or two noble proprietors owning 200 to 300 arpents each, three or four smaller noble and bourgeois proprietors holding between 40 and 50 arpents each, and then a mass of small bourgeois and peasant holdings ranging from 20 arpents (28 acres) to as little as one *pugnère* (.35 acres). At Lacroix-Falgarde, for example, of a total of 82 proprietors, 67 had ten arpents (14 acres) or less, and 48 of these had two arpents (2.8 acres) or less. At Lasalvetat-Saint Gilles there were 94 proprietors of whom 78 had less than 10 arpents and 45 less than 2 arpents. At Issus, besides the three noble seigneurs, only 10 proprietors had more than 10 arpents (none more than thirty) and 45 of the remaining 68 held one arpent (1.4 acres) or less! Examples like these could be multiplied many times. They are sufficient to show how unreal an average holding can be. The peasant properties in particular were composed of a small minority of holdings between 10 and 20 arpents and an overwheming majority of small pieces between two and four arpents. In an average year only farms with over 10 arpents (14 acres) of arable land could produce a marketable surplus over minimum consumption needs.[52] Hence, the holdings of the nobility, small enough by English standards, attain considerable proportion when placed side by side with this mass of small peasant properties. It is in the small village community of a few hundred inhabitants that one realizes what it means for 1% of the population to hold almost one-half of the land.

The *vingtième* tax rolls indicate that only ten noble families leased all or most of their lands at money rents (*fermage*) to tenant farmers. The overwhelming majority administered their estates in the manner of the Marquis d'Escouloubre, that is, in farms of 25 to 50 arpents, each worked by a *maître-valet*

compare with 204 listed on the capitation rolls for the city of Toulouse in 1789.

[52] A. D. C-1337 (Lacroix-Falgarde); C-1338 (Lasalvetat); C-1336 (Issus). Calculating the size of the self-sufficient farm is a delicate process. The best example I have seen is in an article by Pierre Goubert " The French Peasantry in the Seventeenth Century: Beauvaisis," *Past and Present*, X (Nov., 1956), pp. 66-67. M. Goubert describes a grain area slightly more productive than the Toulousan plain in the eighteenth century and concludes that a peasant farmer would need 6 hectares (15 acres or slightly over 10 arpents) to be independent in an average year exclusive of taxes, tithes, and seigniorial dues.

or a sharecropper, and supervised, sometimes with the aid of a salaried steward (*régisseur*), by the noble proprietor in person. Even allowing for some omissions on the tax rolls, there seems little doubt that the typical Toulousan noble was a resident *gentilhomme-campagnard* who managed his estate directly and personally.[53]

In order to ascertain the approximate amount and composition of estate revenues in the Lauragais, I have selected twenty of the more prominent noble families whose tax declarations furnish adequate data to make reasonably accurate estimations. It should be made clear that those estates furnishing the most details of administration, resources, and expenses tend to be the larger ones. The average holding for these twenty selected estates was 403 arpents (564 acres) or about twice the average for the 226 families. However, there is no reason to believe that the *composition* and sources of the revenues and expenses are appreciably different on the "average estate" of 192.4 arpents.[54]

TABLE III

AVERAGE GROSS AND NET REVENUE FROM TWENTY SELECTED ESTATES

Sources of Revenue or Expenses	Amount in Livres	Percent of Gross Revenue
Revenue:		
Grain Lands	3,577	62%
Wood, Meadow, Vines	1,434	25%
Mills, Forges, Ovens	285	5%
Cens, Seigniorial Rights	452	8%
Gross Revenue:	5,748	100%
Expenses:	1,098	
Wages	262	5%
Taxes	836	15%
Net Revenue:	4,650	80%

Again, like the Marquis d'Escouloubre, these noble proprietors drew the bulk of their revenues (92%) from the

[53] A. D. C-1331-1346.
[54] A. D. 1312-1330. Cf. Appendix A. The method of estimating revenues described in Appendix A could be applied with less precision to the hypothetical "average estate." The writer believes it preferable to use actual estates where ample data is present even though these estates are somewhat larger than the statistical average. Cf. n. 59, *infra.*

domain and only 8% from the *cens* and other seigniorial
rights.[55] Unlike the traditional picture of the *grande noblesse*
at Paris, these men were not dependent on seigniorial dues for
a livelihood. Sixty per cent of the gross income came from
grain of which wheat was undisputed king. An additional 25%
of the income came from sales of wood, hay, and wine. The
rents from mills, forges, and brick ovens amounted to only
5%. These proprietors were wheat barons and not *rentiers*
living from seigniorial rights.

Wages to *maîtres-valets* accounted for only 5% of the gross
income. Portions to sharecroppers and harvest-hands, as well
as sufficient seed for the following year, were deducted from
the harvest and are not included here as a " wage." [56] Taxes
were extremely variable since the nobles who held " common
land " paid the *taille* on these lands. There was no set portion
of noble land exempt from the *taille* as in the North. The
Marquis de Grammont-Lanta, for example, paid a *taille* of
700 livres on his 400 arpent domain, and a total tax amounting
to 27% of his gross landed income. The majority of estates,
however, paid at rates closer to those of Marquis d'Escouloubre,
and the overall average for the twenty estates was 13%. Of this
sum, about 10% was for the *taille* and *capitation* and 3% for
the *vingtième*.

Annual repairs, other than special projects such as the *levées*
at Pinsaguel or the dredging of the river Hers, were borne by
the *maîtres-valets* and sharecroppers who availed themselves
of the domain brick field for building block. As at Vieillevigne,
farm buildings throughout the Lauragais were extremely primitive. The hangar-like sharecropper's cottage served as ox-stall,
cart-shed, hen house, hay loft, and hog stye as well as one room
residence. This same narrow, single-story building contained
the store-room for the seed, the kneading trough, the salting-
tub, and even the oven on the back of the chimney. Most of
these buildings were made of *paille-bart*, a mixture of clay and
straw, and only a few were made entirely of brick. The maize
and fodder were left in open ricks and the château served as

[55] *Ibid.* The seigniorial rights were not only fixed but divided among two
or more seigneurs in almost every community. At Montesquieu, to select an
extreme case, there were no less than thirteen co-seigneurs.
[56] Cf. Appendix A.

a warehouse for the wheat. Tools were repaired twice annually at the village forge. The livestock was maintained by the peasant cultivator, the profits or losses from breeding or disease being shared with the proprietor. In short, the expense of ordinary repairs were borne by the peasant occupant with the result that most domains had a minimum of storage facilities, farm implements, and bovine livestock.[57]

The noble proprietors benefited from a system of government compensation paid in the form of tax relief in years of bad harvest. In a bad crop year, the landlord petitioned to the Subdelegate for an indemnity by giving an estimate of his current harvest as compared with his harvest in a " common year." He could plead that his revenues that year were insufficient to cover his current expenses and the additional repairs necessitated by floods, hail, or other natural disaster. It was not considered irrelevant to bolster one's case by emphasizing the cost of a son's education or a daughter's pension, as well as the damages caused by a collapsed barn or a château fire. Indeed, the system of indemnities was calamity insurance of the broadest kind. On more than one occasion, the Subdelegate of Toulouse observed that a noble family, seeking tax exemption, might have incurred a diminution of income, but had not " suffered " relative to its revenues. Nevertheless, indemnities ranging from 25 to 50% of taxes were paid to large numbers of noble families in the 1770's and 1780's. Thus, whenever a seasonal crop failure, flood, or fire threatened the proprietor with extra repair costs or a temporary reduction in his landed income, he was relieved of a large part of his taxes.[58]

The gentlemen farmers of the Lauragais did not live as *rentiers* from seigniorial dues. Their principal income came from an intensely cultivated and closely supervised country estate. Despite primitive methods of farming on domains averaging less than 300 acres, tight management and low costs assured the noble proprietor of a net income between three and 4,000 livres in the 1750's.[59]

[57] For an excellent description of rural buildings on an estate in the diocese of Toulouse, see, Picot de Lapeyrouse, *The Agriculture of a District in the South of France* (London, 1819), pp. 6-10.

[58] A. D. C-112-115. These documents include the petitions of gentlemen for farm relief and the comments of the Subdelegate on the validity of their claims.

[59] Under the administration described above, the hypothetical estate of 192.4

The productive core of the country estate was the domain farm (*métairie*) and wheat its chief money crop. Yet, if wheat was king, why was the domain broken into these relatively small plots, almost half lying fallow? In the following chapter we will indicate what efforts were made by the noble-proprietor toward regrouping the land and reducing the fallow. At this point, it should simply be indicated that the *Midi* of France had its own peculiar geologic and climatic environment that made abandonment of the traditional small farm units and the biennial system of crop rotation extremely difficult.

For any real understanding of agriculture in the *Midi*, two cardinal factors must be borne in mind: (1) the extreme variety of soils, and (2) the sudden changes in the weather. The former factor had taught the peasant farmer, trained by generations of hard experience in the fields, to plant his crops highly selectively. He had learned that his wheat should be planted in a plot of rich loams, his beans in a patch less fertile, and his vines on a piece of marginal rocky soil—in short, each soil its own crop. By doing this, he created a patch-work of near garden culture where it was not exceptional to see a row of vines or fruit trees running directly through a field of wheat or maize. Moreover, the small size and irregular shape of the fields and very lean oxen put a premium on a light maneuverable plow such as the wooden *araire* at the sacrifice of the more deeply penetrating *charrue*. It was not the type of plow that determined the shape of the land parcels, but rather the extreme variety of soils that determined both the kind of culture and the type of plow.[60]

Fundamental to the formation of the peasant's firm attachment to the biennial system—wheat, fallow—was the climate of the *Midi*. It is no exaggeration to say that Haut-Languedoc has no transitional seasons, no real autumn or spring. The winter begins brusquely in November and the crops are threatened by a late frost until Mid-April. In the first weeks of May, the *vent d'autan* blows in violent gusts from the Mediterranean

arpents (267.4 acres) would produce about 250 setiers of wheat and 100 setiers of maize or 3000 livres for the cereals alone at 1750 market prices.

[60] D. Faucher, " Polyculture ancienne et assolement biennal dans la France méridionale," *Revue géographique des Pyrénées et du Sud-Ouest*, V (1934), pp. 241-255; " A propos de l'araire," *Actes du Congrès de la Fédération des Sociétés Savantes (Pyrénées-Languedoc-Gascogne)*, Albi, 1955, pp. 121-124.

and the heavy rains begin. In June the torrid summer of the *Midi* settles heavily upon the red-tile roof-tops of the *pays toulousain*. It is a dry heat, punctuated by sudden hail storms, that parches and destroys all but the most sturdy, well-rooted crops. Under such conditions, spring grains such as barley and oats had a precarious existence in a short season threatened by the dry summer heat. Therefore, only a minimum of spring cereals were seeded. But since these very spring cereals—barley and oats—were the most common second year crops in the triennial system practiced in the North, their near absence in the *Midi* glued the Toulousan peasant and gentleman-farmer alike to the biennial system much longer than in the more temperate North. The *Midi* was faced with making a revolutionary jump from biennialism to artificial meadows, a leap much more difficult to make in the absence of a transitional triennialism.[61]

To this must be added the retardative effect of the vicious cycle of " poor forage, poor cattle, poor manure " which placed a heavy dependence on the fallow both for pasture and for regeneration of the soil. So strong was this cycle based on a few, rugged but lean oxen that new crop courses were regarded with distrust if not with fear.[62] Potatoes were regarded with distaste even as cattle fodder and the poorest peasant would not eat them. Turnips, even when distributed without cost by the Provincial Estates, never took hold. As for artificial grasses, they required a considerable capital outlay and a three year delay before the new grasses made good forage. Moreover, artificial meadows were best planted before barley and not before wheat in a triennial system and this implied a reduction of wheat land from about one-half to one-third of the area cultivated. It was this unwillingness to sacrifice even part of a wheat crop that dominated the thinking of gentlemen-farmers not only in the *Midi* but in parts of the North as well. The Englishman, Young recorded a conversation with a group of noble landholders in which the gentlemen demanded:

Can we sow wheat after turnips and cabbages? (On a certain portion

---

[61] *Ibid.*; D. Faucher, *Géographie agraire, types de culture* (Paris, 1949), p. 64 f.
[62] Montaugé, *op. cit.*, p. 53.

you may have success, but the time of consuming the great part of the crop renders it impossible). That is sufficient, if we cannot sow wheat after them, they cannot be good in France. (This idea is everywhere nearly the same in that Kingdom . . . they thought their own courses more profitable).[63]

What guarantee was there of compensation in the form of better wheat yields in the years to come? For the average provincial of the *Midi*, the answer was simple—only the promises of some meddling English theorists and " *ces gens du nord.*" It is no overstatement to say that the provincial mind, whatever its great qualities, is not noted for boldness in exploring unknown horizons, especially where its pocketbook is in play.

Given such retardative conditions—climatic, geologic, or simply " provincial "—the noble proprietors found it best to work their lands intensively in small plots, hoping to make up in productivity per arpent for the limitations imposed by the variety of the soils and the fallow field. The optimum surface worked by one peasant family and one pair of oxen was about 25 arpents (35 acres). Hence the farm or *métairie* was defined in terms of " pairs of oxen " —a *métairie* of " two pairs " (50 arpents) considered a large plot. Furthermore, the *métairie* represented a quantity of land adequate to nourish one peasant family under the traditional self-sufficient local economy. In the eighteenth century, the *métairie* still furnished enough grain, wine, flax, wood and forage for the peasant's basic annual needs, but an increasing portion of the grain harvest went to the noble proprietor. From an accounting point of view, it was safer for the proprietor to keep his farm units small enough to estimate the division of the harvest as carefully as possible. Better to estimate the shares on many small plots than to risk being cheated on the more variable crop of a larger surface.[64] Moreover, many small peasant sharecroppers or *maîtres-valets* were likely to be more docile in their relations with their proprietor-*maître* than a single tenant-*fermier* who might con-

---

[63] Young, *op. cit.* (Dublin ed., 1793), I, pp. 235-236. In all other citations of Young, I have relied on the Henri Sée edition (Paris, 1931).

[64] C.-E. Labrousse, *Origines et aspects économiques et sociaux de la Révolution française* (1774-1791), (Paris: Centre de documentation universitaire, " Les Cours de Sorbonne," n. d.), pp. 42-43; Aragon, *op. cit.*, p. 95 f.

trol much of the farm capital, including the livestock. Olivier de Serres, the famous early seventeenth century agronomist, whose *Théâtre d'agriculture* was a standard text-book for gentlemen-farmers, had warned against the " rich *fermier* " who profits from " your domain," and " badly repays you for capital advanced." Much better, wrote de Serres, to change to share-cropping.[65] A noble-proprietor's bargaining position was patently much stronger with regard to a small peasant who depended upon his *maître* for livestock and tools, as well as for periodic loans of grain, seed, and coin. Finally, there was a certain prestige attached to having a sharecropper or *maître-valet* that could not be applied to having a tenant-*fermier*. In a world that still valued a certain paternalism, the expression, " *mon métayer*," or " *mon maître-valet* " gave the noble-proprietor the full sense of being a *gentilhomme-campagnard*.[66] For all of these reasons, then, the *métairie* was the classic farm unit and has remained so even to this day.

The land was worked in essentially the same manner it had been worked in the Middle Ages. The floating labor supply was recruited for the harvest in August and a team of about a dozen men and women were assigned to each *métairie*. All harvesting was done with the sickle because the scythe cut the grain sheaves too close to the ground and deprived the poor gleaners of the stubble.[67] The grain was then separated from the sheath by marching mules or horses over it, and it was only near the end of the century that the flail became a popular instrument for threshing (*dépiquage*) in the *Midi*. The grain was cleaned by shoveling it against the wind as in Biblical times, and only a few proprietors practiced hand-cleaning. Lime-washing was unknown even among the more prosperous and progressive proprietors. Before grinding, the seed was set aside for the following year and the harvest hands were paid their *droit de moissonnade*, one-eighth of the harvest. Then the sharecropper or *maître-valet*, under the supervision of the pro-

[65] P. Viguier, *Du colonage partiaire dans le Lauragais* (Paris, 1911), p. 37, and *passim*. Cf. Chapter II, n. 35 *infra*.

[66] Marc Bloch, *Les caractères originaux de l'histoire rurale française*, (Paris, 1952), pp. 152-153.

[67] J. Lebrau, *Ceux du Languedoc* (Horizons de France, 1946). The *droit de glanage*, immortalized by Millet's painting, is practiced even to this day in Languedoc.

prietor or his agent, took his share which varied from 4 setiers (11 bushels) of wheat to a maximum of one-half of the balance of the harvest. The rest was transported to the pro-prietor and often stored in the damp cellar of the château. Sometimes the seigneur had special granaries in local market towns such as Villefranche-Lauragais to serve as depots for his share of the harvest and for his *cens*. But in general, the grain was poorly kept, sometimes not even placed in individual sacks but left in open bins. It was no wonder that the local govern-ment (Royal and Provincial) was not so much concerned with propagating new crop courses as it was with prescribing ele-mentary methods of grain and seed care as well as the use of the flail.[68]

Seed was sown broadcast in September and manuring was done only twice throughout the year. The wooden swing-plow was the basic farm implement. The clevis on this light plow was short and thick and the wrought iron plow-share was irregularly attached to a mold-board that was insufficiently elevated from the ground. The result was that the earth was incompletely turned over and the furrows left irregular and shallow. Many communities clung to the lighter *araire* of Virgil, even more primitive, on which the plow-share was attached to the plow-beam making the furrows even shallower. The other essential farm implements were the harrows and the classic two-wheeled carts, both of wood. There was some scattered use of Duhamel's *semoir à bras* (Tull's seed-drill), but the peasant's most common tools were the spade, the hoe, the mattock, and the shovel. There were no pitch-forks; the handles on the hoes were so short, the field-hands had to work at a back-breaking angle; and the shovel handles were so straightly fixed to the iron rims that even ditch-digging required double effort. In short, even the most simple tools were poorly constructed.[69]

Under such conditions, and allowing for great seasonal varia-tion, the wheat harvest yielded about five to one on the seed or five setiers per arpent (9.5 bushels per acre) in a " common

[68] A. D. C-2428; C-106 " *Mémoire sur la conservation des semences, 1759* "; Montaugé, *op. cit.*, p. 53; Aragon, *op. cit.*, pp. 38-39.

[69] Montaugé, *op. cit.*, pp. 49-52. A. D. C-106, " *Syndic du diocèse aux Etats* " (on the *semoir à bras*).

year " in the diocese of Toulouse. In the Lauragais, yields ran as high as ten to one, but the poorer soils in the directions of Lavaur in the northeast and Muret in the southwest, reduced the diocesan average to five to one. These figures, taken from the royal subdelegate's reports and from private family papers, contrast strikingly with much lower yields declared on the noble tax rolls and the higher yields claimed by proprietors seeking government compensation for bad harvests.[70]

The basis of noble fortune in the diocese of Toulouse was the land. For land was the permanent and solid basis of a livelihood and a mode of life. The wheat fields at harvest time, the sharecropper with his cart, the château on the hill, the parish-church on Sunday—these were the symbols of a stern, patriarchal society, worlds away from the foppishness of a Paris *salon*, and concerned with the serious details of estate management. The Abbé de Bertier expressed a nostalgia for this provincial life when he wrote to his elder brother on the family estate at Pinsaguel:

My first act this morning was to glance out on the terrace to see my de Bertier walking with his pipe in his mouth, clad in his riding coat, and teaching M. Dechaux the art of cultivating the soil and making the farm capital produce.[71]

---

[70] A. D. C-120, Subdelegate to Intendant, 15 September 1786; E-1777 "*Mémoire sur les rendements*," 1772, Saint-Elix-le-Château papers. Contrast with the *vingtième* declarations, C-1312-1330, and the petitions for tax relief, C-114, 115. For the great seasonal variation in harvests see C-119, 120 "*Etat des récoltes*" (Appendix B).

[71] A. D. 6-J, 41. Abbé de Bertier to Marquis de Bertier, March 7, 1756.

CHAPTER II

THE NOBLE AS LANDLORD: ADMINISTRATION
OF THE DOMAIN *

Indisputably, one of the crucial factors in the economic history of France in the eighteenth century is the enormous increase in population. The population of France as a whole rose from 18 to 26 million, or 44 per cent, between 1715 and the Revolution.[1] The rate of population increase varied according to region, and unfortunately there are no reliable population statistics for the diocese of Toulouse during this period. But that the Toulouse area felt this pressure was clearly indicated by a rapid increase in the demand for bread. The royal subdelegate calculated the annual cereal consumption of the diocese in sharply increasing quantities: [2]

Date	Setiers of Toulouse (2.64 bushels)	Bushels
1771	288,000	730,320
1775	384,000	1,013,760
1780	536,000	1,415,040
1786	603,000	1,591,920

The same royal administrator fixed the monthly grain consumption of the city of Toulouse at 12,000 *setiers* (31,680 bushels) in 1759 and at 18,000 *setiers* (47,520 bushels) in 1789, an increase of 50 per cent in thirty years.[3] Allowing for the inexactitude of these estimates, it is patently clear from

* Much of the material in this chapter appeared in slightly altered form in the *Journal of Economic History* (June, 1957), pp. 224-244. I wish to thank the editors of this journal for permitting me to republish this material here.

[1] Marcel Reinhard, *Histoire de la population mondiale de 1700 à 1948* (Paris, 1949), pp. 91-92.

[2] A. D., C-119, 120. No doubt the subdelegate exaggerated his estimates in order to discourage government authorization for grain to leave the diocese. Nevertheless, his upward revision of estimates reflects a steadily increasing demand.

[3] A. D., C-116, 118.

the Toulousan subdelegate's reports to the intendant of Languedoc that grain consumption at the end of the Old Regime was fast outdistancing production and that prices were rising.[4] Wheat sold on the Toulouse market for an average of 9 livres per *setier* during the period 1740-1747, and for an average of 15 livres per *setier* during the period 1780-1787, an increase of 67 per cent in forty years.[5]

In addition to creating an attractive market for the grain producer, the rapid rise in population furnished an abundant supply of cheap labor. After 1750, Toulouse and the surrounding countryside became increasingly swollen with surplus labor. The Toulousan chronicler, Pierre Barthès, wrote more frequently as the century drew to a close of the crowds of refugees from the countryside searching for charity at Toulouse, of bread riots on the Place Royale, and of " the city flooded with country people forced by misery to leave their homes." [6] The church investigation of the country parishes in 1763 presented an equally grim picture of poverty attributed to a superabundance of day laborers who had no land and hence no security against seasonal unemployment and increasing bread prices.[7]

Inevitably wages were low, and leaseholders, fearful of losing their precious land, paid ever higher rents. Wages for *maîtres-valets*, the most fortunate of the rural proletariat, were five *setiers* (13.2 bushels) of wheat, five *setiers* of maize, and

---

[4] This is but another confirmation of the general conclusions reached by C. E Labrousse, *Esquisse du mouvement des prix et des revenus en France au XVIIIe siècle* (Paris, 1933), pp. 170-172, 610; *Origines et aspects économiques et sociaux de la Révolution française, 1774-1791* (Paris: Centre de documentation universitaire, " Les Cours de Sorbonne," n. d.), pp. 2-3, 6-10; and by O. Festy, *L'agriculture pendant la Révolution française; les conditions de production et de récolte des céréales* (Paris, 1947), pp. 12, 36-37.

[5] L. Viala, *La question des grains et leur commerce à Toulouse au XVIIIe siècle, 1715-1789* (Toulouse, 1909), pp. 110-118. The setier of Toulouse was 2.64 bushels. Cf. Appendix C for annual price fluctuations of wheat. This 67% increase in wheat prices compares with Labrousse's estimate of 66% for France as a whole between the base period 1726-1741 and the period 1785-89. Labrousse, *Esquisse*, pp. 170-172. Notice, however, that Labrousse's estimate includes the crisis years, 1788-1789. Therefore, the price rise at Toulouse would seem to be even greater than the national average.

[6] E. Lemouzèle, *Toulouse au XVIIIe siècle d'après les " Heures perdues " de Pierre Barthès* (Toulouse, 1914), February 1766, April 1773, June 1778.

[7] A. D., G-492, " Etat des paroisses " (2 vols.; 1763).

twelve livres in coin annually, plus a cottage, garden, and a provision of wood, salt, and olive oil.[8] This wage was worth 82 livres in 1740 and perhaps 132 livres in 1785. In reality, it was a near-subsistence wage paid in kind, confirmed by local custom, and unaltered until the nineteenth century.[9] Day laborers received about fifteen sous per day in 1750 and approached eighteen or nineteen sous by 1789. Wine workers, women, and children earned less, averaging eight and ten sous per day. The large floating labor supply was absorbed only at harvest time, when the larger proprietors distributed one eighth of the harvest (the customary *droit de moissonnade*) to the seasonal farm hands. Even in a good season, a harvest hand had to participate in more than one harvest to subsist for the year on his portion.[10] In short, farm labor, pressed by numbers, received no more than a near-subsistence wage when there was work available. This low " sticky cost," added to the increasing demand for cereals, created a particularly favorable economic environment for the larger landholders.

This combination of favorable economic factors—an expanding market for cereals, an abundant supply of cheap labor, and an adequate quantity of rich grain land—made the application of a number of administrative techniques by the rural nobleman particularly fruitful after 1750. These techniques included: (1) more precise estate accounting, allied with the enforcement of seigniorial titles; (2) foreclosure of mortgages of indebted peasants as well as purchases from, and exchanges of land with, neighboring proprietors; (3) reduction of labor and middleman costs through progressive changes in leaseholds; (4) the application of more advanced agricultural methods, including forage crops, new crop rotations, irrigation, and clearings, to increase farm production.

With regard to estate accounting significant changes are apparent. The proliferation of eighteenth-century account books and rent rolls (*terriers*) in the local archives does not in itself

[8] A. D., C-1312-1330. These are noble tax declarations for the *vingtième* and include deductions for wages of *maîtres-valets*.
[9] Picot, Baron de Lapeyrouse, *The Agriculture of a District in the South of France* (London: J. Harding, 1819), p. 17. The *maître-valet* on Picot's estate near Toulouse received " by custom " the same wage in 1818.
[10] Théron de Montaugé, *L'agriculture et les classes rurales dans le pays toulousain depuis le milieu du 18me siècle* (Paris, 1869), Part I.

prove increased attention to accounting. Accounts of the sixteenth and seventeenth centuries may simply have been lost.
Nevertheless, there is no question that eighteenth-century
accounts were better organized and more comprehensive than
those of previous centuries. The rent rolls in particular, bound
in sturdy cowhide, are often recopied in an eighteenth-century
hand. For example, in 1752 the Marquis de Bertier made a
careful inventory of all his account books dating back to the
sixteenth century.[11] About 1760 the Marquis de Gardouch
established a " Plan for the Arrangement of an Estate's Charters
and Papers " and issued a directive to his steward to keep five
separate account books, receipts for all sales of produce, and
special explanations for any paper money received.[12] After
1750 the accounts of the Marquis d'Escouloubre become more
exact, some of them written in the Marquis's own hand. The
same general conclusion may be drawn from the accounts of
the noble families Barneval, Fourquevaux, Cambon, Blagnac,
and Riquet de Caraman.[13]

More important than increased precision in accounting is the
use of these books as legal titles for the enforcement of century-
old seigniorial rights and for the collection of rent arrears.
The families of Escouloubre and Varagne-Belesta reasserted
their claims to obligations of local communities within their
seigniorial jurisdictions. In both cases, local customs, dating
from 1235 and 1280 respectively, were recopied and employed
as legal titles to these obligations. They substantiated the lords'
claims to a large share in the community government, to *corvées*
(forced labor) of two days per year, and to more exclusive
rights on the communal meadow. The *cens*, or perpetual
ground rents, were rigorously enforced almost everywhere in
the diocese. Collected largely in kind on almost all of the land
in the Toulousan plain, the *cens* was the most valuable of
seigniorial rights. According to the tax rolls of 1750, about
8 per cent of an average nobleman's income came from the
cens.[14]

[11] A. D., 6-J, 110.
[12] A. D., Gardouch, 1009.
[13] A. D., E-1696, 1712-1713, 1725 (Escouloubre); E-635 (Barneval); E-641
(Fourquevaux); E-642 (Cambon); E-647 (Blagnac); E-1461 (Riquet de
Caraman).
[14] A. D., E-1727 (Escouloubre); Gardouch, 966; C-1312-1330; Jean R.

The important innovation of the eighteenth century, as in other regions of France, was the collection of *cens* arrears. The private accounts of the families Escouloubre, Varagne-Belesta, Bertier de Pinsaguel, Astre de Blagnac, Bertrand de Montesquieu-Volvestre, and Riquet de Caraman indicate careful tabulation of these arrears.[15] No *cens* was too small to be collected. Astre de Blagnac's accounts after 1750 indicate clearly the collection of arrears from a dozen small peasant proprietors who owed only a few livres *cens* annually. Collected en bloc for the previous five or ten years, these arrears amounted to as much as fifty livres per arpent (1.39 acres).[16] In 1724 the Comte de Prat collected from one of his tenants all the arrears for twenty-nine years—a total of three hundred livres, eleven sous.[17]

In addition to *cens* arrears, loans in money, grain, or seed to sharecroppers and small peasant proprietors presented the lord with another advantage. Grain loans were evaluated at the seasonal high plus 5 per cent interest, and careful records were kept. In 1748 Astre de Blagnac lent one of his sharecroppers 204 livres for the dowry of the peasant's daughter. By 1752 subsequent loans and interest had augmented the sharecropper's debt to 881 livres, 18 sous.[18] The sharecropper of the Marquis de Fourquevaux was continually in debt to the Marquis from 1772 until the Revolution. In 1788 he owed the Marquis 100 livres, five capons, eight chickens, and thirteen *setiers* (34.32 bushels) of seed, despite deductions from wages. The Marquis's shepherd was no better off. In 1760 he owed the lord 59 livres, 15 sous in grain and coin; in 1770 he owed 349 livres, 17 sous, according to the Marquis's account.[19] This type of loan, as well as *cens* arrears, could serve as a pretext for land fore-

---

de Fortanier, *Les droits seigneuriaux dans la sénéchaussee et comté de Lauragais, 1553-1789* (Toulouse, 1932).

[15] A. D., E-1713 (Escouloubre); *Archives notariales*, Haute-Garonne, Register 18063, 18082, hereafter, A. Not., followed by register number; A. D., Gardouch, 982; A. D., 6-J, 12; A. D., E-647 (Blagnac); Mlle F. Rocaries, "Un cas de réaction seigneuriale: la communauté et les seigneurs de Montesquieu-Volvestre" (Diplôme présenté à la Faculté des Lettres de Toulouse, 1954), pp. 131 ff.; A. D., E-1461 (Riquet de Caraman).

[16] A. D., E-647. These plots were often less than one arpent (1.39 acres).

[17] A. Not., 91 (August 5, 1724).

[18] A. D., E-647.

[19] A. D., E-641.

closures, since a sharecropper might also own a small scrap of land in the community.

For example, in 1756 the Marquis d'Escouloubre " purchased " three pieces of land totaling under 4 arpents (5.56 acres) from one Jacques Barthelemy for 1,016 livres. In reality this so-called contract of sale was a foreclosure. Escouloubre deducted 1,012 livres in *cens* arrears and paid Barthelemy 4 livres for the land. Although these arrears dated back to 1721, the Marquis calculated a debt of 115 *setiers* (303.6 bushels) of wheat in coin at 10 livres per *setier*, the seasonal high for 1756. In 1784, the peasant Foriez " sold " Escouloubre a scrap of land (¼ arpent) for 206 livres. The entire sum was deducted in payment of a four-year debt of grain to the lord. There are similar examples for 1760 and 1774.[20] How many more of the Marquis's numerous small land purchases between 1756 and 1790 were based on arrears or loans verbally contracted? All debts recorded in the notarial registers of the diocese required the debtor to pledge his land as security. Failure of the peasant to pay his debt after the stipulated period gave the lord a free hand legally, and it appears that he made increasing use of it after 1750.[21]

Keeping in mind always the distinction between the *domaine proche*, land under direct ownership of the lord, and the *mouvances*, semi-independent properties owing *cens* and other obligations to the lord, one can see that the augmentation and consolidation of the estate proper at the expense of the *mouvances* was a key feature of the noble land offensive. Foreclosures based on arrears of debts or dues were one means used to further this process. The seigniorial privilege of *retrait féodal*, the right of option, served the same end. This right permitted the lord to buy any *mouvances* within his jurisdiction that had been recently alienated or exchanged. This meant that the lord would register each of the sales and exchanges within

[20] A. D., E-1712-1713; A. Not., 18082 (Jan. 17, 1756), 18063 (Aug. 7, 1774).

[21] A. Not., 18082 (Nov. 7, 1757). This is a " foreclosure " by Castel-Labarthe. Proof of this type of foreclosure requires either the contract of sale and the cancellation of the debt in the same document or definite evidence that they were related. Such evidence is rare. One can only speculate about the many noble families whose tenants owed them considerable sums and whose domains became subsequently larger.

his jurisdiction and forty days later, under the right of option, could demand the sale of these lands to himself at the contract price.[22]

According to available documents, the Marquis d'Escouloubre purchased thirteen pieces of land between 1767 and 1784 by the application of this right of option on his seigniories of Vieillevigne and Montesquieu-Lauragais.[23]   In 1777 the Confrèrie de la Trinité sold 25,200 livres' worth of land to four individuals at Montesquieu-Volvestre.   Scarcely two months later Antoine-Francois de Bertrand, lord of the community, exercised his right of option and attached all of this land to his own domain.[24]   There are similar examples of the exercise of the right by the Marquis Bertier de Pinsaguel in 1749, 1760, and 1771, and by the Marquis d'Hautpoul-Seyres in 1769.[25] It is significant that clauses explicitly reserving the right of option for the lord are more frequent in leases of seigniorial rights in the second half of the century.   For the first time, in the lease contract of 1755, the Comte Riquet de Caraman stipulated that " in the case of sale of lands of the *mouvance*, the buyer will be held to notify the Lord of Caraman in order that the latter may use the right of option if he wishes." [26] After 1773 the same type of clause appears in the lease contracts of the Marquis de Gardouch.[27]

Besides the use of seigniorial rights to force land sales, the nobles rounded out their domains by ordinary purchase and exchange.   The Marquis de Gardouch, in his " Plan for the Arrangement of an Estate's Papers," assigned a special dossier to acquisitions " either in land or *censives*," either " by purchase or by testament, kept in chronological order and numbered." [28]   Between 1756 and 1790 the Marquis d'Escouloubre acquired thirty-seven scraps of land valued at 37,891 livres in addition to the seigniory of Montesquieu-Lauragais (500 arpents) for 349,000 livres. The " scraps " of land were very

[22] François de Boutaric, *Traité des droits seigneuriaux et des matières féodales* (Toulouse, 1751).

[23] A. D., E-1712-1713; A. Not., 18060-61, 18066.

[24] Rocaries, " Un cas de réaction seigneuriale," pp. 155-160.

[25] A. D., 6-J, 4, 16, 24; A. Not., 18061 (July 2, 1769).

[26] A. D., E-1461.

[27] A. Not., 18066, 18117.

[28] A. D., Gardouch, 1009.

small, often less than one quarter of an arpent (.35 acre). Nevertheless, by such small purchases and exchanges the seigniory of Vieillevigne increased by 48 arpents (66.72 acres) in the forty years before the Revolution.[29]

The general practice was to exchange lands far from the administrative center of the domain for properties close to the principal family château. Where possible, the seigniorial rights were retained both for their immediate revenue value and as a wedge for future expansion along the lines described above. Lands sacrificed were often maternal dowries or donations of distant relatives. As for purchases, noble proprietors either accumulated capital out of income or borrowed from noble acquaintances, usually at 5 per cent. In the French tradition, the Toulousan nobility preferred land to any other form of investment including government *rentes*.[30] The result was two-fold: (1) an absolute increase in the surface of domain land, and (2) a regrouping of the land in consolidated blocks.

A comparison between noble property holdings in 1750 and 1790 measures the success of this policy of aggrandizement. The following table is based on the *vingtième* tax rolls for 1750 and the lists of *emigré* properties for 1790-1792.[31] The table does not include properties outside of the principal seigniorial domain. Hence the surfaces are concentrated within the limits of one community or adjacent communities.

Unfortunately, these sources yield two complete sets of figures for only fourteen families. Among these, however, all but two increased the area of the domain proper. The increases are more impressive when one considers the piecemeal nature of the process of foreclosure, purchase, and exchange. It is

[29] A. D., E-1712-1713; A. Not. 18082. The Marquis paid 149,000 livres immediately in *louis d'or* for Montesquieu.

[30] An investigation of loans by Toulousan noble families to the province of Languedoc, to the municipality of Toulouse, and to the communities of the diocese of Toulouse reveals relatively small investments in any of these *rentes*. A. D., C-2245, 2249, 359, 1516-1517.

[31] A. D., C-1331-1346; Martin, *Documents relatifs à la vente des biens nationaux*, pp. 147-247, 251-315. Unfortunately series Q (*biens des emigrés*) was almost completely destroyed by fire in 1943. Martin's work does not include the district of Villefranche, an important part of the old civil diocese. The Escouloubre papers demonstrate precisely the process of regrouping. A. D., E-1711, 1752.

this process of adding arpent by arpent that Marc Bloch termed the " reconstitution of the domain." [32]

How were these ever larger estates managed? As indicated in Chapter I, the basic agricultural unit was the *métairie*, a block of 35 to 70 acres of grain land with dependent meadow and woodland assembled about a group of brick and clay

TABLE IV

A COMPARISON OF NOBLE DOMAIN HOLDINGS IN 1750 AND 1790

Noble Family	Surface in Arpents de Toulouse (1.39 acres)		
	1750	1790	Gains (+) or Losses (−)
Marquis de Buisson	361	373	+ 12
Marquis de Beaufort	250	260	+ 10
Noble de Caumels	75	62	− 13
Baron de Pagese	329	306	− 23
Conseiller de Rabaudy	211	268	+ 57
Conseiller de Fieubet	226	232	+ 6
Marquis Varagne-Belesta	343	391	+ 48
M. de Barranguet [a]	120	346	+ 226
Conseiller de Comère	50	66	+ 16
Noble de Martin	259	292	+ 33
Marquis Cassagneau-St.-Félix	135	206	+ 71
Conseiller de Celès	175	200	+ 25
Conseiller de Cambolas	123	144	+ 21
Marquis d'Escouloubre	413	524	+ 111 [b]

Source: A. D., C-1331-1346; Henri Martin, *Documents relatifs à la vente des biens nationaux*, pp. 147-247, 251-315.

[a] The De Barranguet family may not be noble. The particule does not necessarily designate nobility.
[b] This " gain " does not include the 500-arpent seigniory bought by the Marquis d'Escouloubre from the Marquis d'Ossun in 1781.

buildings and worked by one peasant family. These farms were administered under one of three forms: (1) *faire-valoir à maître-valet*, (2) *métayage*, or sharecropping, and (3) *fermage*, or money leaseholds.

The system of *faire-valoir à maître-valet* is by definition direct cultivation by wage labor. A peasant farmer was assigned a farm, a few primitive tools, and a pair of oxen. He was given

[32] Marc Bloch, *Les caractères originaux de l'histoire rurale française* (Paris, 1952), p. 140.

a cottage, garden, salt, and olive oil, plus an annual wage of ten *setiers* (26.4 bushels) of grain (half wheat, half maize) and twelve livres coin.[33] Although this *maître-valet* had a certain prestige among the peasants, and his family had often worked the lord's farm for generations, he was in fact a laborer paid a near-subsistence wage. The entire grain harvest of the farm went to the lord's storage bins. Farms managed in this fashion were usually located in the same community as the principal seigniorial château and often supervised by a salaried steward who acted as the lord's accountant for the entire domain. It should be added, however, that many lords managed these farms personally without the aid of paid stewards.[34] The tax rolls of 1750 indicate that this system was preferred on the principal estate of each noble family in the diocese.[35]

In principle, sharecropping provided that the harvest of a farm was to be divided equally between lord and tenant, the latter providing the tools and livestock. In reality, the shareholding contract became weighted progressively in favor of the lord or master. This was due not only to increasing competition among laborers but also to the concentration of the livestock—the principal farm capital—in the hands of the larger proprietors. The sharecropper had to pay for the use of the farm animals as well as for the use of the land. In 1728 Francois Caseneuve, a tenant of Astre de Blagnac, was obligated under his contract for half the harvest, twenty-four pairs of fowl, all the cartage necessary to carry the farm produce to the Toulouse market, and a *prélèvement* (supplementary rent) of eight *setiers* of wheat. In 1757, in addition to the original rents and services, Caseneuve furnished all the seed, paid the lord for all the forage, worked the vines, tended the

---

[33] Montaugé, *L'agriculture et les classes rurales dans le pays toulousain*, pp. 65-69; L. Dutil, *L'état économique du Languedoc à la fin de l'Ancien Regime, 1750-1789* (Paris, 1911); P. Viguier, *Du colonage partiaire dans le Lauragais* (Paris, 1911). Many *maîtres-valets* received only 8 *setiers* (22 bushels) of grain (half wheat, half maize) and 12 livres coin. A. D., E-641, C-1312-1330.

[34] A. D., C-1312-1330. A steward received between two and three hundred livres annually plus maintenance.

[35] *Ibid.* There is some evidence of the extension of this system in the eighteenth century. The Baron de Lapeyrouse, assuming direction of the family estate in 1774, removed all of the sharecroppers and replaced them with *maîtres-valets* on his nine farms. Picot, Baron de Lapeyrouse, *The Agriculture of a District in the South of France*, p .18.

sheep, and paid half-profit on all livestock sales. Of a flock of eighty sheep, Blagnac owned forty-six and the remaining thirty-four were held jointly. Adding the supplementary rents to the usual fifty-fifty arrangement, the actual division of the harvest on this fifty-arpent farm was close to three fourths for the master and one fourth for the sharecropper.[36]

In another case, the Marquis de Fourquevaux's shepherd at Bordeneuve shared at half-fruits the profits of the Marquis's flock of one hundred sheep. These profits included the proceeds of the wool, milk, meat, and skins. Like most of the Marquis's contracts, the agreement was verbal. After 1763 the Marquis took the entire profit on the wool (about one hundred livres per year) and gave the profits of the milk to the shepherd (about thirty livres per year). The forage costs for the sheep were shared in 1763, but borne entirely by the tenant in 1765. Frequently after 1763 the Marquis kept the entire profit on the sales for slaughter as well as the proceeds on the skins. In 1779 the Marquis hired a new shepherd and added a rent in fowl and eggs to the original obligations of the tenant. Again "half-fruits" was a euphemism. The shareholder was in effect a sort of farm hand paid in kind and constantly in debt to the master.[37]

In general, the recorded sharecrop contracts of the period 1685-1725 stipulated the following obligations of the tenant toward the landlord: (1) half of the cereal and wine harvest, (2) a rent in fowl, (3) half the profits of the livestock, (4) provision of half the seed, and (5) a fixed number of cart trips to market. The tenant had free use of the meadow and part of the woodland. The landlord paid all of the property taxes. By the mid-eighteenth century, however, the contracts had altered. More frequently one finds that the tenant owes additional rents and services such as: (1) provision of *all* the seed, (2) a supplementary rent in cereals, (3) unlimited cartage to market, (4) payment of the harvest costs (one eighth of the

[36] A. D., E-647. Assuming a yield of 100 *setiers* of wheat on this parcel, Caseneuve received 21 *setiers* after deductions and the seigneur received 49 *setiers*, or 71 per cent of the net harvest.

[37] A. D., E-641. The rise of the price of wool from about 34 livres per quintal (107 lb.) in 1760 to 58 livres per quintal in 1786 encouraged the Marquis to sell all of the wool on his own account. These are prices at the markets at Villefranche and Montastruc.

harvest), (5) payment for use of the meadow and wood, and (6) payment of half the property taxes. Other legal provisions were drawn tighter. The sharecropper could not be evicted nor could he leave the farm during the term of the lease (six to nine years). The master, however, could sell or exchange the farm at any time. The tenant and his partners (usually his sons or brothers) were held collectively responsible for the upkeep of the farm capital (buildings, tools, and livestock) and the fulfillment of the above obligations. Finally, estimates were made of the annual revenue of the farm, the landlord thus avoiding any " errors " favorable to the tenant in the division of the grain harvest.[38]

Whether worked by sharecroppers or *maîtres-valets*, the domain farm was purposely kept small enough by the noble proprietor to permit it to be intensively cultivated by one peasant family. Hence a farm of thirty-five to forty acres leased to sharecroppers under the conditions described above left little for the tenant. Indeed, it was sometimes even more profitable for the lord to let his land to sharecroppers than to cultivate it with *maîtres-valets*, the supplementary rents leaving the tenants even less than the wage of a *maître-valet*. In any case, sharecropping in the diocese of Toulouse was in fact a system of direct cultivation in which the sharecropper served the same function and received about the same remuneration as the *maître-valet*. As indicated above, the vast majority of estates in the diocese were administered by either sharecropping or *maîtres-valets* in 1750.[39]

Fermage, leases at money rents, were favored by the larger proprietors on farms separated and at some distance from the principal residence, and by some of the judicial nobility on all or most of their properties. Families such as Varagne-Belesta, Riquet de Bonrepos, Fieubet, and Caulet, with heavy responsibilities either in the municipal government or at the *Parlement*,

[38] A. Not., 82, 90-92, 18083-18117 (1757-1786). These references include twenty-four contracts of *métayage*, ten for the period 1685-1725 and fourteen for the period 1757-1786. Cf. Viguier, *Du colonage partiaire*, for eighteenth-century mutations in sharecropping contracts.

[39] A. D., C-1331-1346. This does not exclude the use of leases at money-rents in a few of the farms at considerable distance from the principal domain—those in a neighboring community, for example. However, even this was rare practice.

preferred a simplified administration and leased their land to a single farmer-general. But the money lease had other advantages besides simplicity of administration. It yielded a fixed money return to balance a year of bad crops on lands directly administered. It avoided losses where the lord's absence made close supervision of the harvest difficult. It placed upon the lessee, a bourgeois, the burden of serving the seigniorial titles and collecting the dues from all the inhabitants of the seigniory.

Moreover, frequent adjustments in the terms of the lease compensated for losses from long-run price rises. This is well illustrated by the money leases of the families Varagne-Belesta and Riquet de Caraman:

TABLE V

MONEY LEASES OF THE FAMILIES VARAGNE-BELESTA AND RIQUET DE CARAMAN

M. de Varagne-Belesta, Marquis de Gardouch (781 arpents, 1773)			M. de Riquet de Caraman, Comte de Caraman (170 arpents, 1771)		
Leases	Years	Annual Rents in Money	Leases	Years	Annual Rents in Money
1747-56	9	11,000 livres	1722-24	3	2450 livres
1756-65	9	16,000	1725-31	6	2450
1773-79	6	26,298	1742-48	6	3500
1780-86	6	26,169	1748-54	6	3800
1786-92	6	28,300	1755-61	6	3800
1792-93	1	26,844	1761-67	6	4000
1796-1802	6	Wheat: 2010 setiers Coin: 1500 livres	1777-83	6	6680

Source: A. D., Gardouch, 973, 1002; A. Not., Reg. 18063, 18066, 18073, 18117; A. D., E-1461 (Caraman).

Thus, the Marquis de Gardouch and the Comte de Caraman more than doubled their money rents in the last half of the century. Nor do these figures reveal the complete picture. After 1748 the tenant at Caraman paid the *taille* on the Comte's land, and after 1777 he paid all of the taxes without exception. On both properties the woodland, the *lods et ventes* (mutation fees) and the right of option were explicitly reserved for the lord. At Gardouch the Marquis's lessee paid over three hundred *setiers* (825 bushels) of oats as a suppemlentary rent in kind after 1773. Supplementary rents in fowl were added in the later leases on both properties, as well as transport service and more tree plantings.[40]

It is interesting to observe that in these two cases the money rents alone rose more than twice as fast as grain prices in the same period (that is, a 150 per cent increase in rents as against a 67 per cent increase in grain prices). Perhaps an increase in domain area accounts for part of the rent increase. But it is also probable that the lessee, much like the sharecropper, lost some of his profits with each new lease. Unless he squeezed more profits out of the land, the lessee risked being reduced to a sort of steward paid in kind.[41]

Hence, by the wide practice of direct cultivation by *maître-valet* and by progressive changes in sharecrop and money leaseholds, the noble proprietor increased his income. The sharecropper was reduced to a position little different from that of the wage tenant; both types of peasants delivered the bulk of the grain harvest to the lord's storage bins. In the case of money leases, the noble proprietor exacted fresh rents and services at each new lease, while avoiding the burdens of direct administration and the risks of seasonal crop failures. Judici-

---

[40] A. D., Gardouch, 973 ,1002; A. Not., 18063, 18066, 18073, 18117; A. D., E-1461 (Caraman).

[41] Whether the 150 per cent increase in rent actually reduced the tenant's profit depends on the ratio of total income to rent. For example, if the ratio of income to rent were 3:1, the tenant would show an increase in profit between 1745 and 1785. If the ratio were 2:1, however, he would show a decrease of profit. Consider the following models:

A.		1745			1785	
	Total Income	300	+ 67%		500	(Increase in wheat price)
	Rent	100	+ 150%		250	(Increase in rents)
	Profit	200			250	(25 per cent increase in profit)

B.		1745			1785	
	Total Income	200	+ 67%		334	
	Rent	100	+ 150%		250	
	Profit	100			84	(16 per cent decrease)

Given the size of the estates under examination, the second model would come closer to the facts. It is doubtful that the ratio of income to rent on these two estates could be even as high as 2:1 in 1745. Hence, a progressive diminution of profit seems very probable.

ously mixed, these three forms of domain management complemented one another and offered the lord the double advantage of inflationary profits and assured returns.

What was the role of the *gentilhomme-campagnard* in the augmentation of agricultural productivity? If the role of the English nobility in agriculture is sometimes exaggerated, the role of the French nobility is too often depreciated. To be sure, eighteenth-century Toulousan agriculture remained definitely behind the English standard with regard to crop rotation, suppression of the fallow, plantings of forage crops, and improvement of the livestock. Nevertheless, one must be careful not to judge French progress in this field exclusively by Arthur Young's yardstick.

Despite prodigious government propaganda on the eve of the Revolution, the famous English forage crops—clover, cabbages, and turnips—were scarcely known in the Toulouse area. But the noble proprietors had made successful experiments with their own variety of forage crop, the black vetch, a bean plant particularly resistant to dry heat. The Marquis d'Escouloubre used this hardy forage to great advantage on his fallows at Vieillevigne and Montesquieu-Lauragais. Indeed it appears that in the latter community the families Dupuy-Montesquieu, Rolland de Saint-Rome, Avessens, Decars, and Dalvignier had followed Escouloubre's example by 1785.[42] The Baron de Lapeyrouse and the Comte de Villèle at Mourvilles had equal success with artificial meadows. The consuls of Mourvilles-Basses gave unqualified praise to their lord in a report to the subdelegate of Toulouse: "We consuls must defer to M. de Villèle, who has used forage crops with success on his lands, which embrace two-thirds of our territory. This lord, who has so well practised his theory of agriculture, has been an inspiration to his tenants. . . ."[43]

Without question the nobility had begun experiments with new forage crops, planted on the fallow and serving the dual purpose of providing good fodder for the livestock while reconstituting the soil. But to what extent had the pioneer efforts of Escouloubre or Villèle been generalized? The subdelegate

[42] A. D., C-109, "Responses of the Communities on the State of the Forage," January 1786, Vieillevigne and Montesquieu-Lauragais.
[43] *Ibid.*, "Response of Mourvilles-Basses."

of the diocese in 1786 observed that " the rich proprietors, following the example of Villèle, will turn all their attention toward the establishment of artificial meadows," but he admitted that the poor cultivator had neither the patience nor the resources to wait three years for a good yield of forage, foregoing wheat in the meantime.[44] According to a diocesan inquiry, only 6 communities out of 134 were definitely using artificial meadows with success in 1786.[45]

Must we conclude, then, that the vast majority of noble estates were hopelessly attached to the biennial system—alternate wheat and fallow—and that only half the arable land was productive each year? The answer is no. The cultivation of maize or Indian corn had been introduced in the *Midi* in the late sixteenth century. Admirably suited to the semitropical climate of Haut-Languedoc, this four-month crop doubled cereal production in the eighteenth century and gave the Midi its reputation as one of the richest farm areas of France. The tax rolls of 1750 demonstrate clearly that maize was planted on the fallow. To be sure, the crop division was not uniform. In the majority of cases wheat occupied 45 to 50 per cent of the arable soil, maize and *fèves* (French beans) another 20 per cent, and the fallow the remaining 30 to 35 per cent.[46] A sort of transitional stage between triennial and biennial crop rotation had been effected.[47] The system was generalized especially on noble lands worked by wage tenants and on many shareholds where the " three labors " clause stipulating the rotation of wheat, maize, and fallow was inserted in the sharecropping contract.

Thus, if the Toulousan nobles had barely begun to use artificial meadows, they were already practicing a primitive form of triennial crop rotation. Maize had many advantages. It not only furnished a hardy forage crop for the farm animals but also formed the base of the peasant diet in the Lauragais, the richest part of the diocese. In this way, the money crop, wheat, could be reserved almost exclusively for the market. In

[44] *Ibid.*, Subdelegate to the Intendant, January 11, 1786.
[45] *Ibid.*, " Responses of the Communities."
[46] A. D., C-1312-1330.
[47] P. Féral, " L'introduction de l'assolement triennal en Gascogne," *Annales du Midi*, LXII (1950), pp. 249-258.

the drought of 1785 it was the maize that saved the livestock from mass starvation. Its yield per acre was from two to three times that of wheat. Its roots reached deeper than those of wheat, tending to rest the surface and clean the soil in general. On the other hand, if the soil was not heavily fertilized, maize fatigued it as much as wheat. This fact, however, was not known by contemporary agronomists, Young included.[48]

With regard to irrigation, Arthur Young was much more favorably impressed. Passing through the region of Toulouse, he observed that " irrigation is practised extensively and with great success." [49] In fact, the Marquis de Fourquevaux had diked his trenches, irrigated his natural meadows, and increased his yields of hay and alfalfa. M. de Riquet at Preserville had done the same.[50] The Marquis d'Escouloubre planned an artificial rivulet at Vieillevigne to tap water from the Canal du Midi.[51] The Comte de Tersac assumed all the responsibility for digging a new well at St.-Martin Doides during the drought of 1785. His sudden death threw the town consuls into confusion and halted the work.[52] The Marquis de Bertier built extensive dikes and levees along the left bank of the Ariège River, more for flood control than irrigation. This work diverted the river toward the opposite bank and provoked Noble de Martin to build similar levees at Lacroix-Falgarde.[53] Again, the sharecropping contracts tended to generalize this work with precise provisions for trenching and draining. Irrigation projects were encouraged by the myriad of streamlets and small rivers that flow into the Garonne and Ariège rivers in the region of Toulouse, and many were financed through the Provincial Estates.

Finally, clearings were given special encouragement by the Royal Declarations of July 5, 1776 and August 13, 1766. *Entrepreneurs de défrichements* were accorded exemption from

[48] In 1787 Young and Parmentier discussed the question of the effects of maize on the soil without reaching any definite conclusion. Young, *Voyages en France*, III, p. 1146.

[49] *Ibid.*, II, p. 643. Annual rainfall in the area of Toulouse varies from 20 to 40 inches.

[50] A. D., C-109, " Response of Lanta."

[51] A. D., E-1752.

[52] A. D., C-109, " Response of Saint-Martin-Doides."

[53] A. D., C-1320, " Lacroix-Falgarde "; C-1326, " Pinsaguel."

dîmes, tailles, vingtièmes, and other royal taxes for fifteen years on all lands cleared.[54] In 1773 the subdelegate of Toulouse began to submit résumés of the clearings accomplished in his diocese. According to these reports, 9,645 *arpents de Toulouse* had been cleared between 1773 and 1778, or over 1,900 arpents per year. This figure seems exaggerated since the more detailed reports from 1778 to 1787 indicate an average of only 305 arpents per year. Indeed, all these figures are far from exact. For example, in 114 communities listed for 1784, the subdelegate reported about 5,000 arpents still uncleared; a year later, for 82 communities, he reported 7,680 arpents still uncleared. Given the fact that most of the consuls in the village communities were illiterate, the inaccuracy of the subdelegate's reports is not surprising.[55]

Nevertheless, it is certain that progress in clearings had been made, and that the noble proprietor was among the most active entrepreneurs. The names of De Breuys, Saint Martin, Belesta, Assézat, Villèle, Gavarret, Bellegarde appear often on the lists of proprietors engaged in clearings. Escouloubre cleared less than an acre per year working alone at Vieillevigne; by contrast, at Montesquieu-Lauragais, thirty-two proprietors cleared about one hundred arpents in five years. The Marquis de Gavarret, with the assistance of his son and thirty-eight peasants, cleared twenty-four arpents at Tournefeuille in 1778. There was hardly a seigniory in the diocese that did not register the clearing of at least one to four arpents each year after 1778.[56] Since only 1 per cent of the land in the diocese was in commons, the clearings were made on wood and waste belonging to the larger proprietors, that is, the nobles, and it was they who were their chief beneficiaries.

There were, however, absolute limits to these clearings. The complaint of the consuls of Lanta in 1785 was revealing. " If these clearings are continued," they protested, " soon there will be neither hay nor pasture." [57] The reports of the subdelegate on forage for 1785 indicated that all the land was under culti-

[54] Isambert *et al., Recueil général des anciennes lois françaises depuis l'an 420 jusqu'à la Révolution de 1789* (32 vols.; Paris, 1822-1828), XXII, pp. 461-463.
[55] A. D., C-108.
[56] *Ibid.*
[57] A. D., C-109, " Response of Lanta."

vation at Vieillevigne, Saint-Rome, Saint-Jory, Pinsaguel, Cépet, Labastide-Saint-Sernin, Saint-Sauveur, and that pasture was scarce in most of the other communities of the diocese. Clearings were often made on waste that served as pasture for the small proprietor's livestock and hence accelerated a century-long decay of communal rights in the region.[58] Moreover the increasing shortage of firewood added a second argument against clearings. The city of Toulouse in particular had ever greater difficulties procuring enough wood for winter heating. Consequently, protest was heavy against clearing of woodland. Finally, since most of the diocese was already well cultivated, the new lands cleared were marginal, often of insufficient quality to receive grains with profit. Hence much of the cleared land was put into vines, already overproduced and of secondary value in the eyes of the royal government. Therefore, in 1786 the subdelegate prohibited clearings on lands deemed absolutely necessary for pasture and wood in each community. This greatly reduced the area available for further clearings. Of eighty-one communities, the subdelegate estimated that only six contained more than sixty arpents that could be cleared without danger to pasture and woodland.[59]

The " seigniorial reaction " has often been identified with the increased collection of dues and the appropriation by the local lord of common meadowland. In the region of Toulouse it was much more than that. The eighteenth century witnessed an adaptation of the landed estate to the demands of an expanding market, an adaptation carried out in large part by a new administration of the domain. The success of this effort was measured by enlarged estates, reduced costs, and increasing revenues on the eve of the Revolution. Systematically applied by a class of active and shrewd noble proprietors, a mixture of administrative techniques, both seigniorial and bourgeois, were particularly effective in the years after 1750. Moreover, this agricultural enterprise was not restricted to the administration of the domain. It also included serious attention to the grain trade and abolition of communal rights.

---

[58] Emile Appolis, " La question de la vaine pâture en Languedoc au XVIIIe siècle," *Annales historiques de la Révolution française*, X (1938), pp. 97-132.
[59] A. D., C-108.

CHAPTER III

THE NOBLE AS LANDLORD: THE GRAIN TRADE, THE ABOLITION OF COMMUNAL RIGHTS, THE CONCENTRATION OF LIVESTOCK

I

The transition from a self-sufficient to a market economy in grain was a slow one. Even under the new pressure of population, the local community only begrudgingly and gradually released its grain surpluses to the growing urban market. The small peasant proprietor in particular was unwilling to risk the slim surplus of one year against the chance of a bad harvest the next. But as the price for wheat and maize rose sharply, despite violent seasonal fluctuations, the large landholders who could more safely muster a surplus beyond their household consumption, found it increasingly profitable to transport their wheat to market. These were the owners of the overloaded wagons harnessed to three enormous work-horses, laden with 18 to 20 setiers (48 to 53 bushels) of wheat that rumbled to Porte Saint Sulpice at Toulouse or to any of the local markets—Villefranche, Basiège, Verfeil, Montastruc—in growing numbers as the century drew to a close.

Increased marketing of grain went hand in hand with improved communication, and it is not surprising that the province of Languedoc underwent an accelerated building of roads and canals in the last half of the century. This construction was championed by the entire complex of local assemblies—provincial, diocesan, and communal—whose members planned and financed new and better routes. The province of Languedoc was justifiably proud of what Arthur Young termed its " magnificent bridges," " superb causeways," and " remarkable routes." To be sure, the secondary roads fell somewhat below the high standard set by the post-roads built and maintained by the Provincial Estates. Neverthless, even on the local level, considerable progress had been made.

In the first fifty years of the eighteenth century, the diocese of Toulouse had spent 1200 livres annually for road repair. In 1765 it was spending 40,000 livres, in 1782, 127,000, and in 1786, 198,000 livres annually for road development. Diocesan indebtedness for roads alone rose to 1,885,000 livres by 1787.[1] At the meeting of the diocesan assembly in 1770 it was decided to have four roads continually under construction, and from 1771 to 1790 ten new routes were projected, and work begun. By the end of the century, the diocese was laced with a network of paved roads, 24 feet wide and bordered by neat rows of elm trees. In addition to the excellent royal route from Montauban to Montpellier which traversed the diocese, two paved roads radiated south from Toulouse along the Garonne and Ariège Rivers toward Luchon and Tarascon-sur-Ariège; two others led northeast to Albi and east to Castres in the Cévennes; and still another reached westward toward Auch in Gascony. All of these routes were built between 1750 and the Revolution and all, with the exception of the royal route, were financed by the diocese on the initiative of the diocesan assembly.[2]

Far from neglecting internal improvements, the diocesan assembly had pushed its program so far that the tax-burdened communities protested. The service charges alone on the diocesan debt for public works reached almost 100,000 livres by 1787, a burden of over 20 livres per inhabitant. In February of 1788 the communities of the diocese in an extra-legal assembly, led by the Third Estate, demanded a halt to what they called, " a tendency to achieve the total ruin of the diocese by loans and expenditures arising from expenses regarding the roads, and the habit of turning these funds from their true destination . . ."[3] In 1789, the *cahier* of St. Jory protested

---

[1] In Languedoc as a whole, 9,789,000 livres were borrowed for roads alone in the last 35 years of the Ancien Regime. Two-thirds of this sum was spent after 1781, evidence of the accelerated building program.

[2] L. Dutil, *L'etat économique du Languedoc à la fin de l'ancien régime* (1750-1789) (Paris, 1911), pp. 653-668; J. Coppolani, *Toulouse, Etude de géographie urbaine* (Toulouse, 1954), p. 75.

[3] A. D. C-970, " Déliberation à prendre avant l'Assemblée de l'Assiette par toutes les communautés du Diocèse de Toulouse pour concourir efficacement à arrêter le cours des emprunts et des autres abus qui sont à la veille d'opérer sa ruine totale." February, 1788.

that the new roads served only the local landlord and were "useless to the mass of the inhabitants."[4]

No doubt the larger proprietors were the chief beneficiaries of the road building program. But despite the protests of the communities in 1788, there was no reduction of the diocesan budget for public works. In the same year, the diocesan assembly voted additional loans of 124,000 livres for work on seven separate roads.[5] Although the assembly avowed that the Third Estate was fully represented in its councils, the diocesan body was in fact dominated by the First and Second Estates. Officially, the assembly was composed of a vicar-general, a royal commissioner, three barons of the diocese (de Crêté, Saint Felix, and Lanta), and 24 deputies of the 12 chief towns of the diocese. The deputies were in fact the mayors and consuls of the towns chosen by and even represented by the chief landlord in each community. The names of the deputies leave no doubt that the gentlemen controlled a majority of the assembly and of the chairmanships of all the principal commissions.[6] There seems no question that the local nobility was in an excellent position to combine a civic interest in public improvements with a natural desire to transport its grain to market.

The new routes permitted regular postal and commercial communication between Toulouse and the principal localities within a radius of 60 to 90 miles from the city and thus helped rationalize the Toulousan grain market. Whereas before 1750 only a few merchants controlled the movement of grain to the city, this new network of paved roads permitted a greater number of grain sellers to compete in the wholesale market. It tended to replace the small grain brokers (the *blatiers*) and their limited mule-back supplies with large wagonloads of grain from the Lauragais and even from outside the diocese.[7] Whether more regular communication acted as a brake on increasing bread prices or simply reduced the number of intermediaries and increased the margin of profit for the grain producer is difficult to ascertain. The continued rise in bread prices through-

---

[4] Jean Contrasty, *Histoire de Saint-Jory, ancienne seigneurie féodale érigée en baronnie par Henry IV* (Toulouse, 1922), pp. 217-223.

[5] A. D. C-970, "Procès verbaux de l'Assiette du Diocèse, 1788."

[6] A. D. C-962, 968-970, "Procès verbaux de l'Assiette du Diocèse, 1766, 1787, 1788." These reports of proceedings include a list of the members.

[7] Coppolani, *op. cit.*, p. 77.

out this period, however, and the sums received by local land-lords for their harvests would suggest the second alternative.[8]

The Garonne River was one of the principal arteries of river transport in the *Midi*, handling much more traffic in the eighteenth than in the nineteenth century. Navigation by river boat began some 30 miles south of Toulouse at Cazères. Each year, about 1,600 four-man boats plied their way from this landing to the provincial capital, laden with wool from Spain, wood, stone, and plaster from the Pyrenees, and grain and fruit from the local countryside. North of Toulouse, navigation was seriously hindered by more than 90 water mills before reaching Bordeaux and at least 18 dangerous shoals between the capital and the mouth of the river Tarn, a distance of some 60 miles. Ordinarily it took six to eight days to go from Toulouse to Bordeaux by river boat, pulled by 12 to 15 men. Freight costs and tolls totalled 600 livres for every 30,000 livres of merchandise. The principal items of this trade were cereals, wine, wood, coal, indigo, coffee, sugar, brandy, salted fish, and tobacco. In the late century, an estimated 1800 small boats annually negotiated the tortuous course of the Garonne north of Toulouse.[9]

More efficient water transport was via the *Canal du Midi*, pride of the Province. In 1787 Arthur Young called this water-way linking Toulouse with the Mediterranean " the most beauti-ful thing he had seen in France." The canal was designed and built by Pierre-Paul Riquet in the third quarter of the seven-teenth century and was held as a seigniory by his noble de-scendants until the Revolution.[10] The *Canal du Midi* was supplemented and improved by a new junction with Narbonne, sponsored by the Marquis de Crillon in 1776, and by the *Canal de Brienne* built at Toulouse to circumvent the *Moulin du*

[8] Cf. Viala, I., *La question des grains et de leur commerce à Toulouse au 18me siècle (1715-1789)* (Toulouse, 1909), pp. 110-118; A. D., 6-J, A-35; Villèle Papers.

[9] Dutil, *op. cit.*, pp. 687-699.

[10] The 28 canal shares were held by the Riquet family until the death of Alexandre Riquet de Bonrepos in 1791. At the time of their division among Riquet de Bonrepos's three daughters, these shares yielded an annual dividend of 448,346 livres, making the Riquet family, without question, the richest noble family in the *Midi*. Archives Municipales, Toulouse, Serie G²-42, " Cambon-Riquet." These are the " Forced Loans " levied by the Convention and provide an income statement by all " citizens " of Toulouse in 1793.

Château which blocked the Garonne. In 1786, the King, the city of Carcassonne, and the Riquet family subscribed 115,000 livres to rectify the entire canal course.[11]

Merchandise was transported by horse-drawn barge from Toulouse to Agde or Sète on the Mediterranean, a distance of about 150 miles in 7 days and at the modest cost of 2 livres per *quintal* (110.25 lbs.) in 1750. The barges were 60 feet long, 15 feet wide, and 6 feet deep and could carry 880 to 2000 *quintaux* (110.25 tons) of freight, or twenty times the capacity of the average Garonne River boat. In 1780 there were 170 of these canal craft transporting fish, tobacco, coffee, and sugar from Bordeaux and the West Indies and, above all, grain from the region of Toulouse to Bas-Languedoc and overseas. Significantly, two-thirds of the canal revenues came from the grain trade. Moreover, the return trip brought only 40% of the volume exported southeastward and included no grain—evidence that Toulouse was a center of cereal export. The categories of goods imported indicate the scope of trade made possible by the canal. They included woolens and cottons from Bas-Languedoc, olive oil and wood from Provence, wines from Spain, oranges from Italy, and spices and drugs from the Levant and the Barbary Coast. Canal commerce was evaluated at 652,796 livres, average for the decade 1750-1758, and at 975,282 livres, average for the decade 1780-1788, an increase of 50% in 30 years.[12]

If an improved road system made Toulouse and the local market towns more accessible to the grain producers of the Lauragais, the perfection of the river and canal system opened the possibility of profitable marketing outside of Haut-Languedoc and even outside of the province. Between 1745 and 1768, the value of the grain trade outside of Languedoc rose from six to sixteen million livres.[13] It was not coincidental that this opportunity for an expanded market was joined by a new economic philosophy.

Association of the physiocratic movement with such vague

[11] Dutil, *op. cit.*, p. 700.

[12] *Ibid.* p. 700 ff. It will be recalled, however, that grain prices rose 60% in the same period, so that this increase in the valuation of canal commerce may represent little if any increase in trade volume.

[13] Viala, *op .cit.*, pp. 36-37.

terms as the Enlightenment, has sometimes disguised the fact that Physiocracy was the large proprietor's economic philosophy *par excellence.* The Physiocratic School preached not only that land was the unique source of all wealth, but also that free trade in grain was the best way of increasing farm production under the stimulus of the *bon prix.* And the *bon prix,* in a period of accelerated population increase and of imperfect competition between provincial producers in the interior of France was almost always a high price. Hence, the Toulousan nobility was assisted in its search for a good market by the rapid increase in the local population, by improved communication, and by a new doctrine that proclaimed free grain export outside of the province and even outside of the kingdom.[14]

The Toulousan nobles had many vantage points from which to affirm their sincere adherence to new ideas. The Estates of Languedoc, the Parlement of Toulouse, the diocesan assemblies, the Chamber of Commerce at Toulouse lost no occasion to issue declarations on the " universal benefits of free trade." In 1761 the Estates assembled at Montpellier proclaimed that " the most assured means to animate agriculture is the free exportation of grain, not only from one province to another but also overseas." [15] Not satisfied with the liberal export provisions of the Edict of July, 1764, the Estates proposed automatic renewal of free trade if the price of grain fell below 12 livres, 10 sous per *quintal.*[16]

The years after 1760 brought successes to this campaign. Thanks to physiocratic-minded controller-generals such as Bertin and Turgot, the Monarchy legislated long periods of free trade in grain. From 1763 to 1770, 1774 to 1777, and from 1787 to 1788, national policy favored the *bon prix* and the grain

[14] To be sure, physiocratic ideas with regard to the land tax, the so-called *subvention territoriale,* were received less enthusiastically by the local nobility. Nevertheless, the nobility of Languedoc risked much less than their confrères in the North. The *taille* was *réelle* in Languedoc, and the tax rolls leave no doubt that the Toulousan gentlemen paid property taxes, in some cases as much as one-fourth of their gross landed income. Those who had " noble land," however, were exempt from the *taille,* though not from the 20th tax (the *vingtième*) on landed income. Cf. Chapter I *supra.*

[15] A. D. C-2404. " Procès verbaux de la séance des Etats de Languedoc," October-December, 1761.

[16] *Ibid.,* C-2411. Séance de Novembre, 1768-Janvier, 1769.

producer.[17] Even the Intendant, the Vicomte Saint Priest, had a penchant toward free trade. He wrote in 1758:

I believe that the interior trade must be kept completely free, and that one must simply demand declarations for certificates of release from those merchants who export their grain to Roussillon, Rouergue, and Dauphiné.[18]

In addition to the relaxation of export controls, the abolition of local river and market tolls facilitated the marketing operations of the grain producer. Even before Physiocracy was current ideological coin, the opportunity to float merchandise on the *Canal du Midi* free of all local tolls had diverted a large portion of the grain trade from the seigniorial toll collectors. Local rulings of the Parlement had suppressed these tolls one by one throughout the eighteenth century. The national legislation of Turgot in 1774, freeing the grain trade of all internal customs, merely legalized the atrophy of such tolls in the Toulouse area. The Councilor d'Assézat, seigneur of Venergue, reflected the position of many of the local seigneurs in a letter to the Royal Government in 1750:

I feel the full value of the courtesy with which you honor me by kindly notifying me of the significance of the *Arrêt du Conseil* bearing on the suppression of certain toll rights on the Ariège River which neither I nor my father, nor my ancestors for more than a hundred years have ever enjoyed. Thus, it is nothing more than the suppression of a chimera which had no sort of reality nor existence whatever . . .[19]

There were, however, a number of negligent proprietors who clung to their market tolls into the late eighteenth century. These became the object of more systematic suppression after

[17] Viala, *op. cit.*, pp. 15-23. The Edict of July, 1764 provided for unconditional free trade in grain within the kingdom and free trade overseas until the price of wheat reached 12 livres, 10 sous per *quintal*. The edict was renewed in 1776, although Turgot permitted free interior trade in 1774. After 1777 Necker instituted a pragmatic control policy based on the estimates of the annual harvest. This policy was formed largely as a reflex to increasing numbers of seasonal crisis and was continued, except for a brief interval in 1787-88, until 1789.

[18] A. D. C-116, Intendant to the Subdelegate of Toulouse, December 17, 1758. It is true that the Intendant became less dogmatic after the disastrous crop years of 1771, 1777, and 1781.

[19] J. R. de Fortanier, *Les droits seigneuriaux dans la Sénéchaussée de Lauragais* (*1553-1789*) (Toulouse, 1932), p. 385. Letter of August 12, 1750.

1750. Among the more stubborn seigniorial toll collectors were the local communities who depended heavily on such revenues.[20] The community of Villefranche-Lauragais, whose revenues from market tolls were 900 livres in 1775, fought a prolonged but losing battle against the Treasury Court (*Cour des Aides*) despite a claim based on letters-patent of Francis I. The market towns of Verfeil and Basiège lost their toll privileges of 1 sol per setier of wheat in the same year.[21] At Montrastruc, the Comte de Clarac collected " rights of measure " as late as 1786, aided by his rights of High Justice and the loyal services of the town's archpriest. But, after numerous law cases, appeals, and reversals of judgment, the count finally lost his toll rights.[22] In 1777 there were only five communities that still levied market tolls in the diocese, and by the end of the Ancien Regime only the river tolls at Blagnac, Clermont, Lacroix-Falgarde, and Portet on the Garonne and Ariège Rivers were still collected by the local seigneurs.[23] The abolition of the market tolls on grain undoubtedly stimulated an increase in market fairs, the number of which rose from 120 in 1720 to 180 in 1789.[24]

How was the grain actually gathered from the estates in the Lauragais and sold? French agricultural marketing has won a reputation for its army of intermediaries. The grain trade during the Ancien Regime was no exception. Every summer and fall, the countryside about Toulouse swarmed with the famous grain brokers (*blatiers*), who purchased from the proprietors on the spot in small quantities, often setier by setier. The broker sold in turn to the less numerous commission-

[20] The abolition of communal market tolls served the local landlord in a double sense. It lowered his marketing costs and at the same time lessened the independent influence of the village consuls by weakening community finances.

[21] A. D. C-117. " Concernant les droits sur les grains perçus dans les halles et marchés par les seigneurs," 1775-1777.

[22] *Ibid.* " Suspension des droits d'étalage de mesurage que le comte de Clarac percevait sur les grains vendus à Montastruc "; " Arrêt du Conseil, 1773, executé fevrier, 1786."

[23] Fortanier, *op. cit.*, pp. 384-385; Théron de Montaugé, *L'agriculture et les classes rurales dans le pays toulousain depuis le milieu du 18ᵐᵉ siècle* (Paris, 1869), p. 56. Between 1740 and 1750 the seigniorial tolls were definitively abolished at Auriac, Basiège, Gardouch, Montégut, Montgeard, Venergue, Casselles, Esquelles, Foutens, and Beauville.

[24] Montaugé, *op. cit.*, pp. 55-56.

merchants, the commission-merchants to the merchants and exporters, and these finally to the millers and bakers. The noble
proprietors preferred hard money and it was the commission-
agent who generally supplied the broker with credit. This was
the traditional system of marketing.[25]

Was the noble proprietor, then, relegated to a passive role
in the grain trade? If the broker system was well-geared to
amass the grain surpluses of the small independent proprietor,
it was unsuited for the average Toulousan *gentilhomme-campagnard* of 1750 who had about 250 setiers of negotiable wheat
to market each year. It was to the latter's advantage to avoid
the broker, sell directly to the commission-merchant at the town
market, in bulk, and at the seasonal price high.

The papers of individual families indicate that this type of
marketing was preferred among the Toulousan nobility. In
1751 the Marquis de Bertier sold 100 setiers of wheat in bulk
at the seasonal high of 16 livres per setier—an excellent price
for that year.[26] The Comte de Villèle sold between 600 and
900 setiers per year from his estate at Mourvilles, always at the
seasonal high.[27] The Marquis de Fourquevaux's day to day
accounts for four farms indicate small sales of maize and
vegetables but practically no sales of wheat, suggesting that the
money crop was sold on a separate account, probably *en bloc*.
The small quantities registered were sold at the market at Montgiscard.[28] The Marquis de Gardouch always required a certifi-
cate of sale " at the market " and " especially for grains " from
his steward.[29] Add to these individual examples the fact that
almost all the sharecropping contracts specifically provided for
cartage of farm produce to the market, and it appears conclusive
that the noble proprietor after 1750 did not sell in small quantities to brokers but in large quantities at the local market.[30]

The storage facilities of the larger proprietors gave them

[25] Viala, *op. cit.*, p. 39 f. This is the system described by A. P. Usher,
History of the Grain Trade in France, 1400-1710 (Cambridge, 1933). Usher's
work terminates in 1710, however.
[26] A. D., 6-J, A-35.
[27] Villèle Papers. Thanks to M. Fourcassié, Villèle's biographer, I was able
to look at the comte's rough accounts, 1808-1813. (uncatalogued).
[28] A. D. E-641.
[29] Gardouch, 1009.
[30] A. D. E-647; Archives Notariales, Registers 18083-18117.

the added advantage of awaiting the highest price of the season, or even of several seasons. In 1759 the provincial government ordered an inventory of all the grain warehouses in the diocese of Toulouse in an effort to check "individuals who are not customarily in this commerce and who are suspected of having stocked grain to obtain illicit profits." [31] The subsequent inquest revealed 7,100 setiers of grain in the hands of bourgeois exporters, 8,550 setiers in the hands of Toulousan merchants, only 2,200 setiers in the hands of the grain brokers, 8000 setiers "in the hands of diverse individuals coming from their harvests," and 20,000 setiers in the countryside about the city, also "in the hands of diverse individuals." [32] In short, in January, 1759, five months after the harvest, 62% of the stored grain was in the hands of local proprietors, the bulk of whom were noblemen. In January, 1789, a similar inquiry revealed that 12,000 setiers of grain, one-fourth of the total stored in the city of Toulouse at that moment, was owned by M. Bermont du Loris de Dumay, a nobleman. How many of the other individuals listed on the inventory were agents of local gentlemen, is impossible to ascertain. [33]

Many noble proprietors, not content with speculating in their own grain, speculated with grain of others as well. In the crisis year of 1781, when grain prices at Toulouse rose from 10 livres to 15 livres, 10 sous in one month, the Subdelegate of Toulouse received an anonymous letter which he dispatched to the Intendant. One passage read:

The major part of the grain stock is now [July] in the hands of the wholesale merchants, the speculators, the rich landed proprietors, and the well-to-do who have placed their money in grain at a time when it was cheap in order to market it (s'en défaire) at a favorable moment such as now. [34]

The same letter warned that the small cultivator, unable to amass a surplus, would be forced to begin buying seed in October and November, possibly at 20 livres per setier.

Some of the *Capitouls*, nobility of very recent origin to be

[31] A. D. C-116, Intendant to Subdelegate, January 7, 1759.
[32] *Ibid.* "Etat des bleds, mistures, et féves dans les magazins du Canal avec les noms des propriétaires," January 20, 1759.
[33] A. D. C-118, Subdelegate to Intendant, January 14, 1789.
[34] *Ibid.* Subdelegate to Intendant, July 27, 1781.

sure, were actively engaged in grain speculation. In the same crisis year, Noble Fager and Noble Salruquet sent their agents to Lavaur and Albi where no one knew of the price increase at Toulouse, purchased four to 5,000 setiers of wheat at 11 livres, 5 sous and resold it at Toulouse at 15 livres per setier.[35] A letter of the Subdelegate later in the same year confirmed the unique position of the larger proprietor of grain land. He observed that only the large holders could risk suspension of sale of grains reserved from previous harvests. The mediocre holders needed this grain for their immediate needs, such as household consumption, seed, and taxes.[36] In brief, the noble proprietor of the Lauragais was in an excellent position to make what is commonly known as a " *très bonne affaire.*"

Whatever be the twentieth century opinion of such speculation, the provincial administration of the eighteenth century exhibited a sympathetic mind. In 1758 the Intendant stated that he did not view badly the establishment of warehouses for grain, provided they were known to the government, because they provided " a prompt and sure resource when the markets were insufficiently provisioned." [37] At the height of the seasonal crisis of 1781, the Subdelegate Ginesty elaborated the classic defense of the speculator. He maintained that the speculator provided a ready supply at the critical moment of shortage; he must always " eventually sell "; buying cheap and selling dear was no crime; strong government action would not only " excite the avidity of the landholder," but also alarm the consumer and raise prices still further.[38] In government circles at least the function of the speculator appeared necessary and even desirable.

Thus, by improved means of land and water communication and by a new doctrine of " free trade " in grain, the landlords of the Lauragais expanded their market, reduced middleman costs, and perfected the technique of timely sales of large quantities of stored grain.

[35] *Ibid.*
[36] *Ibid.* Subdelegate to Intendant, September 5, 1781.
[37] A. D. C-116, Intendant to Subdelegate, December 3, 1758.
[38] A. D. C-118, Subdelegate to Intendant, September 5, 1781. No doubt in a period when distribution was most imperfect and the supply only vaguely known, rumor and panic played an exaggerated and independent role in price variation.

II

The diocesan and provincial administration also fostered agrarian individualism with regard to communal rights. In Languedoc, there were two traditional communal rights of pasturage: (1) the right of use by all members of the community of the common meadow, and (2) the right to pasture livestock in the fallow field, wasteland, wood, and meadow of individual proprietors, the so-called vacant pasture.[39]

In the diocese of Toulouse, only 1% of the land was held by the communities in 1750, and most of this was leased at money rents to individuals. The largest town common in the diocese was at Basiège and covered only 39 arpents (55.6 acres). The common at Toulouse, serving thousands of inhabitants, was only 21 arpents (29.4 acres). Many communities such as Auzielle, Quint, and Montariol had less than one acre of common. In some cases, the common existed only in theory, since the local seigneurs had converted the common pasturage into farms for wheat raising. Such usurpations by the seigneurs had taken place at Seyre, Gragnague, and Gargas near the end of the century.[40] In short, the amount of common meadow in the diocese was negligible.

Hence, it was primarily toward the right of vacant pasture on private properties that the local governing bodies of Toulouse turned their attention. The offensive against this right in Languedoc had been initiated early in the eighteenth century by the local communities themselves, represented by their town councils. This anomaly is explained by the fact that almost without exception, the town councils were composed of the most important landholders of each community.[41] These indi-

[39] The problem of the *vaine pâture* or *compascuité* is treated for the entire kingdom by Marc Bloch, " La lutte pour l'individualisme agraire dans la France du XVIIIe siècle," *Annales d'histoire économique et sociale*, 1930, pp. 329-381, 511-556.

[40] A. D. C-1516-1517; G. Richert, " Biens communaux et droits d'usage en Haute-Garonne pendant la Réaction Thermidorienne et sous le Directoire," *Annales historiques de la Révolution française*, 1951, pp. 274-280. Great regional variation is indicated by the fact that in the region of Saint-Gaudens in the Pyrenees about 14% of the land was in common.

[41] E. Appolis, " La question de la vaine pature en Languedoc au XVIIIe siècle," *Annales historiques de la Révolution française*, 1938, p. 99, ". . . les conseils politiques sont formés presque partout de cultivateurs aisés . . ."

viduals were naturally the strongest proponents of the " natural liberty of the proprietor," to use the physiocratic vocabulary, and of the elimination of communal rights on their land in particular. The town councils found a ready sounding board for their appeal in the Estates of the Province, the Parlement of Toulouse, and the Intendant of Languedoc. The Vicomte Saint Priest set the tone of his policy toward the right of vacant pasture when he said:

It is the essence of the administration of this province not to touch, as far as possible, the natural liberty which the proprietors must have to dispose of their possessions as they see fit and that is, above all, because the *taille*, being *réele* [on land], the individual is interested in giving them the full value to which they are susceptible.[42]

As early as 1634, the Parlement of Toulouse had issued a ruling limiting the right of vacant pasture, but it was only after the ruling of March 27, 1725, that the Parlement began to hand down numerous judicial rulings in response to a growing number of individual and community petitions. Under the pretext of maintaining equality for all members of a community, the court in fact defended proprietors who had successfully prevented communal livestock from foraging on their lands. The ruling of 1725 established a general principle: " The Court has made and does make the strongest prohibitions and interdictions to enter or pasture any kind of animal during the entire year in the olive groves, vineyards, newly planted or cut woods, fruit orchards, and other lands bounded by an enclosure." [43]

Among the numerous rulings that followed, four can be cited favoring noble proprietors in the diocese of Toulouse. They were in favor of Charles de Rochefoucard, Comte de Clermont (September 6, 1735), M. de Vignes, councilor at the Parlement (June 26, 1738), M. de Buisson, Marquis d'Aussonne (April 26, 1742), and M. de Célès, councilor at the Parlement (July 23, 1746). All of these *gentilshommes* were engaged in legal disputes with their respective communities over the right of vacant pasture. The substance of these four judgments may be summarized as follows: (1) pasturage was prohibited by any

---

[42] E. Appolis, *Un pays Languedocien au milieu du XVIIIᵉ siècle, Le diocese de Lodève* (Albi, 1951), p. 391.

[43] Appolis, " La question de la vaine pâture," *loc. cit.*, p. 101.

members of the community o nthe seigneur's land and fines for violations fixed at 50 to 100 livres; (2) a survey was projected to estimate the maximum number of livestock each inhabitant could own, outlawing in any case pasturage on lands other than those belonging to each inhabitant; (3) it was prohibited to cut any wood, gather any grapes, or glean before the sheaves had been collected on the seigneur's land; (4) trespassing on the seigneur's land without permission was strictly prohibited; and (5) the pasturage of sheep, goats, pigs, geese, or ducks on the common meadow was prohibited at any time, and the pasturage of oxen, cows, horses, and mules was prohibited before the straw had been collected. More than ending the vacant pasture, these rulings attacked the livestock holder who had little property and even restricted the use of the common meadow.[44]

By 1765, the appeals against the right of vacant pasture had become so profuse that the Agricultural Committee of the Provincial Estates made an inquiry among all the dioceses of Languedoc about this problem. The replies to this inquest, presented before the next session of the Estates by the Archbishop of Toulouse, were almost unanimously opposed to the right of vacant pasture. Subsequently, the Estates voted a general abolition of this right in Languedoc with the proviso that individual communities could vote its retention if they so desired. The Parlement of Toulouse, revealing its fundamental affinity of interest with the Estates, handed down the ruling of June 21, 1766 making vacant pasture illegal " except in those communities which by unanimous vote will judge à propos to retain it. . . ." [45]

Compared to this strong prohibition, the project for a Royal Declaration on the right of vacant pasture sponsored by Bertin, the Controller-General, seemed timid indeed. Bertin's project provided that a maximum of one-fifth of a property be exempted from the vacant pasture and then on condition that this portion be put into artificial meadow and bounded by hedges or ditches. The reaction of Riquet de Bonrepos, Attorney-General of the

[44] A. D., B-1518, f⁰ 652; B-1686, f⁰ 494, f⁰ 543. Series B is the " Archives du Parlement." These are the registers of the *arrêts* followed by the folio number.

[45] Appolis, " La question de la vaine pâture," *loc. cit.*, pp. 111-118.

Parlement of Toulouse, to Bertin's proposal, revealed not only how far Languedoc was ahead of the rest of the Kingdom in the campaign against communal rights, but also the unwillingness of the proprietor beneficiary to accept conditions in exchange for abolition. Riquet, whose extensive landholdings in the Lauragais made him representative of the landed nobility of Toulouse, was quick to point out that Bertin's declaration would still be prejudicial to the " natural right of each proprietor," since it abolished vacant pasture on only one-fifth of a property, while in Languedoc each proprietor had the freedom to prohibit communal pasturage on all of his land if he saw fit. Furthermore, Riquet objected to putting the proprietor to the extra expense of digging ditches and growing hedges when, on the contrary, he should have " the right " to compensation for damages caused by communal flocks and livestock on his land. Finally, Riquet concluded, " it was hardly possible to make general laws for the whole Kingdom on such a matter," and it would be much better that each locality be guided by its own usages as interpreted by the Parlement of its resort. The Intendant Saint Priest, avoiding any conflict with Bertin, simply stated that the new project would encounter no inconvenience in Languedoc " because it conforms to what is already observed here." [46]

Between 1766 and the Revolution, the penalties prescribed by the Parlement for violations of the ruling of 1766 became more severe, especially in rich grain areas such as the Lauragais. Fines varied from 50 to 500 livres for pasturage on another's property, or for exceeding one's quota on the common meadow. The members of Parlement who usually possessed seigniorial rights of justice in rural areas themselves were inclined to delegate the enforcement of the law against vacant pasturage to the seigneurs.[47] The results of this delegation of enforcement powers were manifest in the numerous re-statements of seigniorial rights over the communities. Between 1773 and 1789, numerous are the cases before the Seneschal Court for the diocese of Toulouse in which the local seigneur asserted his

---

[46] *Ibid.*, 119-120. These two letters are found in the Archives Nationales, H-1486, n. 273; H-1486, no. 19; dated August 10, 1766 and July 20, 1766, respectively.

[47] *Ibid.*, 124.

judicial prerogatives, especially with regard to the punishment of communal pasturage on his property.[48] Private contracts also reveal the enforcement of the 1766 ruling. Sharecroppers and tenant-farmers had to pay for whatever wood and straw they were allotted from the seigneur's domain and communal pasturage was strictly forbidden. In short, whether enforced by royal official, Parlementary ruling, or local seigneur, the communal right of vacant pasture had practically ended in the diocese of Toulouse by the end of the Ancien Regime.

From the point of view of increasing agricultural productivity, the abolition of common rights of pasturage on the fallow field was an indispensable step toward the planting of artificial meadows. Artificial meadows demanded enclosure and the right of vacant pasture prevented enclosure. But whether abolition necessarily led to this result is another question. In the diocese of Toulouse, the abolition of 1766 did not lead to profuse planting of artificial grasses before 1786, and probably not before 1800.[49] It seems clear, therefore, that the campaign of the more prosperous landholders against the right of vacant pasture, though an indispensable preliminary to artificial meadows, was not waged with this in mind, and cannot be considered as a technique to increase agricultural productivity. It did, however, indirectly influence the larger proprietor's income by aiding him to gain a firmer hold on the available livestock—the principal farm capital.

The rising demand for cereals encouraged all proprietors, large and small, to plant every available arpent in grain. It was this desire that gave the great impetus to the extensive clearings between 1770 and the Revolution. But clearings were made on meadow and woodland as well as on wastelands, reducing the supply of forage to a minimum. Of 328,435 arpents of land in the diocese, only about 27,000 arpents or 8% were still in natural meadow by 1789.[50] Moreover, the soil of the Lauragais, so favorable for wheat and maize, was too humid in winter, and too dry in summer, to produce high yields of natural grasses. The Subdelegate estimated a yield of 30 *quintaux* (two small cart-loads) of hay per arpent in a common year and 15 or less

[48] Archives Départementales, Aude, Series B-2472-2492. Procès verbaux.
[49] Cf. Chapter II *supra*. A. D., C-109.
[50] Dutil, *op. cit.*, p. 122.

in a dry year.[51] Along the streams, such as the Hers and the Girou, or near the banks of the Garonne or Ariège Rivers, good meadow could still be found, but in the diocese as a whole, cattle forage became increasingly rare.

It was against a background of forage scarcity that the communal right of vacant pasture was progressively suppressed. In a diocese where only 1% of the land was in common, the plight of the propertyless day laborer who owned a few sheep and goats was obvious. But even the mass of the peasantry whose average landholdings in the diocese were 5.8 acres found the problem of pasturage increasingly acute. Clearings had deprived these small proprietors of the wastelands they had used for pasturage; the abolition of the right of vacant pasture barred them from the fallow field, wood, and meadow of the larger proprietors.[52]

The forage reports from the communities during the drought of 1785 emphasized the critical position of the marginal livestock owner. The village of Pujoler reported that it possessed only one meadow on the Girou producing only one-fourth of its usual yield of hay and, as a consequence, the poor were beginning to sell their livestock at a very low price. At Saint-Jory the consuls stated that pasturage was extremely rare and that the meadows near the Garonne belonging to the seigneur were guarded to prevent entrance of community livestock. The consuls of Villandrie reported that only the larger landowners were in a position to buy straw and maize in the neighboring villages and that the other proprietors were forced to use dried oak and poplar leaves wetted with wine as winter forage. The Subdelegate observed that many of the peasant farmers had abandoned their fields entirely because of lack of work-oxen.[53] To be sure, 1785 was a bad year for all proprietors, large and small, but it was the small peasant holder who necessarily suffered most from lack of forage.

With the virtual end of vacant pasture, the larger proprietors

[51] A. D., C-109. Subdelegate to Intendant, January 11, 1786.
[52] H. Martin, *Documents relatifs à la vente des biens nationaux, District de Toulouse* (Toulouse, 1916-1924), pp. 516-517; Richert, "Biens communaux en Haute-Garonne," *loc. cit.*, pp. 280-281.
[53] A. D., C-109. Many communities reported that they had no natural pasturage whatsoever.

had exclusive use of their meadowlands which included the best pasturage in the diocese. M. Rolland de Saint-Rome, for example, had 80 arpents (112 acres) of well-watered pasture along the Hers betwen Saint-Rome and Villenouvelle. At Bonrepos on the Girou the Riquet family had 35 arpents (49 acres) in meadow, leased in 1750 but strictly reserved for the seigneur after 1756. The Marquis de Bertier kept half his domain at Montrabe in wood and pasture, probably for commercial use since the bulk of his work-oxen were at Pinsaguel, over 20 kilometers away on the other side of Toulouse. In the same community, the Baron de Montbrun had half his domain of 100 acres in meadow. To the northeast, M. Picot de Lapeyrouse had 90 arpents (126 acres) of natural meadow along the Girou on his estate near Montastruc.[54]

Without doubt the average noble proprietor had less pasturage than these examples would suggest. Of 50 families taken from the tax rolls of 1750, the average seigneur had about 10% of his properties in natural meadow. As a rule, this meadowland was distributed equally among the domain farms, suggesting the minimum pasturage necessary to feed the work-oxen and other livestock on the adjoining lands under cultivation. Typical was the Marquis de·Gavarret with his 40 arpents (56 acres) of meadowland distributed in 4 arpent blocks among 11 farms.[55] Nevertheless, the noble proprietors were usually able to economize some hay for the market. The Baron de Lapeyrouse observed that the proprietors in the region of Montastruc used the hay of their meadows very sparingly and sold the greater part at Toulouse for a good price.[56]

It would be too much to conclude that the eighteenth century witnessed the complete annihilation of the small livestock-owner in the diocese of Toulouse. The vitality of this class is revealed by the partial re-establishment of communal rights during and after the Revolution.[57] On the other hand, there is little doubt that the bulk of the livestock was in the hands of the larger proprietors who owned most of the available meadowland on

[54] A. D., C-1331-1346; Picot de Lapeyrouse, *The Agriculture of a District in the South of France* (London, 1819), p. 5.

[55] A. D., C-1331-1346.

[56] Picot, *op. cit.*, p. 57.

[57] Richert, *loc. cit.*, p. 284 and *passim*.

the eve of the Revolution. The relatively few registered leases
of farm-oxen by independent livestock-owners in the late century suggest such a concentration. Moreover, not only do sharecropping contracts invariably include a lease of livestock, but
also the progressive reduction of the sharecropper's portion of
the harvest indicates an increasing dependence on the larger
proprietor for farm-capital.[58] The new clearings and, above all,
the suppression of the right of vacant pasture were in large
measure responsible for this dependence.[59]

The livestock accounts of individual noble proprietors were
carefully kept, particular attention being given to natural
increases through breeding as well as inflation in cattle values.
The accounts of the Marquis d'Escouloubre and Astre de Blagnac for 1750 indicate a concern for every ox, calf, colt, and
sheep bought or sold on their farms and the exact division of
profits and costs (to the *sou*) with the sharecroppers.[60] After
1779, the Marquis de Fourquevaux paid more attention to the
division of livestock profits with his sharecropper and after
1783 he kept the entire profit on the stock for himself.[61] The
Baron de Saint Elix possessed an exact inventory of all the
farm animals from an ox to the smallest heifer on each of his
six farms. He calculated an increase in capital value of the
livestock of 1,163 livres between 1739 and 1763, an increase of
40%, largely from natural increases. This entire sum was made
a charge on the leaseholders. In 1772 the baron demanded
his sharecroppers to pay one-half of the capital value of all the
livestock, a sum amounting to over 2,000 livres, or between
200 and 300 livres per sharecropper.[62] No doubt the increase
in the price of oxen, cows, and calves of about 30% between

[58] *Supra*, Chapter II on *métayage* contracts.
[59] The process was accelerated by the severe cattle epidemics of 1775-1783.
The epizootic disease of 1775 took 80,000 head of cattle between Bordeaux and
Toulouse. Thousands more were slaughtered by the provincial administration
in an effort to stem the epidemic by creating a *cordon sanitaire* about the
uninfected area. In the plague of carbuncles (*mal noir*) between 1777 and
1783 the community of Labastide-Saint Sernin lost 29 oxen out of a total of
50 in 32 days. Montaugé, *op. cit.*, pp. 13-45; A. D., C-124.
[60] A. D., E-1713 " Métaire d'Endonnat, 1751 "; E-647 (de Blagnac).
[61] A. D., E-641 " Livre de raison de Fourquevaux, 1753-1789."
[62] A. D., E-1777 Saint Elix Papers.

1775 and 1789 furnished added encouragement to the proprietor to take careful inventory of his livestock.[63]

Sources confirm that the quality of the bovine livestock was distinctly mediocre.[64] Picot de Lapeyrouse spoke for the diocese when he wrote as late as 1818 that nothing had been done towards the improvement of the cattle breeds and consequently they were stunted, lean and deformed. " In all of the canton of Montastruc," he writes, " there is not a single choice bull . . . a pitiful calf of one year leaps on the most beautiful cow. . . . What sort of fruit can one expect? " [65] Good oxen had to be bought outside of the diocese as far as Montauban or Gresoles in Gascony. Horses were not substituted despite the number of available Norman and Andalusian breeds in the Royal Studs of Epinet near Toulouse.

The causes for this neglect were many—overemphasis on cereal production, the neglect of cattle forage, the stubborn attachment of proprietor and sharecropper to traditional methods of agriculture, and the sharecropper's lack of interest in and even suspicion of ameliorations urged by the more progressive noble proprietors such as the Baron de Lapeyrouse. Théron de Montaugé, writing in 1869, states that capital was turned away from agriculture and placed in colonial commerce and provincial *rentes*, although the distribution of noble investments in the Toulouse area would lead to the opposite conclusion.[66] Farm capital, however, was placed in land or clearings rather than into livestock or tools. A letter of the Subdelegate to the Intendant in 1762 was enlightening in this regard. A passage read: ". . . the fear of a heavier tax often prevents the purchase of more livestock in order not to reveal prosperity." [67] No doubt the poor knowledge of veterinary science

[63] Montaugé, *op. cit.*, p. 45. Livestock prices in 1789 were as follows:

1 calf—25 to 30 livres	1 pair of mules—250 livres
1 pair of cows—200 to 300 livres	1 pair of work-oxen—400 to 550 livres

[64] Montaugé, *op. cit.*, pp. 36-48. Dutil, *op. cit.*, pp. 220 f.; A. D., C-106, 107.

[65] Picot, *op. cit.*, p. 27. In his conclusion Picot writes: " It is to be noted that the agriculture of the canton of Montastruc is the same as that of a great number of neighboring cantons. Thus, in the practice of our canton, I have also given that of the canton of Verfeil, Lanta, the center of Toulouse, etc." *Ibid.*, 85.

[66] Montaugé, *op. cit.*, p. 57. Cf. Chapter V *infra*, and, in fact, the whole weight of this study.

[67] A. D., C-106. Subdelegate to Intendant, April 17, 1762.

and the series of cattle epidemics between 1775 and 1783 discouraged many proprietors from investing one *sou* in farm animals beyond the minimum requirements of plowing and fertilizing.[68] In any event, the profits that the noble proprietor realized on his bovine livestock were due largely to scarcity and concentration of available supply, rather than to an improvement of cattle breeds.[69]

Almost all the principal families of the diocese had flocks of 30 to 100 sheep.[70] These flocks were not large enough to be used for extensive sheepfolding since about 300 sheep were required to fertilize 20 arpents (28 acres) of land. But they had the advantage of being small enough to be well surveyed and cared for. The Subdelegate reported that the flocks in the Lauragais were " very well housed," their pens " well equipped, clean, warm, and aired twice annually." He observed that it was " especially in the Lauragais that the best shepherds were found," a factor which, added to the favorable climate, " should give as good a return as in England," provided the local variety were bred with the heat-resisting Spanish Merinos.[71] The larger proprietors were in a position to experiment with new breeds and raise larger than average flocks. The Comte de Villèle took advantage of the experimental sheep farm at Rambouillet to transport Spanish rams over 1000 kilometers (600 miles) to Toulouse. On his estate at Mourvilles-Basses he increased his flock to 300 by the end of the century, and was to double this number in the first quarter of the nineteenth century.[72] After innumerable initial setbacks, the Baron de Lapeyrouse estab-

[68] A. D., C-123. Intendant to Subdelegate, January 27, 1762. In an invitation to the Subdelegate to find students for the new (and only) veterinary school in the *Midi* at Lyon, the Intendant wrote " the treatment of animal sickness has been almost entirely neglected . . . the philosophers and most respectable doctors having scorned occupying themselves with it." A. D., C-124. Note 61 above.

[69] Neglect of farm livestock was not due to a lack of attention on the part of the Estates of Languedoc. In the session of 1765-1767, for example, the Estates reimbursed the Vicomte de Polignac for having brought 42 Swiss bulls into the province. A. D., C-2409 " Séance de 1766-67."

[70] Picot, *op. cit.*, p. 29; A. D., C-1312-1330.

[71] A. D., C-123 " Instruction sur le parcage des bêtes à laine, 1785 "; Subdelegate to Intendant, June 28, 1783, " Réponses sur les bêtes à laine "; Dutil asserts that the Lauragais was not typical of Languedoc, however. Like Arthur Young, he stresses the poor care of the sheep flocks in most of the diocese. Dutil, *op. cit.*, pp. 243-254.

[72] J. Fourcassié, *Villèle* (Paris, 1954), p. 16.

lished a healthy flock by breeding 100 ewes of the local variety
with two Merino rams. To assure this flock of good care, he
sent one of his sons to Rambouillet to procure a " skillful and
docile shepherd." He then built a number of well-aired sheep
pens close to his principal domain including barns for fodder
and litter, brick mangers, stone troughs, and a separate pen for
sick ewes. Between 1780 and 1815 the baron had increased his
flock at Lapeyrouse from 370 to 657 sheep of which 162 were
Merinos.[73]

An official inventory in 1782 indicates the importance of
ovine relative to bovine livestock in the diocese. Given that the
noble proprietors held almost half of the land in each community and that Parlementary rulings permitted only one or
two sheep per habitant, it seems fair to assume that the bulk
of the sheep in each community belonged to the seigneur. Thus,
most of the 1,000 sheep at Saint-Léon belonged to the Marquis
de Gavarret, most of the 810 at Pinsaguel and Portet to the
Marquis de Bertier, most of the 1,075 at Venergue-Vernet to
the Councilor d'Assézat, most of the 950 at Pibrac to the Comte
Dufaur, and most of the 1,100 at Caraman to the Comte Riquet,
cousin of the Attorney-General.[74] These figures indicate a substantial increase over the number of sheep declared by these
gentlemen, on their tax rolls thirty-two years earlier.[75]

Although the noble landlord was more attentive to sheep-
raising than to cattle breeding, in both instances he benefited
from scarcity and concentration of supply. This was due to his
firm hold on the available meadowland, a near-monopoly which
had been made possible by the clearings and the abolition of
the right of vacant pasture. The noble proprietor did not make
appreciable profits from the sales of livestock or subsidiary
products; the Lauragais was neither cattle nor sheep country.
However, control of this important farm capital greatly strengthened the seigneur's bargaining position with his tenants and
his peasant neighbors.

[73] Picot, *op. cit.*, pp. 32-36.
[74] A. D., C-123. Inventory of sheep in the Diocese, 1782. Richert, " Biens
communaux," *loc. cit.*, 285-288.
[75] A. D., C-1312-1330.

CHAPTER IV

SUBSIDIARY ACTIVITIES ON THE ESTATE:
SALE OF WOOD, RURAL INDUSTRIES, VINE CULTURE

I

So well designed was the forestry code of Colbert that its principal provisions were still in force at the end of the eighteenth century. This elaborate edict, including 32 titles and covering almost 100 printed pages, regulated, in the words of the first article, " all water and forest of the Kingdom." Title XXVI provided that " no subject can cut brushwood (*taille*) before 10 years' growth, reserving 16 young trees for each arpent, and forest (*futaie*) can be sold only after 40 years' growth, reserving 10 young trees for each arpent." The third section of this title stated that individuals possessing full-grown trees within 10 leagues (27 miles) from the sea or 2 leagues (5.4 miles) from navigable rivers must notify the royal forestry inspector (*grand-maître*) six months before sale. The fourth section provided that " our subjects may punish delinquents in their woods, rabbit warrens, ponds, and rivers." The ordinance established an elaborate administrative machinery including *grands maîtres*, individual inspectors, lieutenants, guards, clerks, as well as special courts of appeal independent of the Parlements.[1]

Violations of the forestry code were encountered early. An ordinance in 1696 stated that brushwood was being cut at 3, 4, and 5 years contrary to the Ordinance of Water and Forests and prescribed a 50 livre fine per arpent for any trees cut without the permission of the forestry inspector. But the eighteenth century brought an even greater need for wood and fresh violations of the code. The ruling of 1732 attempted to

[1] Isambert, *et al., Recueil général des anciennes lois françaises depuis l'an 420 jusqu'à la Révolution de 1789* (Paris, 1822-1828), XVIII, pp. 218-306. " Edit portant règlement général pour les eaux et forêts, août, 1669."

restrict the wood consumption of ovens and forges by a system of permits. The Ordinance of 1741, in a special appeal for timber for naval construction, ordered a more strict enforcement of all previous rulings restricting wood consumption.[2] In 1756 the Estates of Languedoc appealed for a royal decree to outlaw all clearings of mountain woodland which were "causing the scarcity of fire-wood, the destruction of forests, and the degradation of pasturage."[3] Despite all of these measures, however, the supply of wood in the province in general and in the diocese in particular was being rapidly depleted. In an inquest of 1783 the Subdelegate of Toulouse estimated that there were only 17,507 arpents of woodland, or 5.3% of the total area of the diocese.[4] The *pagelle* (1.25 cubic meters) of cut-wood sold in Toulouse at 3 livres in 1754, at 4 livres in 1770, and at 7 livres in 1789.[5]

As the century drew to a close, the provincial administration became increasingly frantic in its efforts to track down the causes of depletion and, if possible, halt the process. No doubt the Toulousan plain had never possessed those tall oak forests so plentiful in the foothills of the Pryenees to the South, or along the rim of the Montagne-Noire to the Northeast. Toulouse had abandoned wood for city construction by the end of the seventeenth century. Even at this early date the cross-beamed facade was a curiosity in a city built exclusively of red brick.[6] The clearings of the 1780's converted much of the remaining forest and brushwood to grain land and vineyard. Ballainvillier, the last Intendant of Languedoc, observed that the proprietors of Toulouse were particularly active in cutting down trees along the fringes of their estates on the pretext that these trees exhausted the soil.[7]

The Subdelegate pointed to increased consumption as the chief cause of shortage. Although he estimated that rural con-

---

[2] A. D., C-105, Ordinance of May 2, 1696, Arrêt du Conseil de 1732, Ordinance of July 18, 1741.
[3] A. D., C-2398, Session of 1756, Procès verbal; C-2400, Session of 1757-58.
[4] A. D., C-105, " Enquête de 1783-1784 sur le bois du diocèse de Toulouse."
[5] Montaugé, *op. cit.*, p. 24.
[6] Coppolani, *op. cit.*, p. 83.
[7] Dutil, *op. cit.*, p. 216. Ballainvilliers (Intendant 1785-1788), stated in his memoires that the price of wood reached 10 livres per *pagelle* just before the Revolution.

sumption of wood during the winter months was limited to
the burning of "heather, fagots, and roots"—the larger proprietors having moved to the city—he placed the wood consumption of Toulouse at 100,000 *pagelles* per year, over three
times the annual production of the diocese.[8] He deplored the
"taste for luxury" and the "modern habits" of the city
dwellers who maintained roaring fires in their town-houses
during winter. He observed that coal was held to be "neither
clean nor practical in most modern homes." "Despite the
pressing need," he wrote, "no one will use coal" and "coal
will never suit the tastes of the townspeople."[9] This situation
was almost paradoxical, since there was an ample supply of
coal in the neighboring diocese of Albi.[10] Sieur Courtial, a coal
mining proprietor in the diocese of Mirepoix, wrote in 1786:

> The hope of a certain consumption [of coal] in the city of Toulouse
> has been frustrated by the wide-spread prejudice of this city against coal
> smoke, a prejudice which has been fortified by the doctors. . . . This
> prejudice increases despite the high cost and scarcity of wood in such
> a way that no one at Toulouse wishes to use coal.[11]

Corresponding difficulties arose with regard to substituting
coal for wood as a combustible for forges and ovens. Although
no heavy logs were used, the brick ovens of the diocese consumed great quantities of brushwood, fagots, and tree branches.
Coal did not give the same flame, and ovens were not constructed to handle a slower burning combustible. The large
oven of M. de Puymaurin at Auterrive consumed 100 *pagelles*
(125 cubic meters) of wood annually and no substitution of
coal was found possible. The Subdelegate commented that
only one lime oven in the diocese was fueled exclusively by
coal in 1783.[12]

Under such conditions, proprietors were prone to exploit
their woodlands before they reached full maturity. Owners

[8] A. D., C-105, Inquest of 1783-84. The Subdelegate estimated the production
of the diocese at 29,178 *pagelles* or 20 *pagelles* per arpent.

[9] *Ibid.*

[10] It is not surprising that the Chevalier de Solages was finding it increasingly
difficult to market his augmented production of coal from his mines near Albi.
Cf. B. G. Bernis, *Mines de Carmaux, 1700-1900* (Paris, 1918).

[11] Dutil, *op. cit.*, p. 587.

[12] A. D., C-105. Inquest of 1783-84. Dutil claims that coal was used in the
brick factories of the city, however.

felled their trees every 10 years instead of every 15, sacrificing
a third of their growth in order to make an immediate sale in
a favorable market. The Subdelegate commented that a general
law prohibiting such practice was almost impossible because of
the extreme variation in the maturity age of trees. He made
all his calculations of wood production on the basis of current
practice, that is, a cutting every 12 years.[13]

Wood merchants were constantly plagued by all of the problems of marketing a heavy, cumbersome commodity as well as
by government rulings against " illicit associations of wood
merchants attempting to sell at exorbitant prices." [14] In 1758
the Parlement of Toulouse established a schedule of shipping
rates for wood transported on the Garonne or Ariège Rivers
enforced by inspection at all points of trans-shipment. Transport costs were thus fixed at 1 livre, 15 sous per *pagelle* for
wood coming from Cazères, 35 miles from Toulouse, but at
only 5 sous per *pagelle* from Muret, 9 miles from Toulouse.
No insurance was permitted for losses on the rivers and the
stocking of wood destined for Toulouse was explicitly prohibited.[15]

The proprietors of woodlands bore none of the costs and
risks of marketing, and resisted all government efforts to force
them to release their wood to meet the firewood shortage at
Toulouse. In 1754, when the local administration tried to commandeer carts and farm-labor to transport wood from the forest
of Pouze, the noble proprietors confronted the Subdelegate with
effective passive resistance.[16] The attitude of the Marquis de
Gavarret was characteristic. He wrote to the Intendant:

Monsieur, your Subdelegate of Toulouse has asked the consuls of this
community to commandeer all of the carts for the wood of Donneville.
I do not see, Monseigneur, how you could have anything to do with
this; it could only come from the avidity of the merchants who want
cheap cartage. If this were for the King, the nobility would subscribe
to it willingly, since it is devoted as much by duty as by sentiment to
His Service.[17]

[13] *Ibid.*, C-105.
[14] Isambert, *op. cit.*, XVII, p. 71, " Arrêt du Conseil, 23 août, 1781."
[15] A. D., C-105. " Arrêt du Parlement de Toulouse, 29 juillet, 1758."
[16] A. D., C-321. Subdelegate to Intendant, July, 1754.
[17] *Ibid.* Marquis de Gavarret to Intendant, July 20, 1754.

As a rule, the seigneurs did not even manage the cutting of their trees. Tree merchants complained not only of the high prices demanded for uncut trees, but also of the risks of finding a large portion of the timber worm-infected and rotten. One wood merchant claimed that felling and sectioning cost five sous per cubic foot and that half the trees felled were found unsuitabe for lumbering.[18]

The actual process of selling the wood of a noble estate is well-illustrated by the sale of wood on 21 arpents (29.4 acres) of land by the Baron de St. Elix in 1780. Apparently, the price of wood was attractive enough to tempt the baron to sell wood from his park, reserving a certain number of pines, oaks, and other decorative trees which lined his avenues. Therefore, before exploitation, he marked 60 full-grown oaks, 50 young oaks, and all the pines and exotic trees which were to be left uncut. Then, in a written declaration, the baron served notice that:

The seigneur wishes to be paid in coin. The acquirer having paid in coin, can begin to cut his wood, observing to leave 16 young trees per arpent according to the Royal Ordinance. . . . Anyone will be received to make offers.[19]

The offers were submitted at the château of Saint-Elix beginning on Sunday, November 12, 1780. M. Busquet, wood merchant of Toulouse, offered 9,500 livres; Sr. Terredo, wood merchant of Rieux, offered 10,000 livres; and bidding continued on successive Sundays, until Busquet won the auction by offering 10,900 livres, or 529 livres per arpent of wood.[20] The final contract of sale provided that the cutting be finished by April 15, 1781, and the carting completed within six months from that date. The wood was to be exported from three landings designated on the Garonne about 4 miles from the château. The payment was to be made in two installments of 5,450 livres each, at the château, on January 19, 1781 and March 19, 1781.[21]

[18] A. D., C-192, "Mémoire à l'Intendant par les fournisseurs de bois du Haut-Languedoc-Gascogne-Bigorre-Béarn pour la construction des vaisseaux du Roy à Toulouse, Septembre, 1775."

[19] A. D., E-1777. St.-Elix, Sale of Wood, November 29, 1780.

[20] Amortized over 20 years, a generous assumption, this would be an income of 26 livres, 9 sous per arpent, an exceptionally good return.

[21] A. D., E-1777.

Other examples of wood sales by the Baron de Montbrun in 1768, by the Marquis de Bertier in 1755, and by seigneurs in the Comminges suggest that this method of sale was typical among noble proprietors.[22] The seigneurs sold the wood uncut, avoiding all the costs of felling, transporting, and marketing. Unlike their activities in the grain market, their role was essentially passive. It should be noted, however, that wood, unlike grain, required an outside labor force for cutting and carting, constant supervision, and petty bargaining with boatmen. Moreover, wood was more cumbersome to store and to transport than grain. Finally, administrative regulations became more effective at the marketing end of the enterprise. The increment in profit to be realized by excluding the middleman was hardly worth the added effort and risk to the average noble proprietor.[23]

Who owned the remaining woodland in the diocese? The majority of nobles held about 10% of their domains in woodland. Like their meadowland, this proportion was scattered among the domain farms, suggesting an amount necessary to provide the estate with its supply of firewood. The Marquis de Fourquevaux, for example, had 22 arpents of wood serving 7 farms.[24] The accounts of the Comte de Villèle indicate that the household used about 60 *pagelles* of cut-wood, the product of 3 arpents.[25] Hence, each farm of 30 arpents would require about 10% of its area in woodland in order to be self-sustaining.

A substantial minority of the noble proprietors, however, held more than 10% of their domains in woodland. These gentlemen were in a position to exploit their wood commercially. All of them were within a radius of 20 miles of the Toulouse market. They were: [26]

[22] Archives Notariales, Reg. 5891, January 21, 1768; A. D., 6-J, 40, " Comptes pour bois de Palificat, 1755." Marquis de Bertier sold 230 *pagelles* for 1,381 livres or 6 livres per *pagelle* in 1755; A. D., C-192. The wood merchants always bought " on the spot."

[23] There were exceptions. Picot de Lapeyrouse replaced the old hachet with a kind of pick-ax which cut tree-trunks more effectively. He then lodged special workmen capable of using the new tool on his estate and " working only by day " cut two arpents in 20 days. Picot, *op. cit.*, p. 83.

[24] A. D., C-1335.

[25] Villèle Papers. " Fourni par Mourvilles à la maison en nature."

[26] A. D., C-1331-1346. This table represents 17 out of 50 noble domains investigated for their woodlands. The remaining 33 domains had about 10% of their land in woodland.

TABLE VI

Noble Holdings of Woodland in 1750

Name of Proprietor	Domain Surface (in arpents)	Woodland
Picot, Baron de Lapeyrouse	713	108
Comte de Villèle	660	100
Marquis d'Ossun	547	110
Marquis de Bertier	466	104
Riquet, Baron de Bonrepos	467	121
Conseiller Darbon	297	41
Marquis d'Avessens	325	80
Marquis de Gavarret	487	60
Conseiller de Comère	119	65
Marquis de Gramont-Lanta	400	100
Conseiller de Célès	175	80
Marquis St. Félix-Mauremont	262	35
Marquis Dupuy-Montesquieu	770	159
M. de Blandinères, écuyer	204	66
Marquis de Cantalause	366	68
Marquis Cassagnau-St. Félix	135	38
Comte Dufaur de Pibrac	401	44

All of these proprietors could realize a profit of about 6 livres per arpent of woodland in 1750 and about 11 livres per arpent in 1789.[27] This meant a supplement to their landed incomes between 500 and 1000 livres in 1789. Furthermore, there seems little doubt that the nobility of Toulouse held almost all of the remaining forest in the diocese.[28] By the end of the Ancien Regime, the abolition of the right of vacant pasture gave the gentlemen exclusive control over the fruits of this property.

II

Even where commercially feasible, all cut-wood was not sold on the local market for winter heating. In many communities, wood was consumed on the domain as a combustible for brick making, black-smithing, and, in a few cases, for glass-

[27] This estimate is based on a production of 20 *pagelles* per arpent cut every 12 years and selling at 4 livres per *pagelle* in 1750 and at 7 livres in 1789. Cf. Appendix A.

[28] Since about 5% of the diocese was in woodland, and the nobility held 45% of the total surface of which no less than 10% was in wood, this conclusion seems compelling. Cf. A. D., C-105.

blowing. At Auterrive, for example, 2000 *pagelles* (2500 cubic meters) of wood were consumed annually for brick making. At Beaumont, the entire product of 500 arpents of woodland was consumed in the community by various forges and ovens. At Auriac 150 arpents of wood was insufficient to fuel the three brick factories in neighboring Caraman.[29]

The existence of large quantities of red clay and tile in the soil of the Lauragais made the brick-oven a common structure on the noble estate. There were 76 of these ovens in the diocese in 1784 employed to furnish repair materials for farm buildings and building block for construction at Toulouse. In 1781, the Subdelegate wrote his superior:

It is certain that consumption [of brick] has increased very much in the last few years because of the construction of the docks along the Garonne, the church of the Daurade, the hospital of La Grave, and many other private and public edifices . . . so that the present supply of brick is insufficient.[30]

This shortage was increased by the fact that four of Toulouse's eight brick factories were on the point of exhausting the local supply of clay. Brick blocks that cost 50 to 60 livres per thousand " in times past," said the Subdelegate, cost 90 to 100 livres in 1780, a price he termed " exorbitant." Consequently, he urged government approval of new brick ovens in the vicinity of Toulouse.[31]

Despite their high consumption of wood-fuel, the number of new brick factories put to use by the local landlords and approved by the Intendant steadily increased. In 1754, Mlle de Garaud asked permission to reestablish an abandoned brick oven on her estate at Montlaur, basing her demand on the repair needs of the château, five large farms, and the village. In 1774 she wished to place her brick oven closer to the main turnpike in order " to facilitate commerce and exportation of bricks." [32] The Baron de Blagnac, having exhausted his own brick, asked neighboring proprietors to sell him parts of their land containing the necessary raw material. In a letter to the

[29] A. D., C-105, " Inquest on Wood, 1783-1784."

[30] A. D., C-149, Subdelegate to Intendant, May 16, 1781.

[31] *Ibid.*

[32] *Ibid.* Subdelegate to Intendant, July 24, 1754; Intendant to Subdelegate, April 26, 1774.

Intendant, he complained that these proprietors would sell only at an exorbitant price, demanding double the ordinary value. Basing his plea on " the public need for brick and tile," the baron asked that owners of land containing clay appropriate for brick making be compelled to sell it to him at a price determined by experts of the diocese.[33] The seigneur de Cornbarrieu, reconstructing an ancestral brick oven, made a similar plea to use the soils of neighboring proprietors.[34] The Captain de Carrery was so anxious to establish a brick oven on his estate at Vaguière that he wrote a special letter to the cousin of the Subdelegate urging her in strict confidence to help him gain official approval of the project.[35] The Subdelegate's files contain 13 petitions, other than those four cited above, for the establishment of new brick ovens on estates in the diocese.[36]

In their tax declarations of 1750, the nobles indicated that their brick making establishments yielded little or no revenue. Typical was the declaration of M. de Boutaric who claimed that his brick oven at Azas netted him only 36 livres annually.[37] Furthermore, many of the petitions mentioned above come from *petite noblesse* such as the Captain de Carrery, and from the financially desperate, such as the Garaud family, exploiting every available source of income.[38] Nevertheless, the value attached to these brick ovens must not be minimized even among the larger proprietors. The Marquis de Cassagneau-Saint-Felix, for example, admitted that his brick oven produced 1400 livres when the wood was cut every twenty years.[39] In other words, the Marquis's declaration revealed what a continually fueled brick oven could yield.

Nevertheless, the chief value of the brick factory was for local estate repairs. That this brick could be put to extensive use is clearly indicated in the journal of Picot de Lapeyrouse. Upon assuming management of the family estate in 1778, the

[33] *Ibid.* Baron de Blagnac to Intendant, April 21, 1778.
[34] *Ibid.* Subdelegate to Intendant, January 19, 1787.
[35] *Ibid.* Subdelegate to Intendant, April 25, 1772; M. de Carrery to " Madame," September 11, 1771.
[36] *Ibid.* The petitioners include at least 3 bourgeois and one parish priest.
[37] A. D., C-1312 " Azas."
[38] The last Garaud died " ruined." Cf. J. Villain, *La France moderne généalogique (Haute-Garonne et Ariège)*, (Montpellier, 1913), " Garaud."
[39] A. D., C-1325 " Odars."

young baron made general repairs on all of his farm buildings and built many new ones. He wrote:

I began by repairing my residence as a central point of cultivation. I have put in at Lapeyrouse a vast court, a manor-house, large granaries of two stories and well-aired, a store-room and vaulted cellars beneath, stables for draught horses and brood mares, stables for oxen and wedders, wood houses for fuel, cartwright shops, etc. . . . The farm houses were also repaired, the ovens removed to a distance, cart-houses and lofts for fodder added everywhere, and sheep-sheds constructed. Every year I add some improvement to my establishment.

" All this," the baron continued, " is economical for those like myself who have a brick field, large pieces of wood being very expensive." [40]

That the other noble proprietors of the diocese used their brick ovens for estate repairs is indicated by the almost total absence of repair costs as a deductible item on noble revenue declarations. On income tax statements which include detailed repair costs of mills and forges as well as special projects such as the levees at Pinsaguel and Lacroix-Falgarde, ordinary building repairs are curiously absent. The conclusion seems inescapable that cheap labor and the estate brick factory made these costs negligible. Thus the domain brick oven represented an important though disguised asset to the gentleman-farmer.

In the absence of coal and iron, blacksmithing in the diocese was restricted to farm-tool repair on the estate. Forges were usually leased to blacksmiths for rents in kind varying between 5 and 10 setiers (13.2 to 26.4 bushels) of wheat per year.[41] Small deposits of coal and iron in the foothills of the *Montagne-Noire* encouraged a few proprietors to engage in nail making. Sieur Panetier, co-seigneur of Montastruc, used three surface mines to fuel an iron forge in this region. He employed between 30 and 40 workers at wages of 10 livres per year and his sales of nails and iron pins totalled over 500 livres in 1782.[42] However, such enterprises were rare.

Unlike brick making, glass blowing was confined to very modest proportions. Glass blowing consumed greater quantities of wood than brick making, and the royal administration made

[40] Picot, *op. cit.*, pp. 9-10.
[41] A. D., C-1312-1330.
[42] A. D., E-1613 " Livre de comptes de Sr. Panetier."

a special effort to restrict such enterprises. In 1753 there were only 170 glass factories in all of Languedoc and until 1786 there were no glass establishments at Toulouse. The glass factory of the Chevalier de Solages near Albi produced almost 500,000 bottles annually by 1780, and supplied most of the needs of Toulouse.[43] Finally, despite the elaborate legal facade that made glass blowing the exclusive privilege of the *gentilhomme-verrier*, the new glass factories built at Toulouse in 1786 and 1789 were operated by bourgeois owners.[44]

Among the supplementary enterprises on the noble domain was the planting of mulberry trees. Unlike the umbrella pine, the poplar, and other semi-tropical trees, the mulberry was intended for commercial use. In an effort to supply the lagging silk industry at Lyon, the royal administration offered gratuities of 25 livres for every 100 feet of mulberry trees newly planted in the Lauragais.[45] The noble proprietors responded well to this appeal, over 4000 trees being planted in the diocese in 1760 alone.[46] Before the Revolution, wrote Picot de Lapeyrouse, there were many beautiful nurseries of mulberry trees and their cods sold well.[47]

Until 1780 the diocese produced about 250 *quintaux* (13,375 tons) of cocoons and 80 ounces of silk grain annually, but after this date, production dropped sharply, partly because of severe hail storms and early frosts. Throughout the 1780's the Subdelegate reported that the production of cocoons was either " of little consequence " or " of no commercial value." [48] Picot de Lapeyrouse wrote in 1815 that silk had been replaced in popular demand by cotton and wool, and mulberry trees had consequently been abandoned. " I still have 100 of them out of 1,200 which had been planted in 1754." [49]

The semi-tropical climate of the Lauragais was equally favorable to the planting of vines. Despite the efforts of the government to restrict new plantings under the assumption that vines

[43] A. D., C-149; Dutil, *op. cit.*, pp. 589-600.
[44] A. D., C-149 " Letter-Patent, December 5, 1734," Intendant to Subdelegate, October 26, 1786, Subdelegate to Intendant, May 7, 1789; C-69.
[45] A. D., C-110 " Ordinance of September 6, 1752."
[46] *Ibid.* " Sixième état des déclarations sur les mûriers."
[47] Picot, *op. cit.*, p. 38.
[48] A. D., 119-120 " Etat des récoltes, 1764-1788." Cf. Appendix B.
[49] Picot, *op. cit.*, p. 38.

threatened to reduce grain production, the number of vineyards greatly increased between 1750 and 1789. The Subdelegate said that this " enormous production " yielded the vine-grower a " vile price " and he deplored increased wine consumption which he attributed in part to " the luxury that is introduced into all households." On the other hand, he admitted that most of the new plantings were made on soils unfit for cereals, and that they returned a prompt and regular production. Increased consumption of wine, he confessed, was also due to thirty years' increase in population.[50] Pierre Barthès, the petty bourgeois chronicler, often alluded to the cheap *vin ordinaire* which helped compensate the consumer for high bread prices in bad harvest years.[51]

In any case, vine culture occupied less than 10% of the diocese at the end of the eighteenth century. Whether planted in the close rows of the peasant proprietor, or in the wider rows of the noble proprietor, the vineyard served the household and the local market. Its product was too acidic to compete outside the diocese with Bordeaux, Gaillac, or even Montpellier wines. Hence, quality of soil permitting, the planting of wheat and maize was always preferred to vines.

In general, the vines were neither well planted nor well cut, and received only two labors annually. The grapes were often prematurely pressed in large vats under human foot, left many months in the open air, and finally poured into dirty and usually unseasoned casks.[52] An arpent of vine produced an average of two large casks of about 300 litres (66 gallons) of wine, and still left enough mash in the vats for the *demi-vin* and the *arrière vin*, the common beverage of every family. " The *demi-vin*," wrote Picot, " serves the hall, the workmen, and servants." [53] The superior wine in the casks was sold on the local market. On an estate of 713 arpents, Picot had only ten planted in vineyard. Yet he had enough wine for his nine farms, household, seasonal workmen, and 600 litres per arpent for the market. He even used four arpents of vineyard to experiment

[50] A. D., C-110, Subdelegate to Intendant, December 8, 1780.
[51] Lemouzèle, *Toulouse au XVIIIe siècle d'après " Les heures perdues" de Pierre Barthès* (Toulouse, 1914). Cf. his " remarks " on each year, *passim*.
[52] Montaugé, *op. cit.*, pp. 21-23.
[53] Picot, *op. cit.*, p. 70.

with some special wines which he proudly served his guests on feast days at the château.[54] In short, less than 2% of the domain served all of the baron's needs, and even produced a small income.

This arrangement was typical of the noble estates of the diocese. Only 8 of 50 noble proprietors investigated had more than 5% of their domains planted in vines. Of these 8, only two had large areas in vine culture: M. de Boutaric had 43 arpents, and the Baron de Saint Lieux had 172 arpents in vines. Both of these domains were in rocky soils in the northeast of the diocese.[55] For the most part, wine was produced for local, even domain, consumption. Together with soup, vegetables, and perhaps a livre in coin, wine was the common wage of the day-laborer.[56]

Large quantities of fowl were raised on the domain. Each farm of 25 arpents (35 acres) owed a supplementary rent of 12 pairs of chickens, 12 pairs of hens, 12 pairs of capons, and 200 eggs which were delivered to the château on All Saints' Day, Saint Bartholemy's Day, Christmas, and Easter. In addition, each farm furnished the seigneur a certain number of ducks, geese, and pigeons. The stuffing of geese to produce the famous pâté de foie gras was a specialty of the Lauragais. The raising of pigeons was an exclusive noble privilege and the dovecot, which often doubled as a château tower, was a mark of nobility. Finally, each farm raised two pigs, bought by the seigneur, one of which was presented to him at Christmas.[57]

A fraction of every domain was planted in flax and hemp to supply the maîtres-valets and sharecroppers with homespun and rope. Enough wood could be salvaged for clogs. Corn husks and straw took care of matting, litter, and even roofing. Olive oil served as lighting, except at the château, where tallow candles were brought from Tououse. Apart from the château, the domain required very little from outside, except salt.[58]

The activities performed on the landed estate in the Lauragais were extremely diverse. From the point of view of revenue,

[54] Ibid., pp. 68-71.
[55] A. D., C-1331-1346.
[56] Picot, op. cit., p. 82; Montaugé, op. cit., pp. 67-69.
[57] Archives Notariales, Registre 18063, 18089; Montaugé, op. cit.
[58] Montaugé, op. cit., p. 27; Picot, op. cit., pp. 6-10.

the grain lands were the most important. They occupied 80% of the area of the average domain, and produced over 60% of the landed income. Yet the domain was still a long way from specialized agriculture. The marketing of wood and brick, added to sales of hay, accounted for about 30% of landed income. More important, all of the subsidiary activities described above helped free the estate from outside needs and made the income from cereals a clear net gain to the gentleman farmer.

CHAPTER V

THE NOBLE AS *RENTIER*: INVESTMENTS IN PARLEMENTARY OFFICE, PUBLIC SECURITIES, AND PRIVATE LOANS

I

One of France's most renowned economic historians, Henri Hauser, has placed great emphasis on what he terms the " decapitation " of the commercial class by its insatiable desire to invest its accumulated capital in rural property and government office.[1] Nowhere does this generalization seem more apropos than at Toulouse. The seventeenth century had witnessed the decadence of a once vigorous merchant class and the increasing importance of the members of Parlement. The phenomenon was not peculiar to Toulouse, but the lassitude of the city's commercial life made the contrast between a mediocre merchant class and a large and influential magistracy particularly striking.[2] The eighteenth century contributed nothing to reverse this process. On the contrary, the robe families became more firmly entrenched in hereditary office, perpetuating their power and prestige by the revenue of landed property and judicial charges, rather than by fresh infusions of commercial capital.

Of 204 nobles who appear on the capitation rolls of 1789, more than half were nobles of the robe.[3] Attached to the Parlement's six judicial chambers in 1750 were 112 hereditary officers, including one first president, 5 presidents of the subordinate chambers, 15 *présidents à mortier*, 88 councilors, one

---

[1] Henri Hauser, " French Economic History, 1500-1750," *Economic History Review*, IV, pp. 257 ff.; " Réflections sur l'histoire des banques à l'époque moderne de la fin du XVᵉ à la fin du XVIIIᵉ siècle," *Annales d'histoire économique et sociale*, I, 1929, pp. 335-351.

[2] Mme M. Thoumas-Schapira, " La bourgeoisie toulousaine à la fin du XVIIᵉ siècle," *Annales du Midi* (October, 1955), pp. 313-329.

[3] I am indebted to M. Jean Sentou of the University of Toulouse who very generously gave me his complete file of notes on the *capitation noble* for 1789 at Toulouse.

attorney general, and 2 solicitors general.[4] Most of these offices had become the permanent possessions of family dynasties for generations or even centuries.[5] These were the families who, by their number, wealth, and high office, set the tone of Toulousan society and gave cohesion to the noble class as a whole.[6]

Whatever doubt remains concerning other parlements of France, the aristocratic composition of the Parlement of Toulouse appears certain. A study by Jean Egret on the recruitment of parlementarians reveals that at Toulouse all the new presidents and 22 of 27 new councilors between 1775 and 1789 were already noble. Moreover, the conservative aristocratic flavor of the company is indicated by the exceptionally slow renewal of personnel. The Parlement received only 27 new councilors out of a total of 75 in the last 14 years of its existence and only 17 were less than 35 years old in 1790. At Toulouse, as at Nancy, Grenoble, and Aix, the exclusion of non-nobles was effective.[7] Much more exclusive than the Parlement of Paris, the robe nobility of Toulouse was almost entirely a nobility of birth by 1789.

Parlementary office was not only a symbol of noble prestige and power, but also the source of a considerable income. The purchase of an office was an investment yielding a variable return (*gage*) on the purchasing price. The following is a list of *gages* according to office in 1771.[8]

[4] H. Ramet, *Le Capitole et le Parlement de Toulouse* (Toulouse, 1926), p. 129; M. E. Lapierre, *Le Parlement de Toulouse, son ressort, ses attributions, et ses archives* (Toulouse, 1869), p. 6.

[5] The families Rabaudy, Martin, Ayguesives, Catellane, Cantalouse, Cassagneau, Daspe, and Lamothe held offices at the Parlement for generations and the families Bertier, Riquet, Cambon, and Assézat were among those who had owned offices since the seventeenth century. Cf. Villain, *La France moderne généalogique* (*Haute-Garonne et Ariège*) (Montpellier, 1911).

[6] The *noblesse d'épée* of Toulouse were not opposed to reversing the classic progression by entering the robe. The old noble families Aldeguier, Lamote, Sapte, and Daspe had all provided officers in royal regiments, before entering the Parlement. Thus, they joined their nobility of race with that of the magistracy. Cf. Paul de Castéras, *La société toulousaine à la fin du XVIIIe siècle* (Toulouse, 1891).

[7] J. Egret, " L'aristocratie parlementaire française à la fin de l'Ancien Régime," *Revue historique*, CCVIII (juillet-septembre, 1952) pp. 9-10, 12. Of the 27 new councilors, 16 came from the robe nobility, 4 from the old military nobility, 2 from the municipal nobility, and 5 non-nobles from the Chamber of Requests (*petite robe*).

[8] Ramet, *op. cit.*, p. 126 n. The number of councilors was reduced to 75 after 1774.

Number	Office	Gage
1	First President	20,000 livres
15	*Présidents à Mortier*	6,000 livres
5	President-Councilors	4,000 livres
17	Councilors at the *Grand' Chambre*	3,000 livres
71	Councilors at the Chambers of Inquests, Requests and *Tournelle*	2,000 livres
1	Attorney General	6,000 livres
2	Solicitors-General	3,000 livres
5	Substitutes	1,000 livres
117		

It is hard to establish what percentage of the original investment these *gages* represent. If the return was 5%, the official rate, the purchasing price would have been 120,000 livres for *présidents à mortier*, 80,000 for president-councilors, 40,000 for councilors, and 60,000 for solicitors-general. The private accounts of the robe family Cambon-Riquet indicate somewhat lower capital values for parlementary offices. Emmanuel Cambon sold the office of Solicitor General in 1779 for 40,000 livres, and purchased the office of *président à mortier* in the same year for 110,200 livres. In 1777, Cambon received 3,086 livres *gage* for his office of Solicitor General, a return of 7½% on the capital value of the office in 1779. It is, of course, possible that Cambon's rapid parlementary rise from Councilor at the Chamber of Inquests in 1761 to First President in 1787 obliged him to sell his discarded offices at a loss.[9] In any case, it appears that *gages* represented about 5% of the capital value, or sums somewhat above the average for other parlements of France. It is possible that so many of the offices of the Parlement of Toulouse were passed from father to son that the *gages* were based on capital values at the time of their original purchase from the Crown in the seventeenth century. Parlementary offices throughout France sold at higher prices in the reign of Louis XIV, than in 1789.[10]

In addition, the magistrates received the *épices*, obligatory gifts of litigants presenting their cases before the Parlement.

[9] A. D., E-642, " Livre de raison de Cambon-Riquet, 1767-1780."

[10] For a general discussion of this problem, see F. Ford, *Robe and Sword: The Regrouping of the French Aristocracy After Louis XIV*. Cambridge, Mass., 1953), pp. 153-154.

The *gages* were returns on investments; the *épices* were a charge
for professional services rendered. The *épices* were collected in
a common fund and distributed among all the members of the
court by the *receveur des épices*. Although they were high
enough to provoke frequent protests from litigants, the magistrate's share was probably not considerable, especially since the
stamp tax-farm claimed a substantial portion of the common
fund. Without the registers of the *receveur des épices*, it is
impossible to determine the exact amount received annually by
each magistrate. However, judging from the *épices* paid by
the Parlement of Bordeaux and by the Parlement of Rennes,
the individual *président* or councilor did not receive more than
a 1000 livres and probably not more than a few hundred livres
annually. It seems fair to concludes that the robe nobleman's
share of the *épices* approximately covered his *vingtième* and
capitation taxes.[11]

Beside these official revenues, the members of Parlement had
certain privileges of high office, some of real monetary value.
For example, the Parlementary nobles were allowed a certain
quantity of salt free of the salt tax (the *gabelle*) for household
use. A number of them sold the salt among their friends at
a low price, and made the noble class as a whole practically
free of the *gabelle*. The *buvette*, a sort of café at the Palace,
was originally designed to serve *petit déjeuner* to the magistrates, but by 1750 it was serving complete banquets at public
expense, saving the robe considerable sums on their daily expenses. The *buvetier* had become an office worth 7,500 livres,
sold by the First President. About the Palace, and even inside,
the ubiquitous Toulousan hucksters had established their shops
—leased by the whole company of Parlement at a considerable
profit.[12]

A purely economic description does an injustice to the social

[11] At the Parlement of Bordeaux the entire company received only 2,051
livres as *épices* in 1749 and 1761, and in 1750 it received only 987 livres.
Archives Départementales, Gironde, C-4068, 4070, 4076. At the Parlement
of Rennes each councilor received between 84 and 143 livres per month at
court in 1723. Ford, *op. cit.*, p. 155. Castéras fixes the *épices* at Toulouse
at 30, 40, and 50 *écus* per lawcase, but he furnishes no documentary evidence.
Castéras, *op. cit.*, p. 154.

[12] Castéras, *op. cit.*, pp. 155, 158. A royal decree tried to limit the *buvette*
to serving bread, wine, cake, and ice. There is no evidence that it was enforced.

prestige and political influence that an office in the Parlement represented. On the other hand, it emphasizes that such a charge was at once a form of investment, a paying profession, and a convenient way to reduce expenses. Moreover, the revenues were such that the magistrates could afford to work on rotation and extend their vacations away from the Court, beyond the annual two months of recess. This may help to explain how most of the nobles of the robe were able to supervise their country-estates without resorting to money leaseholds.[13] Finally, for some 100 noble families, the revenues of Parlementary office represented a supplement of 2000 to 3000 livres to their annual income in 1789.[14]

II

Before describing the actual practice of loans among the nobility, it is important to emphasize the legal structure in Catholic France, with regard to loans at interest. Without attempting to review the long and complex legal history of the doctrine of usury, a few salient points should be made. First, loans at interest, whatever the rate charged, were officially proscribed until the Revolution (October 12, 1789). It was impossible to recover interests in the ordinary courts, and debtors could even prosecute their creditors criminally for having lent money at interest. Consular judges, however, tended to tolerate infractions of the law, as long as the bills did not stipulate an interest. That is, they did not investigate to see if the interest was included with the principal in the nominal value of the bill. Second, although the scholastic defenders of a rigid definition of *lucrum cessans* (compensation for loss of capital) were clearly on the defensive in the eighteenth century, the most modern French economists (Turgot excepted) never suggested permitting absolute freedom of lending at

---

[13] It should be noted that most of the estates leased in *fermage* belonged to the most important office-holders at the Parlement such as Riquet de Bonrepos, Cambon-Riquet, Caulet, Comère, and Dufaur-Saint Jory. Cf. A. D., C-1312-1330.

[14] To be sure, the *gages* were not always promptly paid. Cf. Cambon's account of his *gages*, A. D., E-642. Moreover, for a new magistrate, the purchase of office represented a considerable capital outlay. However, as we have seen, there were very few new men at the Parlement of Toulouse at the end of the Old Regime.

interest. Even the Revolutionary legislation (September 3, 1807) fixed a maximum of 5% which it took from the legislation of the Ancien Regime with relation to *rentes*.[15]

Long before the eighteenth century, the Schoolmen had permitted a certain form of interest charge (a *rente*) on condition that the capital be permanently alienated. Turgot described this as a rent purchased with a sum of money as one purchases an estate of land.[16] Originally indistinguishable from a quit-rent, the *rente* departed more and more from its initial legal form, and approached a type of loan at interest. By the eighteenth century, the *rente* assumed at least two distinct forms: (1) the perpetual or life rent and (2) the constituted rent. The first was simply the alienation of capital to a governmental, or ecclesiastic institution (municipality, tax-farm, provincial assembly, or " Clergy of France ") in return for a perpetual or life interest, usually between 3 and 5% of the capital sum. Sometimes a perpetual rent was established by the alienation of an estate. The grantor retained a real right over the land, and the grantee became the owner, subject to this charge. In this case, the creditor had the rights of an owner and the transaction was a kind of a sale.[17]

The most modern of *rente* forms was the constituted rent. Instead of land, one party granted another a capital sum, charged with an annual payment in coin.[18] By the eighteenth century, debtors no longer pledged a rent on a particular piece of land as a guarantee of payment, but rather assumed a general obligation on all their possessions. The obligation became attached to the person rather than to the land. In the eighteenth century, regulations concerning constituted rents at Toulouse stipulated that non-payment of rent for two consecutive years gave the creditor the right to demand repayment of the capital. The debtor, on the other hand, could pay back the capital

[15] R. de Roover, *L'évolution de la lettre de change, XIVᵉ-XVIIIᵉ siècles* (Paris, 1953), pp. 123-129; Alexis de Tocqueville, *The Old Regime and the Revolution* (New York, 1955), p. 232.

[16] A. R. Turgot, *Reflections on the Formation and Distribution of Riches* (Paris, 1770), (New York, 1896 edition), pp. 67-68.

[17] This type of alienation was the origin of domain *mouvances*, the grantor claiming *cens* or *rentes féodales*. In the eighteenth century the landowners established such rents only in the last resort. Cf. A. D., C-103-104.

[18] J. Brissaud, *A History of French Private Law* (Boston, 1912), pp. 526-537.

(" repurchase " the *rente*) whenever he wished in coin. Although the debtor could legally refuse repayment on the creditor's request, it was not always wise to do so, and examples exist of creditors calling in their advances. The legal rate for such rents was fixed at 5% by the Edict of May, 1725. Patently, the constituted rent had come close to lending at interest. Only by the tenuous legal fiction that a right to collect a rent had been ". sold " and later " repurchased " were the canonists able to maintain its legality.[19]

To what degree was the law, particularly with regard to the 5% maximum interest rate, still in force at the end of the Ancien Regime? Turgot claims that the actual rate of interest on commercial loans in Angoulême, where he was Intendant, had been between 8 and 10% for the 40 years ending in 1767. He added, however, that in the principal money markets of the Kingdom, it was only 6%. His " Memoire on Money Loans " suggests that the law on *rentes* was relatively effective. He writes:

It is therefore an absolute necessity . . . that the money loan at interest without alienation of the capital, and at a rate higher than the rate fixed for constituted rents [5%] be authorized in commerce.[20]

Among the documentary sources, private and public, concerning loans at Toulouse, I have not found one instance of a loan above 5%, nor any evidence that an added charge was included in the principal. Considering the stagnation of commercial life at Toulouse, this uniform and relatively modest interest rate appears, at first glance, most curious. There was no bank at Toulouse, nor is there any evidence that the tax-farms were lending to private parties. To be sure, the larger merchants performed the functions of bankers as an accessory to their trade, but there were not many of them.[21]

---

[19] *Ibid.*, A. D., E-1726. This *liasse* contains a number of constituted rents " sold " by the Marquis d'Escouloubre between 1752 and the Revolution. Cf. Archives Municipales, G²–42-44, for an extensive list of noble " *rentes*," and Chapter VI, *infra*.

[20] A. E. Turgot, " Mémoire sur les prêts d'argent," *Oeuvres* (Paris, 1844), I, p. 119. Interest rates, maintained Turgot, must be higher than the return on land or the investor would prefer the latter. This observation is another indication that the usury laws were obeyed. *Ibid.*, I, p. 56.

[21] J. Sentou, " Faillites et commerce à Toulouse en 1789," *Annales historiques de la Révolution française* (July, September, 1953), p. 36: ". . . the rate of

On the other hand, Toulouse was one of the most orthodox Catholic cities in France. The Church not only occupied half of the city's area, but also had strong influence in the civil administration.[22] Church views on usury would therefore be heard. The Attorney General, Riquet de Bonrepos, was noted for his religious fanaticism, not only with regard to criminal prosecution of Protestants, such as Jean Calas, or the Grenier brothers, but also with regard to violations of the commercial code. In 1749, a woman was condemned for cheating in commerce, placed half-nude in a cage, lowered by pulleys into the Garonne in mid-winter, and submerged several times before a crowd of spectators on the Pont-Neuf.[23] Why should usury be treated less severely?

If the chronicler Pierre Barthès was typical of petty bourgeois society, the respect for authority and tradition at Toulouse was much greater than frequent bread riots suggest. Barthès was deeply suspicious of irreverent *philosophes*; he regarded the Parlement as the true " Father of the People "; he accepted the severity of capital punishment for theft as necessary, and he hated grain-hoarders, monopolizers, and usurers. Of the latter he wrote: " The usurers become bolder because of the laxness of punishment, and they lend at three times the just value." No doubt Barthès was referring to money-lenders whose clients were men of meager means like himself. Small loans on poor security unquestionably commanded rates above 5%.[24]

However, it appears certain that the principal money-lenders at Toulouse were neither the petty usurers off the rue des

interest practiced from 1770 to 1789 which is 5% . . ." Cf. Archives Municipales, G² 42-44; A. D., E-1726, E-701, E-642 for both public and private constituted *rentes*, invariably at 5%.

[22] The Church had permanent representatives at the Parlement and at the *Capitoulat* and was as active as the Second Estate in the diocesan assemblies and at the Provincial Estates. Cf. Montaugé, *op. cit.*, p. 140 f.; T. Punctous, *Les états particuliers du diocèse de Toulouse aux XVIIe et XVIIIe siècles.* (Toulouse, 1909), pp. 106-121.

[23] Castéras, *op. cit.*, pp. 110-132.

[24] E. Lemouzèle, *Toulouse au XVIIIe siècle d'après " Les heures perdues "* *de Pierre Barthès* (Toulouse, 1914), " Résumé sur 1771 " and *passim*. M. Sentou suggests that some merchants at Toulouse borrowed money at usurious rates, though not openly. Sentou, " Faillites," *loc. cit.*, p. 20. There is also evidence that young noblemen before maturity were borrowing at usurious rates in the Toulousan underworld. Cf. A. D., C-103-104.

Changes, nor the few grain merchants on the Place Dupuy. They were the gentlemen of the Parlement, the Capitoulat, and the St. Etienne quarter. Contrary to the French literary tradition which associates nobility with indebtedness, it would seem that the Toulousan nobility as a whole was a creditor class. It is therefore probable that noble principles and prejudices governed the city's money market and help explain many of its anomalies, including the prevalence of *rentes*, the non-usurious 5% rate of interest, and the shortage of capital for commercial enterprise.[25] It should be borne in mind, that once commercial outlets were eliminated (for whatever the reason), alternate opportunities for investment were limited largely to private loans, government *rentes*, judicial offices, and rural property, tending to lower the price of money. It is this fact, as much as the usury laws, that accounts for a 5% rate of interest.

III

Consider the financial position of three different noble families of Toulouse at the end of the Ancien Regime as revealed in their declarations for the " Forced Loan " of 1793. These balance sheets do not include revenues from offices.

TABLE VII

THE FINANCIAL POSITION OF THREE NOBLE FAMILIES
AT THE END OF THE OLD REGIME [26]

I. *Mme. Adelaide Levis, Marquise de Mirepoix*

		Livres	Sous	Deniers
Real Estate (Revenue)				
1) One house at Toulouse, rue du Temple	1,200#			
2) Lands in Agenois and in the Sénéchaussé of Carcassonne	23,535# 7.3			
Total:		24,735#	7	3

[25] M. Sentou states that the robe nobility was " indisputably the richest class of the region." Sentou, *loc. cit.*, p. 33. Cf. Sentou, " Impôts et citoyens actifs à Toulouse au début de la Révolution," *Annales du Midi* (1948), p. 168 and *passim*. By " principles and prejudices," I mean both a respect for canonical proscriptions and a suspicion of trade.

[26] Archives Municipales, G²–42, 43, 44. The estimates of noble incomes made under the " Terror " must be used with caution. Recall that the seigniorial dues had been suppressed by this date (September, 1793). On the other hand,

Perpetual Rents

1) Capital of 114,000# on the Estates of Languedoc by 8 contracts of 1759, 1774, 1778, 1782 and 1783 at 5%   *5,700#*

2) Capital of 30,000# on the Sénéchaussé of Toulouse by contracts of 1784 and 1786 at 5%   *1,500#*

3) Capital of 12,000# on the Archbishopric of Auch by contract of Jan. 1789 at 5%   *600#*

4) Capital on the *Aides et Gabelles* at Paris by 5 different contracts of Oct. 30, 1721 *   *1,045#17.6*

5) Rent on the *Compagnie des Indes* by contract of Sept. 29, 1720 *   *80# 2.6*

         Total: *8,926#*

---

* These two investments date from the height of the Law Boom, suggesting that the Mirepoix had dabbled in the Paris stock market. Investments such as these after 1722 were extremely rare among the Toulousan nobility.

I. *Mme. Adelaide Levis, Marquise de Mirepoix* (2)

	Livres	Sous	Deniers
Constituted Rents on Individuals			
1) 50,000# on Baynagnet (Carcassonne) at 4% *2,000#*			
2) 33,000# on O'Kelley (Toulouse) at 4% *1,320#*			
3) 7,000# on de Riquet (Toulouse) at 5% *350#*			
4) 7,000# on d'Ormesson (Paris) at 5% *350#*			
5) 20,000# on Gignoux cadet (Valence) at 5% *1,000#*			
6) 25,000# in notes to Mme. Vieuville (Paris) at 5% *1,250#*			
Total:	6,270#		
Gross Revenue	39,931#	7	3

---

the *assignats* had been stabilized at about 50% of their original value by the emergency measures of the *Montagnards*. Cf. J. Godechot, *Les institutions de la France sous la Révolution et l'Empire* (Paris, 1951), p. 330, 336; Henri Martin, " Le papier monnaie sous la Révolution française à Toulouse," *Bulletin de l'Académie de Législation*, III, 1919, IV, 1920.

Interest on Debts and Liabilities **

1) ⅓ of pension for widow Gerly, (my two brothers-in-law pay other ⅔)   666#13.4
2) 12,000# due Guillaume at 5%   600#
3) 6,000# due Lassalle at 5%   300#
4) Life pension due Madeleine Bribal, legatee of my husband by testament of June 21, 1779   50#

Total Liabilities:	1,616#	13	4
Net Revenue:	38,314#	13	11

** The Marquise is exceptional in that she had no obligations other than those arising from the family settlement. Guillaume and Lassalle were probably the two cadet brothers-in-law.

II. *Louis Palarin, Baron de Castelnau* (*Robe*)

Real Estate (Revenue)

1) House and estate at Castelnau d'Estretefonds   6,645#16.8
2) Land at Brujères   2,999#11.11
3) House at Toulouse (rented)   1,500#

Total:	11,145#	8	1

Perpetual Rents

1) Capital of 116,766# on the Province of Languedoc and the Sénéchaussée in 27 different contracts. Rente reduced to 3%   3,403#
2) Capital of 55,000# on the City and Commune of Toulouse, reduced to 4%   2,200#

Total:	5,603#

Constituted Rents on Individuals

Capital of 125,591# 14 sous on eight individuals (including at least 2 merchants and 2 émigrés) at 5% and 26,000# capital to two individuals at 4%

Total:	7,319#	10
Gross Revenue:	24,067#	18	1

II. *Louis Palarin, Baron de Castelnau* (*Robe*) (2)

	Livres	Sous	Deniers
Interests on Debts and Liabilities			
1) Pension to Anne-Françoise Palarin, sister-in-law, by testament of her husband Raymond Palarin	3,150#		
2) Pension to the servant of Raymond Palarin	100#		
3) Capital of 25,900# to four individuals at 5%	1,295#		
4) Capital of 25,000# owed to Bahassage, sister, by family arrangement at 5%	1,250#		
5) Foundation established by the quarry of the City.. .. ..5#			
Total Liabilities:	5,800#		
Net Revenue:	18,267#	18	1

III. *Marquis Pierre de Gavarret* (*Military*)

	Livres	Sous	Deniers
Real Estate (Revenue)			
1) Lands in communities of Villefranche, Cassals, St. Vincent, Vallegue, and Lux	4,807#13.8		
2) House at Toulouse, rue du Croix Baragnon (of my wife)	1,350#		
Total:	6,157#	13	8
Perpetual and Life Rents			
1) Rent on the Royal Treasury	1,100#		
2) Two contracts on the Province of Languedoc, one of 4,000# and one of 3,000# at 5% (of my wife)	350#		
3) Two life rents on the Royal Treasury, payable at Paris (of my wife)	336#		
Total:	1,786#		

Constituted Rents on Individuals

1) 10,000# at 3% (6 years)	*300#*	
2) 8,000# at 5%	*400#*	
3) 6,000# at 5%	*300#*	
4) 15,000# at 5% (to Receiver of the National Lotery)	*750#*	
5) 15,660# at 4½%	*697#10*	
Total:	2,447#	10
Gross Revenue:	10,391#	3 8

III. *Marquis Pierre de Gavarret (Military) (2)*

	Livres	Sous	Deniers
Interests on Debts and Liabilities			
1) 20,000# in two sight drafts at 4% to M. Fornier	*800#*		
2) 2,000# to Mme. Ginesti at 5%	*100#*		
3) 13,000# in a bill of exchange to Duprat de Moissac at 5%	*640#*		
4) 4,000# to Lafage de Rieux at 4%	*160#*		
5) 3,000# by note to de Castres at 4%	*120#*		
6) 4,000# by note to Villeneuve-Lacroisalle at 4%	*160#*		
Total:	1,980		
My wife owes:			
1) 9,000# to M. Luppé at Auch at 5%	*450#*		
2) 4,800# to M. Montigny at Paris at 4%	*192#*		
3) 2,000# to M. Cazan at Toulouse at 5%	*100#*		
Total:	742#		
Total Liabilities:	2,722#		
Net Revenue:	7,669#	3	8

The Levis de Mirepoix, by their political activity and considerable wealth, approach the rank of *haute noblesse.* The Castelnau and Gavarret, with revenues between 10,000 and 25,000 livres were more characteristic of the diocese. Obviously, families such as the Du Barri, with an income of 70,000 livres

for special services rendered to the King, or the Riquet de
Caraman, with an income from the *Canal du Midi* of over
300,000 livres, cannot be classified as typical. In general, old
military families, such as Gavarret, Fourquevaux, Hautpoul,
Grammont, or Escouloubre, had less of their money in *rentes*
than did robe families, such as Castelnau, Dadvizard, Bertrand,
Baranguet or Bastard. But almost all noble families had a
portion of their capital in *rentes*, and most of them lent more
than they borrowed.[27]

About half of the *rentes* " purchased " were perpetual rents
on the State with a marked preference indicated for *rentes* on
the Estates of Languedoc. There is no question that this institution commanded more confidence than the National Treasury
at Paris. The system of provincial and diocesan estates maintained its interest rate at 5% almost to the end of the Ancien
Regime while the National Government earned the reputation
for repudiation of debt and gyrations of interest throughout
the century.[28] The determination of the diocesan assembly to
maintain a good credit standing was revealed in its reaction
to a complaint of the Third Estates in 1788:

If one suspends the interests and reimbursements of capital, the communities and dioceses will be hurt by allowing their debts to accumulate,
a situation which is diametrically opposed to the principles of all good
administration.[29]

At least 55 of the 105 creditors of the Estates of Languedoc

[27] *Ibid.* All of these names, except Escouloubre, appear on the Declarations
for the " Forced Loans." For the Marquis d'Escouloubre, cf. A. D., E-1710,
E-1726, and E-1696-1754 *passim* (" Escouloubre Papers.")

[28] A. D., C-2432 " Compte-rendu des Etats de Languedoc, 1789." Of
28,474,128 livres Provincial debt, about 15 millions were at 3% and 13,500,000
livres at 5%. Cf. Punctous, *op. cit.*, pp. 298-302 for a very favorable account
of the local administration of finances and especially the reimbursement of loans
and the maintenance of a 5% interest. For a detailed account of national
finances, A. Renaudet, *Etudes sur l'histoire interieure de la France de 1775 à
1789; La finance*, " Les cours de Sorbonne " (Paris, 1946). " As for voluntary
loans, we have seen that the government places them through the intermediary
of a body whose credit is more solid than its own, which are more respectful
of their engagements that it is itself; it borrows via the *Hôtel de Ville de Paris*
or via the Provincial Estates," p. 37.

[29] A. D., C-970.

for the year 1759, were Toulousan noblemen.[30] The great majority of them were attached to the Parlement of Toulouse. With the single exception of the President de Maniban who drew a *rente* of 4,350 livres from the Estates, none of the Toulousan noblemen received more than 1,000 livres, and few of them received more than 500 livres, indicating capital investments of about 10,000 livres maximum. Significantly, many of the beneficiaries were female members of well-known Toulousan families. Dame Anne Dufaur de Pibrac for 100 livres *rente*, Dame Hélène de Marette, widow of M. de Lamothe, for 150 livres, and Dame Catherine de Bertier, widow of M. de Benoît, for 150 livres, were typical creditors. Subsequent loans to the Estates for public works, advances on taxes, and army supply have the same characteristics. Wives, daughters, and widows of the families Anceau, Cambon, Escouloubre, Bertier, Fourquevaux and Dufaur are frequently inscribed for *rentes* between 100 and 400 livres. This suggests that many of the noble families found such *rentes* a convenient way to pay jointures for widows and annuities for unmarried daughters. Thus, landed property was spared some of the burdens of the family settlement.[31]

In 1789, the Estates were paying 1,108,921 livres in *rentes* to their creditors, most of whom were Toulousan and Parisian nobles.[32] Compared to this sum, the 73,648 livres paid by the Municipality of Toulouse seem little indeed. Here again, the subscribers were predominantly noblemen, although exclusively from the region of Toulouse. The loans were extremely small, returning between 20 and 200 livres in annual *rentes*. However, many of them dated back to 1650 and, even at 2%, they had paid for themselves twice over.[33] Finally, even in the villages of the diocese, the seigneurs were drawing 2% *rentes* on loans of a few hundred livres, usually for royal taxes, to their respective communities. Like the *rentes* on the Municipality of

[30] A. D., C-2245. Another 16 subscribers were probably Toulousan noblemen. Only 12 of the total 105 were definitely non-noble. The robe nobility of Paris and Toulouse account for three-fourths of the creditors listed.

[31] A. D., C-2245, C-2249. "Créanciers de la Province de Languedoc," 1759, 1785-89. Cf. Chapter VI, *infra*.

[32] A. D., C-2432.

[33] A. D., C-359, "Rentes payés par la Ville de Toulouse, 1743."

Toulouse, those on the village communities were returns on loans of long standing. Unimportant outlets for investments, these loans probably represented a desire on the part of the seigneur to control the finances of the village community.[34]

Constituted rents present a more complex picture. One discovers a network of loans among noble families, rather than a pattern of loans between bourgeoisie and nobility. For example, Dupuy lent Rabaudy 10,000 livres at 2%, Grammont lent Riquet 17,000 livres at 5%, Escouloubre lent Hautpoul 4,000 livres at 4%, and Bussy lent Fourquevaux 6,000 livres at 5%.[35] It is a curious interchange of loans, suggesting mutual assistance to meet specific needs of liquidity, rather than long term investments. In May, 1752, Escouloubre borrowed 5,000 livres and repaid the full amount in September, 1754.[36] Likewise, Varagne-Belesta borrowed 6,600 livres in 1762, and amortized the debt over seven years.[37] In both cases, the gentlemen were far from insolvent, but needed liquidity for family dowries. The interest rate charged sometimes fell below 5%, further evidence of a gentlemen's agreement. Considering the shortage of specie at Toulouse,[38] and the practice of keeping money placed, dowries of 30,000, 60,000, and sometimes 100,000 livres could not be amassed without borrowing from many sources.

A few nobles like Bussy lent substantial sums to merchants and even millers and bakers, as well as to other noble families. Others, like Hautpoul and Rolland de Saint-Rome, owed between 6,000 and 8,000 livres in interest, although their landed incomes were more than adequate to amortize some of these obligations. Both had over twenty creditors to whom they owed capital sums of 5,000 livres each. The fact that these two gentlemen drew almost all of their income from the land, and that Rolland de Saint-Rome purchased Church property during the Revolution, suggests that every spare livre went back into the land, and that small loans were contracted only for immediate family needs. Hautpoul's creditors included 12 noblemen,

[34] A. D., C-1516-1517 "Rôles des impositions de toutes les communautés du diocèse de Toulouse, 1789" Two volumes.
[35] Archives Municipales, G² 42-44. Hereafter, A. M.
[36] A. D., E-1726.
[37] A. D., Gardouch, 1009.
[38] A. D., C-110 Subdelegate to Intendant, December 8, 1780.

among them Anceau, Catalane, Montégut, Palastron, Monbel and Escouloubre.[39]

In any case, it is certain that the nobles did not lend large sums—a loan over 10,000 livres was exceptional—nor did they invest in commercial ventures. Those few *rentes* on the *Compagnie des Indes* date from 1720 and were paying less than 2% in 1789. Aristocratic Toulouse was a far cry from commercial Bordeaux. Handsome profits on West Indian sugar, coffee and indigo were not made in the capital of Languedoc. Aside from a few cloth merchants, business was confined to small dimensions—drugs, confectionary, wine, candles, hat-making. In short, business ventures in Toulouse were risky and offered small returns.[40] Moreover, the prejudices of an old landed gentry held particularly firm in a thoroughly agricultural area. Comte de Villèle expressed the views of many of his class when he wrote:

All that I have seen . . . leaves me with the opinion that all men with an acquired fortune who desire only to conserve it, must keep at a distance from people, of whatever class or profession they be, who strive to make a fortune; he must avoid all business, all relations with them, because they will not fail to make him their dupe. Furthermore, to each man his *métier* as the proverb says: look at the proprietor trying to speculate, and at the merchant trying to enter agriculture. . . . Never have I participated in the least speculation. . . .[41]

The nobility of Toulouse, outstripping the local bourgeoisie in influence and wealth, dominated the local money market. Consequently, its investments assume a peculiarly non-speculative nature. Their principal *rentes* were on the Estates of Languedoc, giving them an assured income which they often used to pay pensions and jointures. The constituted rents represented loans to other noblemen, apparently to meet immediate needs for liquidity. The Toulousan nobleman was a *rentier* in the sense that he preferred a guaranteed return of 5% to a risky commercial venture.

[39] A. M. G² 42-44.

[40] Sentou, " Faillites et commerce à Toulouse en 1789," *loc. cit.*; George V. Taylor who has done extensive research on the bourgeoisie of Toulouse concludes that commerce was not very respectable among a class that sought social status through ennobling office.

[41] Comte de Villèle, *Mémoires et Correspondance* (Paris, 1888), I, pp. 187-188.

Allowing for considerable individual variation, investments in public securities and private loans yielded perhaps 2000 livres net revenue to a noble family. Adding the returns from Parlementary office, a robe nobleman might expect at least 4000 livres. In general, then, a Toulousan gentleman (robe, sword or *cloche*) could count on a supplement to his income of about 3000 livres from non-agricultural sources at the end of the Old Regime.[42]

---

[42] Landed income from the " average estate " was established at 3000 livres in 1750 and 5000 livres in 1789. Cf. Chapter I and Appendix I.

CHAPTER VI

THE FAMILY SETTLEMENT

The transmission of a noble estate to the succeeding generation was settled by the contract of marriage of the eldest son and by the will of the father, head of the family. By the contract of marriage of the eldest son, the bride's dowry and mode of payment were fixed and her claims to the estate in widowhood established; the prospective husband received either maintenance or part of the estate; and the eldest son to be born of the marriage received half of the family estate by entail. Maintenance meant either an allowance or, more frequently, an apartment in the family château with servants and a carriage. Occasionally, the prospective husband received the entire estate by donation of his father in the marriage contract, but he pledged half of it in turn to *his* eldest son.[1] The subsequent testament of the father willed the rest of the estate either to his widow or to the eldest son. If the widow received the estate, she was obliged to convey it to the eldest son when he came of age or when she died. In this case the widow served as the encumbered heir (*héritière grevée*). When the eldest son received the estate, he was obliged to pay portions (*légitimes*) to his sisters and younger brothers when they came of age or married, as well as the jointure of his mother.

The portions were capital sums paid in coin; only in rare cases were they paid in kind. A ruling of the Parlement of Toulouse stated:

The child is obliged to take his portion in coin when, for the honor of his illustrious family, the land of the heredity must be conserved

---

[1] Sometimes a father would entail a specific piece of property, usually the paternal domain, to his grandson by testament. This was infrequent, however. Among twenty-five families, I have found only four cases of this kind of entail. The perpetual entail was even more rare. I have found only one case. The entail was usually couched in the marriage contract. Cf. A. D., *Testaments séparés*, 11809-11858; *Insinuations*, 34-38; *Contrats de mariage séparés*, 11802-11805; and Appendix D.

en bloc . . . since this dignity can not be conserved if the lands are divided.[2]

The portions were estimated on the "unsettled" half of the estate in equal shares to each of the children.

When a father, marrying his son, gives a certain part of his property to the first child to be born of this marriage, and if more than one are born, they will not take their portions on that part, which has never belonged to their father, but only on the other property of the father.[3]

That is, given an estate worth 300,000 livres at the death of the father, and five children, half of the patrimony would have been entailed by the contract of marriage of the eldest son to *his* eldest son and the remaining 150,000 livres would be divided into five portions of 30,000 livres each. However, if there were only four children (or less), only a third of the total estate would be divided for portions, or 25,000 livres each in the above case.[4]

The eldest son had a claim to a portion along with his sisters and younger brothers even though he was the heir to one-half or two-thirds of the patrimony. If the value of an estate increased between the payment of a portion at the time of a daughter's marriage and the death of her father, the daughter had the right to a supplement to her portion. Conversely, if the value of the estate decreased, the dowry could be judged " excessive" and reduced, though only after the death of the husband. If a son or daughter died before coming of age or marrying, his or her portion might be re-divided among the surviving brothers and sisters.[5]

Although a wife's claims on the family estate were very limited during her husband's lifetime, as a widow she had the right to her dowry plus a supplement depending on the terms of her marriage contract. For example, given a dowry of 20,000 livres, 12,000 might "bear" a supplement (*augment*) which was fifty percent in the region of Toulouse, or 6000 livres in this case. The remaining 8000 livres were considered

[2] A. Despeisses, *Oeuvres ou toutes les plus importantes matières du Droit Romain sont méthodiquement expliqués et accomodées au Droit Français* (Lyon, 1750), II, p. 374.

[3] *Ibid.*, II, p. 368.

[4] *Ibid.*, II, p. 361.

[5] *Ibid.*, II, pp. 352, 375.

" paraphernal " or property on which the husband could enjoy only the income during his lifetime. The wife always had free disposal of the paraphernal property. As a widow, she also had the right to her personal belongings (clothes and jewelry) as well as maintenance in a furnished apartment of her choosing usually in the family château or townhouse. Finally, she had the right either to a fixed sum for " the year of mourning " or to a life annuity (*pension viagère*). In principle, the annuity was paid only until the capital of her dowry and supplement was repaid. However, since a widow usually continued to live with her eldest son in the family château, this capital was rarely paid. The annuity, therefore, represented approximately the interest on the dowry and supplement. It was usually readjusted upward or downward, depending upon the family fortune, by the will of the husband or by agreement with the eldest son when he succeeded to the estate.

The two examples below represent the claims of two widows of the families Cadillac and Bertier. Madame de Cadillac was a Riquet and exceptionally well dowered; Madame de Bertier may be considered more characteristic of the nobility of Toulouse.

The Claims of Mme. de Cadillac on Her Husband's Estate [6]

Paraphernal Property:	110,000	*Total:*
Dotal Property:	40,000	176,000
Increase (*Augment*):	20,000	Livres
Personal Possessions:	6,000	
Furnished Apartment in the Château de Cadillac		
Annuity (until capital paid): 10,000 livres		

The Claims of Mme. de Bertier on Her Husband's Estate [7]

Paraphernal Property:	5,000	*Total:*
Dotal Property:	12,000	26,000
Increase:	6,000	Livres
Personal Possessions:	3,000	
Furnished Apartment in the Townhouse, Place St.-George		
Life Annuity: 1500 (Increased to 3000 in 1752)		

[6] A. D., *Contrats de mariage séparés*, 11803, January 20, 1722.
[7] A. D., 6-J, 43, " Contrat de mariage entre Adrien de Bertier et Dame de Gramont," November 28, 1712.

These claims, in addition to any legacies she might have received, constituted the fortune of a widow. On her death portions were estimated in the same manner as on the paternal property. Almost invariably half of the widow's possessions had been entailed to her eldest son in her contract of marriage. The maternal portions were calculated on one-half or one-third of her fortune depending on the number of children. Since daughters received their portions at the moment of marriage, dowries were composed of both maternal and paternal portions.

How were these portions paid? There were three possibilities: (1) by selling part of the estate, (2) by borrowing, or, (3) by saving from current income. In practice, all three of these methods were employed, though the first, selling, in relatively few cases. Current income was sufficient to cover the interest on portions or annuities, but capital payments, especially for daughters' dowries, usually required some form of borrowing. Borrowing might take the form of a loan unattached to land or it might take the form of a mortgage. In reality, the two forms of borrowing were not always distinct since a bill of exchange or other promissory note could be transformed by court action into a lien or claim on landed property. Even the entailed half of the estate could be called upon to serve as security for such loans (i. e., for the payment of the interest) though ordinarily this half could not be sold.

The liability of the entailed property was open to controversy. The jurist, Despeisses, in an authoritative synthesis of Roman and French law applicable to the *Midi*, stated at one point that " in making an entail the testator wishes to prohibit all sorts of alienations whether by exchange or sale of the lands entailed." However, a few lines later he commented, " Such a prohibition to alienate does not prevent the creditors of the deceased from selling the lands." [8] The Attorney-General of the Parlement, Riquet de Bonrepos, asserted in a lawsuit in 1754 that " permission to alienate a part of the entailed properties is an exception to the nature of the entail and is valid only by the express will of the testator. . . . The law does not give the encumbered man the liberty to destroy the trust in order to free the patrimony [of debt] but only a facility to be able to borrow in case of need. . . . To mortgage is not to alienate.

[8] Despeisses, *op. cit.*, II, pp. 137-138.

The mortgage is only a guarantee of security." [9] The Royal Ordinance on Entails (August, 1747) stated that if the moveables and the unsettled property were insufficient to pay the debts and charges on the estate, then the entail could be broken by court order (Title I, Articles 38 and 44; Title II, Article 17). But the ordinance also stated that " all entails made by marriage contracts or donations in life and duly accepted can neither be revoked nor indebted (*chargées*) even with the consent of the beneficiary " (Title I, Article 11). Finally, with characteristic evasiveness, the ordinance read, " whether it is more advantageous to the entail to pay the arrears of interest and charges or to reimburse the capital, we leave the [local] judges to decide." (Title II, Article 11).[10]

Despite a certain ambivalence in the law, it can be said with reasonable assurance that the entailed properties were not completely outside of the reach of creditors. Moreover, as we have seen, only one-half of the estate was entailed; the other half, the so-called " *biens libres,*" could be mortgaged or sold without question. It is also certain that an entail could be broken or modified by a legal act of the father. For example, his will or codicil might state explicitly that the entailed properties be alienated if necessary to pay the debts of the family. Finally, entailed property could be sold by a ruling of Parlement if the unsettled part of the estate was insufficient to pay creditors, legacies, or family charges. In August, 1780 the entailed lands of the family Castelnau d'Estretefonds were released for sale by an *arrêt* of Parlement in order to pay family debts and charges to a maximum of 190,000 livres.[11]

Thus, there was a considerable gap in the legal defense of estate indivisibility by entail. However, although the estate did not escape mortgaging, the general use of a special form of mortgage loan tended to lessen the danger of foreclosure. This special form of mortgage loan was the constituted rent which stipulated that the capital could be legally exacted only

[9] A. D., 4-J, " Mémoire pour M. le Procureur-Général, 1754."

[10] Isambert, et al., *Recueil général des anciennes lois françaises depuis l'an 420 jusqu'à la Révolution de 1789* (Paris, 1822-1828), XXII, pp. 193-216.

[11] A. D., *Insinuations*, 38, fol. 572. The entail was valued at 300,000 livres. The *métairies* sold were to be those farthest from the château. No seigniorial rights could be sold. Technically, the entail had not been " broken," but its value had been greatly reduced.

if the debtor defaulted on his interest payments for two successive years. This type of loan contract made it possible for noble
families to borrow extensively (usually in Parlementary circles)
without great risk of foreclosure.[12]

Furthermore, by a rigid family discipline and by careful
attention to the amortizing of debts and their payment at the
end of each generation, the danger of estate decimation by
foreclosure and sale could be avoided. Such regular payment
was not beyond the means and ingenuity of the local nobility.
Technically, it was a question of keeping portions and family
charges within the bounds of resources and spreading the payments over long periods.

II

There was nothing to prevent the fixing of portions by family
agreement below the amount authorized by the local law. The
"Renunciation" was the common legal instrument by which
a daughter or cadet renounced all future claims on the estate
in return for a dowry or a pension. An inventory of the family
fortune was taken only at the end of a generation, and whether
a daughter's dowry represented her full portion depended
almost entirely on her father's word. The establishment of an
exact inventory was itself the source of many family lawsuits,
sometimes degenerating into petty struggles over the keys to
this or that cabinet. In 1780 the Bastard sisters literally seized
the family château and defended it for several weeks against the
solicitors of their cousin, the new heir. Later they based a
lawsuit on 120,000 livres supposedly found in their father's
desk.[13]

Under the law all members of the family who entered the
regular clergy, including Chevaliers of the Order of Malta,
were automatically excluded from portions. The ruling of the
Parlement was very clear on this point.

The said monks and nuns are not counted among the number of
children of whom they form no part even though the father has left
them a life annuity because such an annuity is a sort of alms or charity
rather than a portion (*légitime*) for which they are ineligible.[14]

[12] Cf. Chapter V on constituted rents.
[13] A. D., 2-J, "Mémoire pour Jean de Bastard, comte d'Estang contre Dame
Marie-Louise de Bastard et Dame Guillemette de Bastard, 1784."
[14] Despeisses, *op. cit.*, II, p. 364.

This proviso made it easier to keep the legally recognized number of children at four or less and thus subject only a third of the estate to portions. Entry into orders also necessitated a testament which willed the personal property of the novice to the family. These legacies were seldom more than a thousand livres. It was customary in the Caulet family for a *Chevalier de Malte* to leave his modest inheritance to a cadet nephew to pay for his reception into the same order.[15] If a daughter entered the Church even preferential legacies were revoked. Marquis d'Hautpoul wrote in his will:

. . . however, if my eldest daughter enters into a convent, I revoke the above legacy. If she has professed after the age of twenty-five and has already received the said sum of 8000 livres, which from the moment of her profession will belong to my heir, she will reimburse him.[16]

For many daughters who did not enter a convent, spinsterhood was their destiny and the picture of the prudish recluse tucked away in the family château is not pure caricature.[17] Under these circumstances it was relatively easy to convert a portion into a life annuity or to forego the portion altogether. President de Caulet's will directed that portions be paid when the boys reached twenty-five and when the girls married, " and until then they will be maintained (*nourris*) on my estate which will represent the interest on their portions." [18] Presumably the President's two daughters did not even receive annuities. It was probably not pure verbiage when a Caulet spinster wrote in her testament:

I beg my other brothers and sisters not to be disappointed because I give them no exterior proofs of my attachment to them. The little property that I have does not permit me to follow the movements of my heart.[19]

François d'Espie was even more precise. His will read that

[15] A. D., *Testaments séparés*, 11820, March 5, 1681; Insinuations, 37, fol. 253.
[16] A. D., *Testaments séparés*, 11840, August 2, 1780.
[17] The Dubarry sisters, who made spinsterhood actually " racy," must be excepted from this generalization. But the Dubarry family was notoriously eccentric.
[18] A. D., *Testaments séparés*, 11820, September 6, 1722.
[19] *Ibid.*, Will of Henriette de Caulet, November 22, 1732.

portions would be paid only "on condition that my two daughters marry." [20]

The Army and the Church were the common vocations of younger sons. Once placed in either of these institutions, a cadet could expect little financial help from the head of the family beyond his portion. "We cadets," wrote Antoine de Bertier to his elder brother on the death of their father, "will be the victims. I shall do whatever you wish." [21] Of the military, few had the resources for marriage unless they could find an heiress. Most of them retired early to the family manse decorated with the *Croix de St. Louis*, sometimes supplemented by a modest royal pension. Bachelor cadets willed their possessions to the head of the family, and often contributed to the dowries of their nieces. As for cadets in the secular clergy, Abbé de Riquet observed, "It is customary for ecclesiastics to be drawn from cadets *peu riches*." [22] Abbé de Bertier wrote to his father from a Paris seminary, "You have treated me like a disinherited son. All I ask is 40 *ecus* (120 livres) per year so as not to be disgraced before my superiors." [23] If a cadet abbé was treated as a family liability, a younger son who became a Prince of the Church might ultimately prove a family asset. Jean de Caulet, Bishop of Grenoble, willed his nephew, head of the family at Toulouse, 380,000 livres in land and contracts on the Clergy of France, an impressive inheritance even by Paris standards. [24] But few cadets of Toulousan noble families ever attained these heights. A canon of Saint Sernin, a bishop of Lavour, an abbé of Auch—such was the career of a cadet who entered the Church. Théron de Montaugé wrote that younger sons in the region of Toulouse remained bachelors and became men servants of the eldest, or else emigrated. [25] Although this conclusion appears too strong, there is no question that the eldest son felt little obligation towards his younger brothers once their portions had been paid.

How many younger sons and daughters married? The fol-

[20] A. D., *Insinuations*, 37, fol. 554.
[21] A. D., 6-J, Antoine de Bertier to François de Bertier, May 25, 1752.
[22] A. D., 4-J, Abbé de Riquet to Mme. de Riquet, May 4, 1749.
[23] A. D., 6-J, 41 *bis*, Abbé de Bertier to Adrien de Bertier, January 7, 1735.
[24] A. D., *Contrats de mariage séparés*, 11805, "Articles de mariage entre Tristan de Caulet et Madeleine de Mesples," May 24, 1762.
[25] Théron de Montaugé, *op. cit.*, p. 118.

lowing table demonstrates the relative consistency of marriage policy among a limited number of noble families. Table VIII represents the number of children of fifteen prominent families over four generations, arranged according to sex and marital status.

TABLE VIII

THE CHILDREN OF FIFTEEN NOBLE FAMILIES OVER FOUR GENERATIONS
1670-1790

Code: T.—Total Number of Children   D. Y.—Died Young
S.—Number of Sons   Ch.—Entered Church
D.—Number of Daughters   D. U.—Died Unmarried
M.—Married

Family	T.	S.	D.Y.	Ch.	D.U.	M.	D.	D.Y.	Ch.	D.U.	M.
Escouloubre	21	8	2	–	1	5	13	–	3	2	8
Varagne	19	9	2	2	1	4	10	–	5	1	4
Hautpoul	13	9	–	2	2	5	4	–	–	1	3
Fourquevaux	10	5	–	1	–	4	5	–	–	2	3
Riquet de Caraman	24	13	2	1	1	9	11	–	2	–	9
Villèle	19	8	1	1	1	5	11	2	–	2	7
Maniban	12	7	1	1	2	3	5	1	–	–	4
Bertier	21	10	2	2	1	5	11	–	4	–	7
Cambon	23	13	–	2	7	4	10	–	3	4	3
Résseguier	19	9	–	2	2	5	10	3	1	4	2
Caulet	25	11	1	3	2	5	14	1	1	8	4
Cambolas	18	5	–	–	–	5	13	–	5	–	8
Assézat	9	6	–	–	3	3	3	–	–	2	1
Comère	10	5	1	–	1	3	5	–	–	4	1
Aldéguier	31	16	–	4	8	4	15	1	3	10[a]	1
Total:	274	134	12	21	32	69	140	8	27	40	65
" Average Family " [b]	4.58	2.23	.2	.35	.53	1.15	2.35	.13	.45	.67	1.10

[a] Although there is no evidence of marriage of any of these ten girls, some of them may have married.

[b] The " average family " is the " Total " divided by sixty generations.

Source: The table is based on the genealogy of J. Villain, *La France moderne généalogique* (*Haute-Garonne et Ariège*), (Montpellier, 1911) 4 vol. The fifteen families represent the most prominent in terms of wealth and public function. The first six families are of the sword and the remaining nine from the robe. No members of the municipal nobility (*Capitouls*) are represented.

As one would surmise, the number of sons and daughters is about equal, though the total size of families is perhaps smaller than the romantic image of the *gentilhomme-campagnard* and his numerous progeny.[26] Notice that, with the exception of the Riquet de Caraman family, the number of married sons is invariably five or less. Five married sons indicate that one younger son married in four generations; four indicate that only one son, presumably the eldest, married; and three indicate that the male line ended in the fourth generation. Most of the sons in the category, "Died Unmarried," were officers in various Royal regiments. The number of married daughters is more variable, but (the Riquet family again excepted) never more than two per generation, and one or less marriages per generation for ten of the fifteen families.

Table IX represents the total number of children of the same fifteen families arranged generation by generation. Table X represents an average noble family generation by generation based on the preceding totals. Both tables are intended to suggest a certain evolution in family policy regarding the younger generation.

TABLE IX

THE CHILDREN OF FIFTEEN NOBLE FAMILIES GENERATION BY GENERATION

(Use the same code as in the previous table.)

Generation	T.	S.	D.Y.	Ch.	D.U.	M.	D.	D.Y.	Ch.	D.U.	M.
1670-1700	74	33	1	5	11	16	41	4	10	8	19
1700-1730	90	40	5	11	7	17	50	2	12	17	19
1730-1760	60	36	3	5	8	20	24	2	5	8	9
1760-1790	50	25	3	–	6	16	25	–	–	7	18

TABLE X

AN "AVERAGE NOBLE FAMILY" GENERATION BY GENERATION

Generation	T.	S.	D.Y.	Ch.	D.U.	M.	D.	D.Y.	Ch.	D.U.	M.
1670-1700	4.92	2.2	.07	.33	.73	1.07	2.72	.26	.66	.53	1.27
1700-1730	6.0	2.67	.34	.73	.47	1.13	3.33	.13	.80	1.13	1.27
1730-1760	4.0	2.4	.21	.33	.53	1.33	1.6	.14	.33	.53	.6
1760-1790	3.33	1.67	.2	–	.4	1.07	1.67	–	–	.47	1.2

Source: Villain, op. cit. By "Average Noble Family," I mean simply the totals for each generation divided by fifteen.

[26] The Mémoires d'outre tombe of Châteaubriand have perpetuated this image which had better be limited to Brittany. Unfortunately, some historians, notably L. Funck-Brentano and P. Gaxotte, have applied Châteaubriand's sentimentalized picture of the hobereau to all of France.

After 1730, there is a definite decline in the total number of children, suggesting perhaps a conscious effort to limit the size of families by some primitive method of birth control, certainly not unknown in the eighteenth century.[27]   This is especially interesting given the general rise in population during the eighteenth century. Second, after the same date, there is a marked decline in the number of daughters and younger sons placed in the Church. In the last generation before the Revolution there were no children among the fifteen families in either the regular or secular clergy. This suggests that anti-clericalism may have had adherents among the Toulousan nobility. There is no doubt that the consolidation of the monasteries and convents in all of France, sponsored by Brienne, Archbishop of Toulouse, was provoked by a decline in candidates at the end of the Ancien Regime. Third, the number of married daughters, except for the generation 1730-1760, remained constant. It was customary for one of the daughters to marry. Finally, the number of married sons remained about the same throughout the four generations, suggesting an effort to keep the number of marriages among younger sons at a minimum.

To be sure, the averages in the last table must be used with circumspection. The first and second tables are more meaningful because they do less violation to family variations. One conclusion seems incontestable, however. Younger sons did not marry; usually one daughter did. This meant that a younger brother's portion would be at least partially returned to the family when he died. A cadet usually placed his portion in land or *rentes* so that the capital was intact on his death. A sister's dowry, on the other hand, became part of her husband's property and was lost to the family. Moreover, it was easier to deal with a dependent younger brother than with an independent brother-in-law. The former might settle for a life annuity or at least a schedule of payments convenient for his elder brother; a brother-in-law was likely to demand prompt payment of his wife's dowry in full.

---

[27] F. A. Pottle, Ed., *Boswell's London Journal, 1762-1763* (New Haven, 1950), Entry of May 16, 1763. For obvious reasons, details on this point are hard to come by.

III

At least one of the daughters married and received a substantial dowry even above the amount of her legitimate portion. These dowries represented the greatest single burden on the family fortune and deserve careful attention.

In reply to his younger sister's protest at receiving a dowry considerably less than her elder sister, Adrien de Bertier avowed that 10,000 livres in the larger dowry was not a portion but a preference legacy (*préciput*) willed by their father for the eldest daughter "to facilitate a good marriage." [28] Such a marriage was important to the prestige of a noble family and was worth a financial sacrifice. Madame de Cadillac expressed it this way:

It often happens that a family announces many advantages for a marriageable daughter uniquely in order to attract rank, and when the time comes for concrete proposals, it would like to reduce them. But after the first propositions it is not honorable to bargain. [29]

Regarded from the point of view of the prospective husband's family, it is difficult to say which was more important in arranging a marriage, the rank of the bride's family or her dowry. Madame de Cadillac's views on this question are worth quoting at length:

There is a question of a marriage for my son. Some mutual friends have proposed this girl and M. de Cadillac has replied evasively. Here is a young lady of very good birth since she is a Duras and her mother a Larochefoucaud. She is 19 years old, has 150,000 livres in coin, and has one brother who is 19 and has a regiment which is with the Army of Flanders. The father is 86 years old and has 40,000 livres income. This father is Marquis de Sivrac. He has land in Saintonge and a domain near Cadillac. . . . Marshal de Duras likes this old man and his whole family very much and takes care of their advancement. It is he who said that this girl was not rich enough to marry at Paris and that she must establish herself in the provinces. [30]

The letter is informative in a number of ways. One thing stands out clearly. The dowry and indeed the general financial position of the prospective wife's family were of great import-

[28] A. D., 6-J, Lawsuit between Adrien and Catherine de Bertier, 1749-1751.
[29] A. D., 4-J, Mme. de Cadillac to Mme. de Riquet, August 31, 1746.
[30] *Ibid.*, August 13, 1746.

ance in making a good marriage. The fact that this branch of the Cadillac family was not rich suggests also that marriageable bachelors were scarce.

Since the marriage of a daughter was a reflection of status for a noble family, the problem was a delicate one. If a family aimed too high in the social hierarchy, the burden of the dowry might assume dangerous proportions. The families Riquet or Varagne de Belesta could afford dowries of 150,000 livres and therefore might search outside of Haut-Languedoc for eligible bachelors. But the more typical Toulousan families of robe and sword—the Escouloubre, Hautpoul, Gavarret, Fourquevaux, Bertier, Caulet, Assézat, or Résseguier—could not afford such dowries, and, for the most part, contented themselves with local marriages within their own class at dowries between 20,000 and 80,000 livres. Such dowries represented between three and four years income.[31]

Yet even these more modest symbols of *éclat* had to be carefully managed. Here the composition of the dowry, the schedule of payments, and the determination of a son-in-law to collect the entire sum were important factors in the burden to the family. Only a small proportion of the dowry would be paid immediately in coin; another portion would be promised at the death of the bride's parents, with or without interest; still another portion might be paid by transferring claims on individual debtors of the family or on public institutions such as the Provincial Estates or the Royal Tax Farm. Often the entire family from bachelor uncles to obscure spinster aunts would be mobilized to make contributions filling out the dowry to an impressive round number. Furthermore, paid portions of the mother's dowry were used to pay the dowry of the daughter, and often the marriage of the daughter was the occasion for a judicial condemnation of the mother's parents or brother to pay her dowry directly to the new son-in-law.

The composition and mode of payment of the dowry of Marie-Anne d'Escoulobre in 1739 combined a number of the elements mentioned above. The dowry of 22,000 livres was composed as follows:

[31] A. D., *Contrats de mariage séparés*, 11802-11805. Dowries among families of *Capitouls* and the *petite noblesse* of Toulouse averaged 10,000 livres. These estimates are based on fifty marriage contracts, of which fifteen represent noble families of recent origin.

1. 3000 livres "Donation in Life" by François d'Escouloubre de Sainte Colombe, uncle, to be paid without interest on his death.
2. 1000 livres "Donation in Life" plus a *rente* of 40 livres by François d'Escouloubre de Castelos, uncle, to be paid immediately.
3. 4000 livres, Preference Legacy by the Marquis d'Escouloubre, father, by testament of 1734 "to be taken on his lands and heredity."
4. 6000 livres, Paternal Portion, "to be taken on the lands and heredity of the Marquis, father."
5. 8000 livres, Maternal Portion, 6000 to be paid immediately and 2000 on mother's death without interest.

On this occasion Dame d'Escouloubre, widowed mother of Marie-Anne, finally received 7600 livres as a payment on her mother-in-law's dowry by a contract of marriage of 1683, fifty-six years before. She added 400 livres to this sum and gave it to her son-in-law, presumably as a payment on the paternal portion and preference legacy of the bride. Then she borrowed 6000 livres from one Jean de Foucaud, Chevalier of St. Louis, at 5% and paid the maternal portion. For Dame d'Escouloubre the burden of the dowry was only 400 livres and the interest on the 6000 livres borrowed. The 2000 livres still due on the paternal portion before her death could be echeloned in small payments.[32]

This optimistic picture is somewhat blemished by the dowry provisions of a second daughter married in 1750. Lucrèce-Gabrielle d'Escouloubre also received a dowry of 22,000 livres of which 5000 were contributed by her uncle and sister. However, the balance of 17,000 livres was paid immediately in *louis d'or*. In this case the money was raised by selling the domain of Buillabrats to another noble family for 20,000 livres.[33] The land sold was part of a great-uncle's inheritance.[34]

Contrast the dowries of Catherine and Françoise de Bertier. Catherine, the younger, received a dowry of only 10,000 livres,

[32] A. D., E-1709, "Contrat de mariage de Marquis Duston et Dlle Marie-Anne d'Escouloubre," November 25, 1739. Foucaud could demand his capital only if Dame d'Escouloubre failed to pay the 300 livres interest for two successive years.

[33] *Ibid.*, "Contrat de mariage de M. de Durand de Nogarède et Dlle Lucrèce-Gabrielle d'Escouloubre," January 24, 1750.

[34] A. D., E-1707, "Donation de Gaston-Louis d'Escouloubre, Seigneur de Balesbax," August 11, 1708.

representing her paternal and maternal portions. By written accord with her eldest brother, Catherine renounced all future claims on the family estate and agreed that her portion could not be paid in land. She received 3000 livres in coin and 3000 livres in provincial *rentes* at her marriage in 1714; the remaining 4000 livres were due after the death of her mother and were paid by 1724.[35] On the other hand, Françoise, the older, received a dowry of 30,000 livres in 1711 composed as follows:[36]

1. 6000 livres, Paternal Portion.
2. 8000 livres, Maternal Portion and Preference Legacy.
3. 6000 livres, Legacy of Comte de Chastelus, uncle, by testament of June, 1709.
4. 10,000 livres, Preference Legacy (supplement based on inheritance of uncle, June, 1709.)

This larger sum, her eldest brother found more difficult to pay. For four years he paid an interest of 1000 livres. Then in 1716 and 1717 he sold two pieces of land, one for 9000 livres and another for 22,500 livres. But the purchasers did not pay immediately, and in 1732 Adrien de Bertier still owed his sister 14,192 livres capital in addition to interest arrears of 14 years totalling another 9,934 livres.[37] By 1752 this obligation had been liquidated, but, as we have seen, not without resort to small sales of land.

By her contract of marriage of 1722, Anne-Victoire, eldest daughter of Riquet de Bonrepos, received 20,000 livres in coin and the promise that the remaining 130,000 livres be paid within six years.[38] Twenty years later, 40,000 livres were still unpaid. A partial account of payments between 1745 and 1757 reveals that Anne-Victoire's mother was amortizing the debt and interest by paying for numerous small purchases of her

[35] A. D., 6-J, 36, "Accord entre Adrien de Bertier et Dlle Catherine de Bertier, sa soeur." December 14, 1714; *Ibid.*, 32, "Procès entre Adrien et Catherine de Bertier," 1749-1751.

[36] *Ibid.*, 43, "Contrat de mariage de M. de Bertier-Mailhas et Françoise de Bertier Pinsaguel," February 27, 1711; *Ibid.*, 75, "Transaction entre Dame d'Anglar de Rochedagous et Adrien de Bertier, son fils," February 27, 1711. Adrien attempted to avoid these preference legacies by hiding the testament of his uncle.

[37] *Ibid.*, 43, "Mémoire de Mme de Comère pour comptes avec M. de Pinsaguel, son frère," 1711-1732.

[38] A. D., *Contrats de mariage séparés*, 11803, January 20, 1722.

daughter. For example, in 1746 Madame de Riquet paid 4,206 livres, mostly to merchants at Toulouse for such items as a writing table (104 livres), dresses and skirts (108 livres), a tapistry (167 livres), mourning clothes (608 livres), and a " suit for *M. le chevalier* " (335 livres). The total was deducted from the amount due on the dowry. In this manner, Madame de Riquet was able to pay 17,000 livres in capital between 1746 and 1751. This was tantamount to paying out of current revenue. However, after Madame's death in 1754, her eldest son became responsible for family portions. He began by making a payment of 14,000 livres, but had to borrow 4000 from the Church Hospice at Toulouse and 10,000 from one M. de Pardaillon.[39] By 1772, fifty years after the marriage, the dowry of Anne-Victoire had been liquidated.

Unfortunately, Anne-Victoire had not been satisfied with the generous provisions of her dowry. Coming from one of the richest families at Toulouse only to find her husband in rather serious financial difficulties, she made repeated claims on the family for supplements to her portion. In a letter to her mother she expressed a spirit common among the women of the Riquet family. " The conservation of my rights is perhaps chimeric but, as you say, one must treat business as business. . . ." [40]

In her contract of marriage in 1722 Anne-Victoire had formally renounced all future claims on the family in return for her 150,000 livre portion. In 1724, when her younger brother, Adrien, died at the age of ten without leaving a will, she demanded a division of his portion among the surviving children, received a supplement of 18,000 livres, and made a second renunciation. Later in the same year her two younger sisters entered the Church and willed Anne-Victoire another 25,000 livres on condition that she make no further demands on the patrimony. In 1731, by formal convention with her mother, she received a gift of 6000 livres and declared herself " entirely paid." Still unsatisfied, in 1748 she re-opened the case of Adrien's portion, demanded a new estimation of the Riquet fortune, and threatened the head of the family with a long and expensive lawsuit. Anne-Victoire settled for 40,000 livres and again renounced all claims on the Riquet estate. It is not

[39] A. D., 4-J, " Comptes avec Mme. de Cadillac, 1745-1757."
[40] *Ibid.*, Mme. de Cadillac to Mme. de Riquet, August 26, 1747.

surprising that her son used the same legal arguments in the next generation to add another 25,000 livres supplement to his mother's portion.[41] Altogether, Madame de Riquet de Cadillac amassed a portion and supplements of 239,000 livres. Nevertheless, by 1772, her brother, Baron Riquet de Bonrepos had paid all but 50,000 livres of this sum.[42]

This accomplishment is less startling when we realize that Riquet de Bonrepos's revenues from the *Canal du Midi* alone were over 100,000 livres yearly.[43] His fortune was certainly well over two million livres in 1760, and had an accurate estimation been made for portions, Anne-Victoire would have had the right to every *sou* of the amount she finally did receive. Moreover, such a revaluation of the estate would have entitled the remaining cadet, Abbé de Caraman, to a similar sum. Hence, given the resources of the family, the daughter's dowry and supplements can not be considered an excessive burden. In fact, Anne-Victoire's periodic claims permitted the spacing of payments over fifty years.

IV

This is not to say that the Riquet, prosperous as they were, met their family charges without effort. No sooner had one generation been paid portions than another took its place. In 1769, when Riquet had almost liquidated his sister's portion, his daughters began to marry. His agent wrote to one of his debtors:

M. le Procureur-Général [Riquet de Bonrepos] has kindly asked M. le Marquis to make arrangements for his reimbursement. If Monsieur can not pay all at once, M. de Riquet is willing to accept it in parcels. M. le Procureur-Général is not an unreasonable creditor since this debt has run over twenty years and the interest has doubled the capital. The considerable expenses that M. le P. G. has had both this year and last on the occasion of the marriages of Mlle de la Gardes and Mlle de Marcel and the money that he has had to pay his two sons-in-law obliges M. le P. G. to call in the sums that are due him.[44]

[41] A. D., 4-J, "Mémoire à consulter," 1774; "Transaction du 6 septembre, 1748"; "Transaction du 28 août, 1776." Under the law, a renunciation was irrevocable only after ten years. Cf. Despeisses, *op. cit.*, II, p. 352.

[42] A. D., 4-J, Receipts of Riquet de Bonrepos, 1772.

[43] A. D., 4-J, "Etat de recette et dépense du Canal, 1753-1754." The net revenue of the canal in 1754 was 421,491 livres. Riquet de Bonrepos held about one-fourth of the shares in 1755.

[44] *Ibid.*, Agent of Riquet de Bonrepos to Marquis de Cadillac, July 13, 1769.

Between 1760 and 1769 three of Riquet's daughters married
with dowries of 150,000 livres each. In 1772 the total obligations of the family appear as follows:

TABLE XI

THE OBLIGATIONS OF RIQUET DE BONREPOS, 1772 [45]

Obligation	Capital	Interest
1. Portions owed one sister and three daughters	397,000 (100,000 non-interest bearing)	14,850
2. Life Annuities to Individuals	20,940[a]	1,047
3. Perpetual *Rentes* to the Church	2,000[a]	100
4. Notes owed to Individuals, 20 at 5% and 2 at 3%.	249,500	11,787
Total:	646,500	27,784

[a] These sums were not payable and hence are not added in the total.

The Procurer-General's income was quite ample to cover the
service charges and it appears that no interest arrears were
accumulating. The amortization of portions at this date was as
follows:

TABLE XII

CAPITAL PAYMENTS ON PORTIONS BY RIQUET, 1772 [46]

Member of Family	Amount Paid	Since	Total Portion
1. Madame de Cadillac, sister	189,000	1722	239,000 livres
2. Madame de Buisson, daughter	30,000	1760	150,000
3. Madame de Cambon, daughter	38,000	1768	150,000
4. Madame Dadvizard, daughter	35,000	1769	150,000
Total:	292,000		689,000

There is no evidence that these capital payments necessitated
any sales of land or canal shares. On the contrary, in 1745
the family had purchased the Marquisat of Lavalette for
53,000 livres on which they still owed 13,500 in 1772.[47] As

[45] *Ibid.*, Receipts of Riquet de Bonrepos, 1772.
[46] *Ibid.*
[47] A. D., 4-J, Mme. de Riquet to M. de Riquet, 1745; *Ibid.*, Receipts of Riquet de Bonrepos, 1772.

for the canal shares, Riquet de Bonrepos held 6⅓ and his cousin, Riquet de Caraman, the other 21⅔ in 1791.[48] On the other hand, many of the capital sums borrowed from individuals had been used to make payments on portions. Some of the loan contracts make it quite clear that the capital was to be employed in this manner. It seems probable that many of the other loans were used for portions as well. Of Riquet's twenty-two creditors about half were noblemen who had lent him capital sums between 5000 and 10,000 livres.[49] It is also worth noting that family obligations in 1791, twenty years later, reveal about the same ratio between paid portions and notes owed individuals.[50] It seems reasonably certain, then, that Riquet was paying his family charges by borrowing. Rather than rapidly reducing the overall estate indebtedness, he was shifting his obligations from family charges to many small loans.

The following loan contract should explain why Riquet, and many of his class, pursued this policy. In August, 1770 Riquet borrowed 24,600 livres from Marquis de St. Sernin at 5%. The contract read:

M. de Riquet de Bonrepos, Marquis de Lavalette, of his own free will has sold, created, assigned, and constituted on all and each of his properties, moveables and immoveables, present and future, and notably and expressly on his share of the revenues of the Canal de Languedoc, the annual and perpetual *rente* of 1230 livres in favor of M. Benoit de Berel, Marquis de Saint Sernin.[51]

The interest or *rente* was to be paid directly by the Receiver and Director-General of the Canal out of Riquet's revenues. The contract also stipulated that the 24,600 livres capital be transferred immediately to Riquet's daughter, Madame de Buisson, as a payment on her dowry. The key clause followed:

It is agreed that the Seigneur de Bonrepos can never be constrained to reimburse the said sum of 24,600 livres except in default of payment of the said *rente* of 1230 livres during two successive years. On the

[48] *Ibid.*, " Etat du patrimoine de M. de Riquet de Bonrepos, 1791.
[49] *Ibid.*, Receipts of Riquet de Bonrepos, 1772.
[50] *Ibid.*, " Etat du patrimoine de M. Riquet de Bonrepos, 1791." The total estate indebtedness was 443,000 livres in 1791 or 203,500 livres less than in 1772.
[51] A. D., 4-J, " Contrat de constitution de rente, 2 août, 1770."

other hand, he is permitted to repurchase the *rente* whenever he wishes in one single payment in gold or silver coin, excluding any kind of bills or other paper created or to be created by Edicts or Declarations of the King. . . .[52]

In October of the same year and in January of 1775, Riquet borrowed another 21,000 livres from two noblemen on the same terms to make a payment on the dowry of his other daughter, Madame Dadvizard.[53]

This type of loan contract exposed an estate to much less danger of foreclosure than did claims for portions. An Anne-Victoire de Riquet could threaten her eldest brother with a lawsuit if he did not pay her legitimate portion, but a creditor like the Marquis de Saint Sernin had no case whatever unless Riquet fell behind for two consecutive years in his interest payments. Add the practice of spreading these individual borrowings thinly among many creditors, and the danger of a sudden foreclosure and forced sale of land would be minimized.

To be sure, bills of exchange and other promissory notes with a definite time limit for the repayment of capital existed at Toulouse. But one finds them generally in the hands of small merchants and speculators, suggesting debts accumulated by the purchase of goods. The bulk of the debts of the Marquis de Maniban were of this sort and were the principal reason for the court action which led to the sale of his domain at Cayras.[54] Borrowings for portions, on the contrary, were negotiated as much as possible among other noblemen and under the terms of the constituted rent described above. The declarations for the Forced Loan in 1793 establish this practice beyond doubt.[55]

Only when a noble family went outside of its circle in the Parlementary quarter in search of *louis d'or* did it encounter

[52] *Ibid.*, Notice the aversion to any kind of paper money. This clause dates from the *Système* of John Law in 1720.

[53] *Ibid.*, Contracts of Constituted Rents, October 5, 1770 and January 19, 1775.

[54] A. D., 2-J, Correspondence between M. Pugens and Marquis de Maniban, 1782-1783.

[55] *Archives Municipales*, G² 42-44. Cf. families Hautpoul, Cambon-Riquet, Castelnau, Caulet, Castellane, Polastron, Puylaroque, Dubourg, Nogarède, and Bertrand. All these noble families were either creditors or debtors of other nobles by *rente* contracts at 5%. There were a few exceptions. The Bastard family preferred bills of exchange to *rentes*.

other forms of loan contracts. These occasions were likely to be provoked by financial needs other than family charges. A loan destined for townhouse embellishments, a new berlin, Norman horses, or other forms of conspicuous consumption required another kind of contract and another kind of creditor. In 1745 Baron de Riquet went to Paris to procure a parlementary office and apparently let few of the advantages the capital offered for good living pass him by. He soon found it necessary to look for ready coin outside of the usual family money market. His wife at Toulouse was well aware of the dangers this entailed.

You have addressed yourself to that scoundrel Saget for money, but I have intercepted the letter. . . . If you need money, I prefer to send you what I borrow among my friends who do not make me pay a large interest. I am very displeased with your bad conduct.[56]

The constituted rent was a mixed blessing since it encouraged borrowing. Employed to make the initial payments on a daughter's dowry or to pay the legacies in the first year after a father's death, the constituted rent had obvious advantages. But used to pay all of the portions and legacies without a plan for amortization, even this form of mortgage loan could become risky. Once a gentleman began defaulting on his interest, the danger signals were up. Fortunately, by law and by custom, family debts were paid at the end of each generation, placing a definite check on excessive borrowing. Debts had to be amortized out of current income in order to avoid sales at the moment of the succession. The noble families at Toulouse appear to have followed this practice since their principal family domains, as we have seen, tended to become larger rather than smaller as the century progressed.[57]

To be sure, the inheritance of a mother or an uncle was often sacrificed to clear the paternal domain of debt. The Escouloubre sold part of a great uncle's inheritance south of Carcassonne to pay a daughter's dowry in 1750.[58] Adrien de Bertier sold his uncle's inheritance in distant Auvergne in 1719 for 180,000

[56] A. D., 4-J, Madame de Bonrepos to M. de Riquet, January 20, 1745.
[57] Cf. Chapter II above.
[58] A. D., E-1707, Donation of August 11, 1708; E-1709, " Contrat de mariage du 24 janvier, 1750."

livres which may account for his modest debts in 1752.[59] In 1745 Dame de Caulet sold the domain of Gragnague acquired by marriage two generations before in order to clear the paternal domains of Tournfeuille and Gramont of all charges.[60] Dame Dupuy de Castelnau instructed her heir to pay the estate charges by selling the domain called " de Bernoye " if necessary, but none of the other lands of her inheritance.[61] The Marquis de Castelnau d'Estretefonds directed his heir to pay all the portions from the domain ot Valour, keeping the paternal domain of Castelnau " always free of debt." [62]

The number of eldest sons who married heiresses was too great to be ascribed to fate alone. Sons of the families Hautpoul, Gardouch, Campistron, Caulet, Cambon, Bertier, and Riquet all made alliances with at least one heiress in the course of the century. Jean-Mathias de Riquet and Adrien de Bertier achieved similar results by marrying three times and harvesting three successive dowries.[63] Such inheritances and dowries formed an important reserve from which to meet estate charges and they protected the paternal property from mortgages.

Hence by the adroit use of several techniques—the constituted rent for initial payments, amortization out of current income facilitated by careful spacing of payments, accumulation of an expendable reserve through advantageous marriages, and a final clearance of charges at the end of each generation—a noble family met the burden of family charges.

V

The precise manner of settling an estate at the end of a generation is recorded in the papers of the Bertier de Pinsaguel family. In 1752 Adrien de Bertier, Marquis de Pinsaguel, patriarch of seventy-three years, died leaving seven children.[64] Among the sons, two were in the Army and one in the Church;

[59] A. D., 6-J, " Livre de raison de M. Adrien de Bertier, 1709-1723."

[60] A. Not., 1137, " Transaction du 28 juillet, 1745."

[61] A. D., *Insinuations*, 37, fol. 450.

[62] *Ibid.*, 36, fol. 200. The paternal domain was valued at 300,000 livres in 1770.

[63] Villain, *op. cit.*; A. D., 2-J, Campistron de Maniban genealogy; A. D., 6-J, 43 and 75 (Contracts of Marriage of Nov. 28, 1712, March 2, 1711, and Nov. 29, 1698).

[64] Cf. Genealogy of the Bertier de Pinsaguel with dowries added.

THE BERTIER DE PINSAGUEL FAMILY IN THE EIGHTEENTH CENTURY

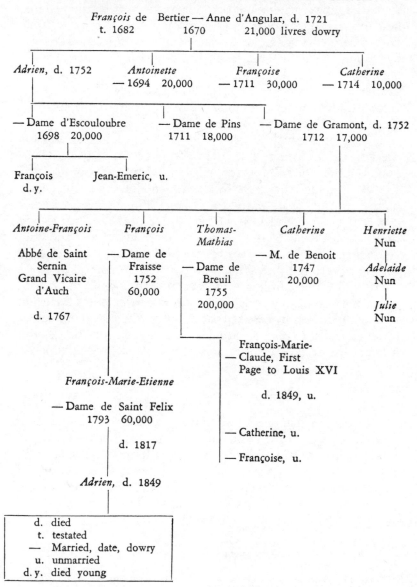

François de   Bertier — Anne d'Angular, d. 1721
        t. 1682   1670   21,000 livres dowry

Adrien, d. 1752   Antoinette   Françoise   Catherine
            — 1694   20,000   — 1711   30,000   — 1714   10,000

— Dame d'Escouloubre   — Dame de Pins   — Dame de Gramont, d. 1752
    1698   20,000   1711   18,000   1712   17,000

François   Jean-Emeric, u.
d. y.

Antoine-François   François   Thomas-   Catherine   Henriette
                                        Mathias   Nun

Abbé de Saint   — Dame de   — M. de Benoit   Adelaide
    Sernin   Fraisse   — Dame de   1747   Nun
Grand Vicaire   1752   Breuil   20,000
    d'Auch   60,000   1755   Julie
                                    200,000   Nun
    d. 1767

                                        François-Marie-
                                    — Claude, First
                                        Page to Louis XVI

                                        d. 1849, u.
François-Marie-Etienne

    — Dame de Saint Felix   — Catherine, u.
        1793   60,000

        d. 1817   — Françoise, u.

        Adrien, d. 1849

        d.   died
        t.   testated
        —   Married, date, dowry
        u.   unmarried
        d. y. died young

among the daughters, the eldest was married and three others were in convents. The Marquis's will was a model of sobriety. He willed 150 livres for funeral masses and 200 livres to his servants. To his three daughters in orders he gave life annuities of 40 livres each " not to be paid to their superiors but to my daughters." To Abbé Antoine-François, Grand Vicar of Auch, he willed " his portion according to the law " and expressed the desire that the Abbé be received at the family château as always and that he be respected as a second father by his two brothers. To Thomas-Mathias, chevalier, he willed his portion and a preference legacy of 25,000 livres payable by the heir ten years after the latter took possession of the estate, paying 5 percent interest until the capital was paid. By this legacy, Thomas-Mathias was to renounce the donation made to him by his half-brother, Jean Emeric, who had died four years before.[65] To Catherine, married daughter, he willed her portion, subtracting 13,000 livres dowry already paid. The Marquis confirmed the donation of half his estate, made in his contract of marriage of 1712, to his eldest son not in orders. Then he willed the rest of his property to this son, François, (*héritier général et universel*), to be received after the death of the Marquis's widow, to whom he gave a life-interest.[66]

The will directed that the inheritance be kept intact, including the livestock, buildings, farm tools, and the moveables on the domains of Pinsaguel and Montrabe. Only the liquid assets, including the ready coin and the product of the harvest, were to be used to pay the legacies, the debts, and even the portions.

I wish that my heredity be rendered entirely free of debt, even of the portions and other charges when they can be validly paid before any placement, acquisition, or augmentation of my heredity be made.[67]

Adrien died in April, 1752 and in August the four Bertier children who had claims to portions assembled at the town-

[65] A. D., 6-J, 6, " Mémoire pour Thomas-Mathias." Jean-Emeric was Adrien's son by first marriage. The Marquis was very angry with him for having willed his property to the cadet, Thomas-Mathias, instead of to François, as he had asked him. " All properties must be reunited to form a good house," said Adrien.
[66] A. D., 6-J, 44, " Testament de M. Adrien de Bertier, Marquis de Pinsaguel," February 17, 1750.
[67] *Ibid.*

house on the Place Saint George to settle the estate.[68]   After some discussion over the donation of the deceased half-brother, Jean-Emeric, the three cadets agreed with François, the heir, that the patrimony was worth 300,000 livres, including 20,744 livres for the moveables inventoried the month before and 13,000 already paid on Catherine's dowry.   Deducting first the debts on the estate totalling 51,657 livres, the patrimony on which portions were to be estimated was reduced to 248,343 livres.   Since there were only four children with claims to portions, only one-third of the patrimony entered into calculation.   The third was then divided into four equal portions, that is, one-twelfth of the total patrimony for each child or 20,685 livres.   François, the new head of the family, promised to pay the portions to each of the three cadets in gold or silver, remitting a five percent interest until the capital was paid.   He also promised to pay the 25,000 livre preference legacy to Thomas-Mathias.   The 13,000 livres already paid on Catherine's dowry were deducted from her portion.   The three cadets then renounced all claims on the estate and even to a supplement should its value increase.[69]

Thus, the new Marquis de Pinsaguel inherited an estate worth 300,000 livres on which he had to pay:

Debts and Legacies	51,657 livres
Portions to Cadets	49,065
Total:	100,722 livres

This was no small charge on an estate returning about three percent or 9000 livres per year.[70]   A closer inspection of the debts, however, reveals that the burden was considerably less. One third of the total obligation (30,000 livres) represented the claims of Adrien's widow, Dame de Gramont de Bertier. These included her dowry (17,000 livres), the supplement (6000), her personal possessions (3000), and two promissory

---

[68] Recall that, under the law, the three sisters in orders had no claims to portions.

[69] A. D., 6-J, 67 "Transaction sur la composition du patrimoine de M. Adrien de Bertier," August 7, 1752.

[70] *Ibid.*, François claimed that the revenues represented "scarcely three percent." The private correspondence of Madame de Riquet confirms this evaluation for the mid-century at Toulouse. Cf. A. D., 4-J, Mme. de Riquet to M. de Riquet, July 9, 1745.

Louis-Marie-Cécile de Campistron, Marquis de Maniban

Victor-Maurice de Riquet,
Comte de Caraman

Joseph de Caulet,
President of the Parlement of Toulouse

Château of Marquis d'Escouloubre at Vieillevigne

Château of Baron de Saint Elix

Château of Marquis de Bertier at Pinsaguel

Townhouse of the Assézat family,
Councilors at the Parlement of Toulouse

(Editions Labouche-Frères—Toulouse)

notes (4000), all payable only in the case of separation of widow and son.[71] Moreover, Dame de Bertier died four months after her husband, changing an estate charge into an asset.

The will of the Marquise was as sober as her husband's. She willed 200 livres for funeral expenses, 150 livres to the servants, life-annuities of 20 livres to each of the three daughters in the Church, portions to the other four children, and the rest of her property to François, the new head of the family.[72] Thanks to a legacy of 20,000 livres owed by her brother, Baron de Lanta, the Marquise had a fortune of 44,207 livres. The three cadets claimed portions and legacies totalling 21,551 livres which François covered by " assigning their claims on the Baron de Lanta," who in addition to the 20,000 livre legacy owed interests of 1500 livres.[73] The death of François's mother reduced the charges on the estate by 30,000 livres and even added 7000 livres in promissory notes and personal possessions to the new Marquis's fortune.

Another 5,446 livres of the charges were in non-mortgage loans (*dettes cherografères*). They were distributed in small sums and owed to merchants and solicitors for goods and services rendered. The list included funeral expenses (563 livres), cost of will and inventory (780 livres), " to Dauriac, merchant, by his account " (107 livres), " to Debrier, upholsterer (65 livres), and other similar debts. François was not obliged to pay these sums immediately and they did not represent a lien on the estate. To be sure, by ruling of Parlement, they could be converted into mortgage loans, but this required at least a year's time and considerable legal expense. Since none of the nineteen individual debts amounted to more than 1300 livres, and only three were over 300 livres, there was little danger from this quarter.[74] In any case, the new Marquis

[71] *Ibid.*, 67, " Accord entre Mme. de Gramont de Bertier et François, son fils," August 29, 1752.

[72] *Ibid.*, 44, " Testament de Dame Henriette de Gramont de Bertier," (Died August 14, 1752).

[73] *Ibid.*, 67, " Composition du patrimoine de Mme. de Gramont de Bertier," August 16, 1752; 44, " Transaction sur le patrimone de Mme. de Gramont de Bertier," August 16, 1752. The portions were fixed at one-twelfth the total fortune or 3,683 livres. The cadets did not receive their money from the Gramont de Lanta family until 1761. *Ibid.*, " Quittances, 30 mars, 1761."

[74] High legal costs always encouraged a creditor to seek a private arrangement with his debtor.

liquidated over half of these secondary obligations in the first two years after his father's death.[75]

The mortgage obligations (*dettes hypothéquaires*) totalled 13,407 livres, including 6000 owed to one M. de Saubeils, 6600 to three Church orders, and 807 to two old servants. M. de Saubeils, the old Marquis's only important individual creditor, continued to receive his interest at 4 percent. Since Church orders preferred perpetual *rentes*, it is probable that only the interest on the 6600 livres was owed. There is no mention of the two old servants on the young Marquis's list of payments. The total interest on these three sums was only 610 livres.[76]

Finally, there were the family charges, including two legacies of 2800 livres and the portions for the three cadets totalling 49,065 livres. The manner of payment of these obligations depended to a large degree on the financial position and even the temperament of the cadets.

Abbé Antoine-François had become Grand Vicar of Auch in 1742, a benefice worth 5000 livres per year. This income obliged the Abbé to spend much of his time in Auch, the remoteness of which he often keenly felt. Confessing that his brother François's life would have been more to his liking, he varied his own existence by making excursions in a handsome carriage-and-four worth over 2800 livres to the watering spa of Bagnères-de-Luchon where he took apartments at some expense. His correspondence and inventory at death suggest a man with more than modest inclinations for fine glass, silverware, an extensive library, considerable furniture (both at Toulouse and Bagnères), not to mention gaming, hunting, and eating, pleasures he pursued at Auch. Before his death in 1767, he had accumulated about 22,000 livres in debts, a respectable sum for a country abbé.[77] It is not surprising that Abbé de

[75] A. D., 6-J, 67, " Etat général des dettes dues par la succession de M. Adrien de Bertier"; 12 " Etat des payements faits par M. de Bertier depuis 1752 à la liberation de la succession de M. son père," 1754. It is certain that François paid 2882 livres of the total and it is probable that he paid another 1600 by 1754. The items on the list of payments are not always identifiable on the list of debts.

[76] *Ibid.*

[77] A. D., 6-J, 41 *bis*, " Correspondance de l'Abbé de Bertier, 1732-1769." Cf. letters of February 26, 1741, 18 May, 1752, 13 December, 1755, and March 7, 1756; *Ibid.*, 5 " Succession de l'Abbé de Bertier," September 8, 1767. After the Abbé's debts were paid, there remained only 6,498 livres.

Bertier was quite firm in his demand for his portion, for, being a man of taste, he knew how to use it. The first item of François's list of payments after 1752 was " 13,843 livres paid to Monsieur l'Abbé." [78]

Similarly, Madame de Benoît, François's sister, received 9,683 livres in the first two years after her father's death, representing the balance of her portion and legacy. We know little about Catherine, but she appeared inclined to accept her eldest brother's advice to stay away from the " sophisms " of the law.[79]

The third cadet, however, Thomas-Mathias, received only 6,695 livres and 700 livres interest annually on the 14,000 still due. The chevalier was a minor at the moment of his father's death and isolated by the arrangements made among his brothers and sister. He was also wary of a lawsuit which might cost him the greater part of his portion.[80] Moreover, in 1755 he married an heiress whose two seigniories in Périgord were valued at 200,000 livres.[81] Unlike his provincial brother at Auch, Thomas-Mathias became a *grand seigneur* in Périgord and had a son who reached the giddy heights of First Page to the King.[82] In brief, Thomas was not pressed for money and François could delay payment of his portion. A proliferation of private loans by Thomas after 1772 and his elder brother's interest in the terms of the contracts suggests that the portion and legacy were finally paid.[83]

Despite the directives of Adrien's testament, the portions could not be paid from the liquid assets alone. Even though the payments were spread over ten and even twenty years, some borrowing was necessary. Although the accounts are incomplete, François borrowed 15,000 livres from five individuals in 1756 and 6000 from still another in 1757, both sums at five percent.[84] To be sure, some of the *écus* may have been employed

[78] *Ibid.*, 12, " Etat des payements," 1754.
[79] *Ibid.*, 36, François de Bertier to Catherine de Benoît, November 10, 1775.
[80] *Ibid.*, 12, " Etat des payements," 1754; *Ibid.*, 6, " Mémoire pour Thomas-Mathias."
[81] *Ibid.*, 6, " Fortune de Françoise de Breuil de Bertier," October, 1773.
[82] *Ibid.*, 62, Letter to M. de Bertier, May 23, 1776.
[83] *Ibid.*, Constituted Rents, April 17, 1772, July 5, 1774, June 5, 1774; M. Monna to Marquis de Bertier, August 22, 1774.
[84] *Ibid.*, 67, Constituted Rents, March 26, 1756, July 22, 1757. The five

for the rebuilding of the château at Pinsaguel, though the fact that the young Marquis undertook this project only four years after his father's death suggests that family obligations were not burdensome.[85] In any case, the loan contracts followed the classic model. They pledged the estate as security for the interest, but the capital could not be recalled except in default of interest for two consecutive years.

Twenty-four years later, in 1781, one of François's creditors by the contract of 1756 needed his capital of 8000 livres in order to pay for a family lawsuit. He proposed that Bertier pay 5000 livres in coin and a life annuity of 400 livres to liquidate the debt. However, since the terms of the contract did not oblige Bertier to pay the capital, he drove a hard bargain and settled for a repayment of only 4200 livres in coin and the life annuity of 400 livres.[86] Given the prevalence of this type of loan, there is reason to believe that this kind of arrangement (involving a considerable reduction of the capital sum) was frequent. How favorable a practice for an eldest son with portions to pay! Under optimum conditions, he could borrow, pay the portions, and later liquidate the debt by repaying only part of the capital.

Unfortunately, it is not until 1817 that we find another family settlement among the Bertier papers. Although this date falls outside of the scope of this study, the ideal plan of payment of estate charges is so clearly stated that one might assume it was applied in the eighteenth century. The obligations of the Bertier estate in 1817 totalled 112,000 francs. By careful spacing of payments, the " pressing obligations " were reduced to 18,100 francs for the first year. The Marquis's plan called for payment of this sum "without being obliged to sell the next grain harvest if the market be low." [87] The principal method of repayment was summarized as follows:

creditors by the first contract included one "bourgeois," one *ancien Capitoul*, and three noble ladies.

[85] *Ibid.*, 67, Contract and Receipt of August 24, 1757. In August, 1757, François made his last payment of 6000 livres (in *écus*) for the rebuilding of his château, the total cost of which was 24,080 livres. In 1754, he also purchased a carriage and horses for 1600 livres, *Ibid.*, 12, " Etat des payements."

[86] *Ibid.*, 67, Accord of April 16, 1781.

[87] *Ibid.*, " Plan pour le payement des dettes de la succession," 1817. Rather than sell the harvest immediately, the plan suggested renting the third floor

Thus, Adrien [de Bertier] can very easily make his *payments period by period without borrowing or selling anything* by adopting the plan outlined above, and with a little reasonable economy; only the will is needed, since the means are clear.[88]

No doubt this ideal was not always possible to attain. Borrowing became necessary especially when cadets were numerous and determined. It is nonetheless clear that the Bertier family scarcely increased its nominal indebtedness between 1752 and 1817. On the contrary, given the doubling of grain prices between these two dates, the relative burden of indebtedness had greatly lessened. The financial position of the Bertier house at these two dates might be compared as follows:

TABLE XIII

THE ESTATE OF BERTIER DE PINSAGUEL [89]

	1752	1817
Area	462 arpents	471 arpents (1800)
Debts	100,722 livres	112,000 francs
Revenue	9,000 livres	22,982 francs
Taxes	1,095 livres	3,000 francs

The Bertier example demonstrates the application of the methods of debt payment described in the preceding section. Both Adrien and his son François made advantageous marriages; their wives' dowries were substantially above their sisters' portions. The Bertier borrowed money by means of the constituted rent, amortized their debts over long periods, and cleared the estate of old charges at the end of each generation.

However, meeting estate charges was not simply a matter of technique. Fundamentally, it was a matter of serious temperament and disciplined habits. Indeed, there were moments when an aristocratic family pushed its pecuniary discipline perhaps to excess. In 1746, after the death of her father-in-law, Madame de Cadillac wrote to her mother:

---

of the townhouse, if Bertier's mother moved. "*Par bon plan, on peut faire face à tout,*" concluded the plan.

[88] *Ibid.*, Italics mine.

[89] *Ibid.*, Cf. 67, "Transaction sur la composition du patrimoine de M .Adrien de Bertier," August 7, 1752, 84, 87, 110; A. D., C-1326, 1324 (*vingtième* rolls).

Finally, my dear *maman*, the great ceremony of opening three testaments is finished. . . . The first was totally in favor of M. de Cadillac. . . . I shall tell you very confidentially that there are two more testaments that we could produce in case of need. They are sealed in good form, but we won't mention them until we find it necessary.[90]

On the other hand, private correspondence also furnishes many examples of a more honorable pecuniary discipline. The letters of Madame de Riquet to her husband abound with stern admonitions regarding the payment of obligations.

One must live austerely to meet all obligations and I ask you to do your part.

Our affairs do not permit us to hire such an expensive cook, when I recall that we have six or 7000 livres debt to pay from our revenue. We don't have money to throw out of the window.

Of course you are not in a position to take a house in Paris. You have a few debts to pay first.

No question about it, the canal is going marvellously; we must manage our affairs with even greater economy.[91]

In similar fashion, Madame de Cadillac was the real manager of family finances. In 1747 she planned to sell a domain for 130,000 livres so that " while paying all the debts of the house, there will be enough left over to buy a smaller domain in the neighborhood which will bring the same revenue as the one we are selling. The difference in price results from the fact that our domain is titled " (i. e., seigniorial rights attached).[92] Abbé de Riquet confirmed the business acumen of still a third female member of the family, Madame de Riquet de Caraman, daughter of the First President of the Parlement of Paris. Commenting on her proposition that he sell his canal share, the Abbé wrote:

. . . she is naturally given to little details and *petits détours* . . . and she knows I need money.[93]

The following passage has the merit of telling us something,

[90] A. D., 4-J, Madame de Cadillac to Madame la Présidente Riquet, January 2, 1746.
[91] *Ibid.*, Madame de Riquet to M. de Riquet, October 10, 1744, November 24, 1744, February 17, 1745, April 19, 1745.
[92] *Ibid.*, Madame de Cadillac to Madame la Présidente Riquet, November 28, 1747.
[93] *Ibid.*, Abbé de Riquet to Madame la Présidente de Riquet, May 20, 1747.

not only about M. de Riquet, but about the Bertier brothers as well. After Comte Thomas-Mathias de Bertier had been repaid the 7,300 livres lent to Mlle. de Gavarret, his agent at Toulouse wrote:

It is time for another placement without loss of interest. I have contacted your brother [for advice]. . . . I placed the 7300 livres in favor of M. de Riquet because I know his solvability, his integrity, and his great exactitude. Your brother advised me to keep the interest aside for your stay at Toulouse.[94]

Shrewd and economical, this provincial nobility had long since abandoned the aristocratic tradition of *largesse*. As with other expenses, the burden of the family settlement was met in a businesslike manner.

[94] A. D., 6-J, 62, M. Campas to Thomas-Mathias de Bertier, May 26, 1790. It would appear that at this date the Revolution had scarcely touched the economic activities of the nobility at Toulouse.

CHAPTER VII

EXPENSES AND MODE OF LIVING AT TOULOUSE

I

The Baron de Montesquieu once defined the grand seigneur as a man who sees the King, speaks to ministers, and has ancestors, pensions and debts.[1] Well might a former *président à mortier* of the Parlement of Bordeaux and a gentleman-farmer of the Garonne valley poke fun at a Parisian courtier. For how different was the life of a provincial gentleman from that of the *grande noblesse* at the brilliant capital! In stronger terms, from his estate in rugged Provence, the Marquis de Mirabeau attacked the "civilized brigands," "bloodsuckers," and "vampires of society" who were the financiers and court nobility of France. Champion of the *gentilhomme-campagnard*, the famous physiocrat hated frivolity and urbanization with a vehemence that called forth all of the polemic and enthusiasm of the *Midi's* Italian frontier. Mirabeau's satire of the urban nobility is worth quoting in full:

They (the provincial nobility) are not to be compared with us (the urban nobility), because we know the rules of the theatre, the essential difference between Italian and French music; we know geometry or take our course in botany or anatomy; we know each other by our carriages, by varnish, by snuffboxes, by chinaware; we are ignorant neither of vanity nor of intrigue, nor of the art of business, nor of demanding charity, nor, above all, of what is the relative value of silver and silver-plate. They, on the contrary, make their entire science consist of seven or eight articles: to respect religion, not to lie, to hold their tongue, to do nothing base, to suffer no insult, to ride well, to fear neither famine nor thirst, and to shoot a pistol.[2]

Country life might produce fewer musicians, geometricians, poets, and parade actors, but was this the function of a nobility?

[1] Charles de Secondat, Baron de La Brède et de Montesquieu, "Lettres Persanes," *Oeuvres* (Paris, 1875), Letter 88.
[2] Marquis de Mirabeau, *L'ami des hommes ou traité de la population* (Paris, 1756), (ed. 1883), p. 85.

It was the resident nobleman who lived a " merry and hard life willingly, cost the State little, and produced more for it by residence and tending to the land." [3]

With little less verbosity than their Provençal cousins, the nobles of Toulouse were gentlemen of similar prejudices. The Villèle family, 12th century nobility, were the Mirabeau of the Lauragais. The Comte de Villèle, despite his attainment of the premiership under the Restoration, remained true to his father's provincial inclinations. He regarded the management of national finances as a defense of France's billions against the infamous bankers of Europe.[4] His success (indeed a small miracle) in balancing the national budget after the Napoleonic wars can be attributed in large measure to his earlier training on the family estate at Mourvilles. At Paris the young count was continually informed of the affairs of the domain by the clear, crisp correspondence of his father.[5]

Villèle's distaste for frivolity and his attachment to King, Church, family, and estate management were evident throughout his life. With his political conservatism one could take issue, but none could deny the consistency and even courage of his convictions. When Napoleon came through Toulouse on his way to Spain in 1809, Villèle wrote:

But at no price, neither I nor any member of my family would consent to take one step to see him, so much were our views contrary to his usurpation. His high capacities and his military successes in our eyes cannot furnish *bon droit*.[6]

As for religion, Villèle's biographer tells us that, without being either fanatic or devout, Villèle was a practicing Catholic. He was too practical to take an interest in metaphysics. For him, Catholicism was the accepted faith, completely interwoven with the society he knew. Like the typical Toulousan, he loved a religious procession, especially if it was sponsored by the Archbishop to pray for good weather. Yet it sometimes happened that the Count " missed a mass." [7]

[3] *Ibid.*

[4] Comte Joseph de Villèle, *Mémoires et corréspondance* (Paris, 1888), I, p. 188.

[5] Jean Fourcassié, *Villèle* (Paris, 1954), p. 16.

[6] Villèle, *op. cit.*, I, p. 191. The count addressed his memoires to " the legitimate heir of the two kings that I have served, Henri V, Comte de Chambord."

[7] Fourcassié, *op. cit.*, p. 57.

As for family life, Villèle's father had set a rather austere patriarchic standard. His mother would have preferred him to be a page in the house of a prince, but his father entered him in the naval school of Alais at the age of fifteen. The young Joseph took a competitive examination, proved his four generations of nobility, and received 300 livres annually in appointments plus a 600 livres pension from his father. Far from leading the life of a court fop, Joseph earned his modest 900 livres on the frigate *Engageante* stationed at Brest in cold Brittany.[8] He was not to return home for 18 years.

Such training was not lost on the young count. Family and naval discipline made Villèle the "friend of order" in every corner of his life. He was the perfect *père de famille*, and had ten children; and the most vitriolic pamphleteer of his later public life never accused him of having a mistress.[9] As the administrator of Mourvilles, the young count husbanded the fruits his father had sown. His father had been a pioneer in the movement toward the suppression of the fallow and the establishment of artificial meadows,[10] and Villèle supervised the family estate with the same minute attention to every detail.[11] It was typical of Villèle's outlook to regard any extra expenditure with skepticism. The elder Villèle had spent the winter months at a townhouse on the rue Sainte Claire, but the younger Villèle considered this an unnecessary luxury and stayed at an inn when he came to Toulouse. In 1812, when the estate returned a net revenue of about 30,000 francs, the Villèle family bought a barometer and a clock, both of which he labelled "fantasies."[12]

The Villèle were but one noble family of the Lauragais. The complexity of individual response, even to the same heredity and environment, must caution one against overgeneralization. Nevertheless, it can be demonstrated with reasonable certainty that an austere outlook and a frugal mode of living were characteristics of the aristocracy of Toulouse.

[8] *Ibid.*, pp. 16-20. Villèle's memories about this portion of his life are far from enthusiastic.
[9] *Ibid.*, p. 49.
[10] Cf. Chapter II.
[11] Villèle Papers—Journal from 1809 to 1831.
[12] Fourcassié, *op. cit.*, pp. 13-14, 49-50.

To be sure, qualifications exist. The mores of the robe nobility differ in some measure from those of the sword nobility. Moreover, no history of the Toulousan nobility would be complete without allusion to the notorious Du Barri family and the equally extravagant Marquis de Gudanes. Yet, qualifications once made, the moral center of gravity of the noble class falls clearly on the side of family discipline, ordered finances, and relatively modest distractions and expenditures. The Toulousan noble would disprove the maxim of La Bruyère and remain independent both personally and financially.[13]

II

Six to nine months of a gentleman's year were spent in the countryside tending to estate affairs. Earlier chapters have demonstrated how diverse and time consuming these affairs were. Life on the estate was punctuated by the harvest, the religious holiday, the meeting of the town elders, inspection of the farms, summer evenings on the terrace, and fall evenings by the roaring fire. In a diocese that possessed little forest or game, even the hunt was reduced to modest proportions.

During eight or nine months of the year château life could be very pleasant. Madame de Riquet's walks at Bonrepos, the family château a few miles from Toulouse, always put her in a good frame of mind.[14] Her daughter wrote on more than one occasion:

Here is admirable weather made especially for going out into beautiful countryside like yours. Enjoy the fresh air at Bonrepos![15]

The Bertier were equally content at Pinsaguel, and their correspondence refers frequently to tours of the estate and copious family dinners.[16] Château life permitted many moods. Madame de Cadillac wrote from her country estate:

Madame de Gontau and some other people are visiting. . . . They

[13] La Bruyère. *Oeuvres* (Les Grands Ecrivains de la France. Paris, 1865), I, p. 326. "A noble, if he lives at home in his province, is free but without support; if he lives at Court, he is protected, but he is a slave."

[14] A. D., 4-J, Madame de Cadillac to Madame de Riquet, October 21, 1747.

[15] *Ibid.*, September 3, 1747.

[16] A. D., 6-J, 41, Abbé de Bertier to François de Bertier, March 7, 1756, December 8, 1741, December 26, 1741.

dance and play comedies. . . . I prefer solitude where I can be alone with my books and writing table. I go from one to the other.[17]

Winter in the countryside, however, was much less agreeable. The château at Bonrepos was never as warm as the townhouse on the rue Velane, and the Riquet family stayed at Toulouse from November to March.[18] Alone in her château in the late autumn of 1748, Madame de Cadillac alluded to " the terrible wind that shakes the entire mansion, like a witch " and obliged her to change her bedroom three times in a single night.[19] In November, Madame de Cadillac, like others of her class, " looked forward to her establishment at Toulouse." [20]

The winter season at Toulouse began after Saint Martin's, (November 12th), and lasted until March. After the reopening of Parlement, the Faculties of Law, Medicine, and Theology suddenly became alive, and the rue des Lois, center of the student quarter, again echoed with shouts, disputes and raucous laughter. In the more respectable quarters—Saint Etienne, Dalbade, Saint Bartholomé—the evenings were more sedate. Only the increased number of bobbing lanterns of the sedan-chairs on the rues Ninau, Croix Baragnon, or Sainte Claire indicated that the older generation of gentlemen had also returned from the country.

Without question the geographic position of Toulouse was an advantage in maintaining a gentlemanly existence. Toulouse was a week's coach ride from Paris, a trip requiring time, effort, and expense which deterred most noble families from dissipating their resources in the " bottomless pit " on the Seine. For Paris had a way of demoralizing even the strongest characters. When Adrien de Bertier went to the city on horseback in 1710, he not only purchased whigs, shirts, cravats, umbrellas, shoe buckles, silk stockings and *mouches*, but also incurred a gambling debt of almost 2000 livres in one evening. Fortunately, the Marquis did not linger there too long.[21] The Abbé de Riquet, attending seminary at the capital, was scandalized by the habits of one Parisian noble family.

[17] A. D., 4-J, Madame de Cadillac to Madame de Riquet, March 26, 1746.
[18] *Ibid.*, September 3, 1747.
[19] *Ibid.*, October 18, 1748.
[20] *Ibid.*, November 16, 1748.
[21] A. D., 6-J, " Livre de raison, 1709-1723," January 30, 1710.

They hire useless servants and discharge the necessary ones; they have rented a country-house where they never live and are always looking elsewhere for another house. . . . One comic but inconceiveable thing is their borrowing in order to pay their debts.[22]

Clearly, it was advisable to avoid the contamination of such a city.

The climate of the *Midi*, despite its intense summer heat, was infinitely more agreeable to a people that loved open air than the damp, cold climate of the North. A trip to Luchon to take the waters or a visit to Albi would adequately supplement the three months' season at Toulouse. Versailles had its brilliance, to be sure, but a reception at the *Salle des Illustres* of the Municipal Palace, the colorful nautical parade on the rue de la Pomme, or the fireworks at the opening of Parlement after Saint Martin's—all had a compensatory *éclat*. The chronicler Pierre Barthès captures some of this color and pomp in a description of the investiture of the new Capitouls:

They all left the *Hôtel de Ville* in full dress as usual, except for the mousquetaires who have been eliminated; the old *Capitouls* dressed in their princely robes, their hoods on their shoulders, the newly elected having theirs also in black. They paraded straight to the Sénéchal in two files, one old and one new. . . . They returned to the *Hôtel de Ville* in the same order. Once arrived, the old *Capitouls* transferred the seals of their office to their successors to the shouts and acclamations of a crowd of people, gathered to enjoy a spectacle of nomination blessed with good weather and promising an administration more satisfactory for the city. . . .[23]

The nobility—robe, sword and *cloche*—were the élite of the provincial capital in every sense, political, social, and economic. To be "presented" at Versailles might carry a certain social prestige, but most of the gentlemen of Toulouse were aware of the high price exacted for the King's kiss. At Toulouse there was no court pomp, but neither was there a host of arrogant financiers, or ambitions bourgeois merchants, or unpolished nouveaux riches, only too well known at commercial centers such as Bordeaux, Nantes, or Paris. In short, at Toulouse there was no new challenge to the traditional order of society. Here a nobleman's position was secure in all of the hierarchies

---

[22] A. D., 4-J, Abbé de Riquet to Madame de Riquet, May 10, 1750.
[23] Barthès, "Les heures perdues," *op. cit.*, July, 1778.

whether based on blood, office, or material resources. Here he could spend modestly and still play the grand seigneur on the steps of Saint Etienne or in the front bench of the parish church without rubbing shoulders with the " vile bourgeoisie."

Not that gentlemanly pleasures were restricted to religious and municipal celebrations or Sunday promenades in the *Jardin Royal*. Toulouse, like other provincial towns of the Kingdom, was a little Paris in the cultural and social sense. It had its theatre, academies, salons, banquets, balls, and gambling houses. The ladies set the tone at social gatherings, and proper society had so far been spared the Spanish cigarette and that vulgar English import, the Club. The words " Dandy " and " Lion," later identified with a parvenu to the refinements of civilization, had not yet entered the local vocabulary.[24]

III

By 1750, provincial privilege had broken the Parisian monopoly on the organization and supervision of the theatre. In 1756 a grand ballet was executed at Toulouse by the troupe of M. Deshayes, privileged comedian of Monseigneur, Duc de Mirepoix.[25] Twenty years before, however, a theatre hall had been established in the municipal palace with mezzanines, loges, galeries, decorated ceilings, and even running water. To the new theatre was attached a permanent troupe of singers and comedians. The better seats were occupied by the elegant class of the city and province, gathered to see the chief works of Corneille, Racine, Molière, Voltaire and the new opera by M. de Beaumarchais " *Le barbier de Seville.*" [26] A good seat for the season cost 144 livres and the parlementary nobility in particular was well represented.[27]

After 1750, theatre censorship was administered by the *Capitouls*. The *Capitouls*, it will be recalled, were often en-

[24] Jean Fourcassié, *Toulouse, trente ans de vie française* (Paris, 1953), p. 50 f. Another English import, however, would have a great success in the Restoration, horse-racing.
[25] Max Fuchs, *La vie théâtrale en province au XVIIIe siècle* (Paris, 1933), I, p. 127 n.
[26] P. Castéras, *La société toulousaine à la fin de l'Ancien Régime* (Toulouse, 1891), p. 42.
[27] A. D., E-642. An item in President de Cambon's account book, dated May, 1779, reads: " *Mon abonnement à la comédie—144 livres.*"

nobled, men of some business inclination, austere *pères de famille*, devout Catholics, often lacking in literary accomplishment, and with a certain zeal for good morals. All of these qualities are revealed in an anecdote dating from 1751:

Capitoul: The last time you played " *L'Avare*," a comedy setting a bad example, in which a son steals from his father. Who wrote this Avare?

Theatre-
Manager: Molière, Monseigneur.

Capitoul: Is this Molière here? I will teach him to have morals and to respect them. Is he here?

Theatre-
Manager: No, Monsieur, he died about 77 years ago.

Capitoul: So much the better. But, my dear man, make a better selection of the comedies you perform here. Can you only perform the plays of obscure authors? No more Molière, please. Try to give us comedies that everybody knows.

Needless to add, the theatre manager appealed to the Parlement and a ruling was handed down authorizing representation of " *L'Avare*." The nobles of robe and sword were not to be deprived of their Friday night's entertainment by the awkward manoeuvres of their foster cousins, the *Capitouls*.[28]

Conveyance to such a social event was not ostentatious. Carriages were rare at Toulouse and confined to the richest noblemen for special occasions. The evening dress of good society, consisting of silk or velvet, buckled shoes, white or light colored stockings, and short breeches, made negotiation of the mud, sewage, and rainwater on the narrow streets most hazardous. Consequently, even the best families bowed to practicality and used the sedan-chair which served a double purpose. It avoided the inconvenience of walking in the filthy streets of Toulouse by permitting the occupant to mount and alight within the entrance hall.[29] It permitted the gentleman all the honors of livery at a modest price. Whereas a coach-and-four cost at least 1,000 livres, a sedan-chair, complete with coat-of-arms could be had for only 250 livres.

The Marquis de Bertier had two sedan-chairs, a small

[28] Castéras, *op. cit.*, pp. 44-45.
[29] *Ibid.*, pp. 29-30.

phaeton and two black horses in his stables at Pinsaguel and Toulouse, representing an investment of 450 livres.[30] Even the Du Barri sisters, installed on the rue de la Pomme, after their return from Versailles, gave up their coach for a sedan-chair.[31] President Cambon, probably the richest man in Toulouse after his marriage to Dorothea Riquet, contented himself with a cabriolet worth 552 livres until 1779, when he bought an English berlin. The coach may have been second hand, for it cost only 306 livres plus 372 livres for new harness and train, 48 livres for painting, and 300 livres for other miscellaneous repairs. An expense of about 1,000 livres was modest indeed for a man with an income of 50,000 livres.[32] The most parsimonious of all was Sentous-Dumont who, in order to place his son, voyaged to Paris in a sedan-chair. He left Toulouse June 1st and arrived in Paris June 17th at the total cost of 350 livres.[33]

Gambling is often considered an aristocratic vice, since it presumably reflects *largesse*, and a disdain for livres, sous, and deniers. In any case, it was as much a social prerequisite of the eighteenth century as bridge is a prerequisite of the twentieth. Despite the efforts of the *Capitouls* to execute local ordinances against it, gaming at Toulouse was not confined to sinister haunts like the "*Vert Galant*," half hidden in the maze of narrow, dark alleys behind the ramparts. It was practiced in some of the most respectable townhouses of the city, particularly in the *salons* of old marquises and spinsters. One of the best known was the *salon* of Mme. de Fontenilles, a countess well in her eighties. Her tables were frequented by such distinguished company as the Marquise d'Aussonne, the Dames de Clermont and La Beaumelle, Maurice du Bus de La Mothe, the Baron and the Chevalier de Najac, the Chevalier de Larrague, a generous scattering of abbés—Panat, Divieux, Dulaur

---

[30] A. D., 6-J, 110, "Inventaire d'Adrien de Bertier, juillet, 1772." One of these sedan-chairs, garnished with the Bertier coat-of-arms, still stands in the *foyer* at Pinsaguel. (1954).

[31] Armand Praviel, *Monsieur Du Barri et sa famille* (Paris, 1932), p. 149.

[32] A. D., E-642.

[33] A. D., E-701, "Cahier de famille de Sentous-Dumont, 1730-1742." Sentous-Dumont was the descendant of a *Capitoul*, a member of the *petite noblesse* with an income of about 1,500 livres.

—and even a Councilor at the Parlement, M. de la Caze, uncle of the infamous Jean du Barri.[34]

Equally famous was the gambling *salon* of the Du Barri sisters, No. 27 rue de la Pomme. Here we find young gentlemen whose names appear on the Subdelegate's list of indebted noblemen, the Marquis de Fauga, the Marquis de Faget, M. de Roune; the former *Capitouls*, Chirac and Bernier; Mme. Colombier, Mlle. de Bonafour, and M. de Savy-Gardiel among others.[35] The *Maison Besinier* on the rue des Paradoux was fined on a number of occasions for " having permitted card playing among students after eleven o'clock." [36] Gambling debts were certainly contracted, though not by *salon* hostesses and gentlemen like La Beaumelle who invariably " kept the bank."

IV

Although the gentlemen of Toulouse constituted a creditor class, there were indebted individuals among them. Many of the indebted were found among the younger noblemen who borrowed on their father's name and who often compounded their indebtedness by frequenting the usurers of the Porte de Bazacle or the rue du Peyrou. The Subdelegate of the diocese wrote about one of these indebted gentlemen in 1781, " Sieur de Gillety is one of a number of those young people of good family who contract debts and mortgage their capital before reaching the legal age required to alienate it." Pursued by his creditors to whom he owed about 10,000 livres, Gillety was conveniently attacked by a " nervous disorder " and retreated to his château. His mother, taking advantage of this respite in the youth's spending, economized and satisfied most of the creditors.[37] The young Marquis de Senaux promised to sell his townhouse to pay off 18,000 livres of debts for clothing and furniture, and immediately half of his creditors agreed to wait.[38] Noble de Montbrun explained to the Intendant that his father's income of 20,000 livres was more than adequate to pay off a

---

[34] A. Feugère, " Le Capitoul David et les jeux défendus," *Annales du Midi* (1932-33), pp. 305-306.

[35] Praviel, *op. cit.*, pp. 149-150.

[36] Feugère, *loc. cit.*, pp. 310-311.

[37] A. D., C-103, Subdelegate to Intendant, January 17, 1781.

[38] *Ibid.* Marquis de Senaux to Subdelegate, July 10, 1786.

debt of 18,000 livres to merchants and usurers, but, "not willing to disturb him at his age," the youth asked for a royal stay
(*sauf-conduit*) and apparently received it.[39] In 1780, Joseph
de Meritens went to the West Indies with his cavalry regiment,
leaving behind over 8,000 livres in debts, partly for household
provisions, wines, *eaux de Cologne*, and glass ware. Although
he had received a number of stays on the promise that he would
sell some property, his mother finally paid off the bulk of the
debt out of current income.[40]

Consider the case of the Sieur de Vignes de Colomiers. The
Subdelegate described him as a "young man of very good
family with a weakness, unfortunately too common, for de-
voting himself to the foolish expenditure of young lords." To
please his young wife, he had contracted debts with usurers and
in a short time amassed obligations totalling 50,000 livres.
The royal official was certain that all would be well if Dame
de Vignes, an active and intelligent woman, could have a free
hand at arranging her husband's affairs. Unfortunately, she
was pregnant, and her husband kept most of his follies from
her. Nevertheless, through her intervention, the debt was reduced to 32,000 livres without touching the domain of Colomiers or the lands of de Vigne's two former wives valued at
137,500 livres, debts deducted.[41]

Indeed, some of the ladies appeared more adept at handling
family finances than their often reckless sons or young husbands.
On more than one occasion, they rescued the estate from
mortgage or diminution by sale. Judicious fathers often substituted when sensible women were lacking. Of course, some
profligacy was beyond redemption. The youth of M. de Fajole,
Marquis de Pordeau, was characterized by the Councilor de
Rolland as "a true dissipation, in the full meaning of that
expression." With an inheritance of 663,785 livres, the young
Marquis exhibited an amazing imagination for expenditure in
a provincial town. In a few years he had spent 141,752 livres
and was involved in a mass of lawsuits over annuities, jointures,
and dowries. Gambling was his dominant passion. In one day,
he was reported to have lost 14,000 livres. Since half of Fajole's

[39] *Ibid*. Noble de Montbrun to Intendant, November 10, 1782.
[40] A. D., C-104, Subdelegate to Intendant, May 17, 1783.
[41] A. D., C-104, Subdelegate to Intendant, June 18, 1785.

estate was entailed, and most of the other half sold, he found it difficult to pay even his principal debts which totalled 60,000 livres. Needless to add, his farms were badly neglected.[42]

Examples like Fajole will always caution one against bold statements. Nevertheless, the bulk of noble debtors exaggerated their plight in order to put off indefinitely repayment of capital sums and avoid selling any property. In most cases, their appeals for royal stays did not reflect any incapacity to meet their obligations but rather a desire for a convenient mode of repayment.[43]

Sieur de Monclar wrote in alarm that his financial situation was so critical that he could not face coming to town to straighten out his affairs. The Subdelegate commented that he was the victim of a brother who dissipated the estate while the elder was in service. Upon closer inspection, however, it appeared that Monclar owed only 7,000 livres and possessed lands valued at 120,000 livres. Reluctantly, he sold one small domain to pay his debts.[44] Other nobles with similar financial problems refused to sell even the smallest domain under the pretext that the buyers offered only half the full value of the property. M. de Puylarin owed 10,000 livres but, according to the Subdelegate, " he has given no indication of selling and according to all appearances he will give none, unless he is pressed." [45] M. de Mascarville, who had received a number of royal stays on the promise to sell some of his land, ended by cancelling his project to sell, claiming that the family estate was held in trust. His debts totalled 18,000 livres, and his annual pension was 3,800 livres.[46]

The Marquis de Brueys owed 15,000 livres and asked for a stay to gain time to satisfy his creditors " without being obliged to alienate his properties at a vile price." The Subdelegate observed that M. de Brueys's well tended estate was worth 150,000 livres, not including his constituted rents which amounted to another 20,000 livres capital. Moreover, the

[42] *Ibid.* M. de Rolland to Intendant, October 20, 1781.
[43] Cf. Appendix D, Printed Form of a Royal Stay.
[44] A. D., C-103, Sieur de Monclar to Intendant, April 3, 1784, Subdelegate to Intendant, June 19, 1784.
[45] A. D., C-104, Subdelegate to Intendant, May 6, 1782.
[46] *Ibid.*, Subdelegate to Intendant, June 10, 1786; Subdelegate to Intendant, May 9, 1787; Subdelegate to Intendant, June 27, 1788.

Marquis refused to permit his father-in-law to pay the interest on his wife's dowry to his creditors, despite this provision in the loan contract. Many of his creditors were artisans and inn-keepers who had furnished the Marquis with provisions, and none had the courage to prosecute a personage of his quality. The Subdelegate concluded that a stay would only encourage him to borrow more.[47]

The Castelnau pushed the prestige of their house even further at the expense of their chief creditor, M. de Halles. In an episode reminiscent of Molière's "*George Dandin*" or the "*Bourgeois-Gentilhomme*," M. de Halles writes:

I have had the weakness, not only of lending Dame Comtesse de Lascarie-Castelnau all the remains of my small fortune, but also of fixing my signature to different bills of exchange.[48]

The bills included 5,000 livres " for the support and incidental pleasures of the Marquis de Castelnau," brother of the countess, and some 8,000 livres for her own. The Castelnau estate was worth at least 200,000 livres.[49]

These examples of indebted nobles, taken from the Sub-delegate's files of petitioners for royal stays against constraint by their creditors, suggest a number of conclusions. First, the gentlemen were able to obtain royal stays delaying repayment of debts, and, above all, avoided sales of land with relative ease. Second, there were not many heavily indebted noblemen. Debts over 20,000 livres (about two and one-half years' average income in 1789) were rare. With few exceptions, their re-sources were such that, given a steady eye on the account book, they could amortize their debts out of current revenues. Third, it appears that most of these debts arose out of a series of petty expenditures for clothing, furniture, wines, household pro-visions, and, only in a few cases, from gaming. Most of them can be ascribed to the follies of youth. They were not the colossal sort of debts that arise from a building mania, a retinue of valets, secretaries and carriages, and all that goes under the general classification of a magnificent style of living. Finally, there are very few nobles of the robe on the Subdelegate's list

[47] A. D., C-103, Subdelegate to Intendant, July 11, 1789.
[48] *Ibid.* M. de Halles to Subdelegate, September 15, 1783.
[49] *Ibid.* Subdelegate to Intendant, October 4, 1783.

of petitioners. Of twenty-five noble debtors investigated, only four were from robe families.[50]

V

Professional pride and austerity still characterized the robe nobility in the eighteenth century. The Marquis de Maniban ordered that his son pursue a career in the robe on threat of disinheritance. His will directed that the young Joseph-Gaspard obtain an office in the Parlement of Toulouse as soon as possible

... in order that he follow the example of his ancestors who have fulfilled their functions with honor and firmness ... [and] if he does not enter the profession of the Robe he will be reduced to a simple portion and my inheritance will go to Councilor Lancelot de Maniban, my brother, or his heirs ... provided they be of the Robe.[51]

It would be a mistake to underestimate the internal discipline of this Parlementary nobility and its sobering effect on the noble class as a whole.

The older generation of magistrates clung to their taste for the Latin Classics, filled the Chambers of the Palais with ponderous citations from the famous glossators of Roman Law, and looked with disdain on the belles-lettres, poetry and philosophy of some of their contemporaries. Only the younger councilors and presidents added Molière and Voltaire to their Aristotle, Cicero, and Plutarch. Recall that in 1789 there were only 17 councilors under 35 years old at the Parlement, and the Calas affair hardly earned the company a reputation for " enlightenment." [52] In a speech at the reopening of Parlement in 1748, the Marquis d'Orbesson, *président à mortier*, captured the pride and conservatism of the Toulousan magistracy. " Yes, you are gods on earth," he said, " but your formidable charge demands eminent virtues." [53]

---

[50] A. D., C-103-104. The robe debtors were the younger Senaux for 18,000 livres, Comtesse de Castelnau and her brother for 13,000 livres, M. de Vaisse for 5,000 livres, and M. de Parazals for 239,000 livres. M. de Vaisse was disinherited by his father and left a pension of only 800 livres by his mother. M. de Parazals was burdened with a debt of 86,000 livres in capital and interest for his office of advocate-general and three unpaid family pensions totalling 130,000 livres capital.

[51] A. D., *Insinuations*, Reg. 34, fol. 73, Testament of Jean-Guy de Maniban, December 22, 1700.

[52] Egret, *loc. cit.*, p. 12.   [53] Castéras, *op. cit.*, p. 143.

First President Emmanuel de Cambon was perhaps the best representative of the eighteenth century robe nobility. Contrasted to his father-in-law, Riquet de Bonrepos, Cambon was tolerant of protestants, moderate in his interpretation of law, and affable and elegant in proper society. His well furnished townhouse off the Place Saint Etienne was open in summer and winter to receive his colleagues and friends. His proud and dignified wife, Dorothea Riquet, maintained a *salon* famous for its exquisite tone.[54] Cambon's household account included a " philosopher " at 300 livres per year.[55] The picture one conjures of President de Cambon dancing the menuet with Madame de Bonfontan or conversing with Madame de Grammont appears more distinguished and cultivated than the card tables and backgammon boards of the Du Barri sisters on the rue de la Pomme.

Cambon's outstanding *salon* was imitated by other robe noblemen such as Daguin in his baroque *Maison de Pierre* on the rue Sainte Claire. The councilors Catelan, Lahage, Lamote, Mourlens also had *salons* in the winter season. Here, under glittering chandeliers, one discussed all subjects, often with barbed comments and always with *esprit*. Occasionally, conversation departed from politics, literature, or the latest scandal at Paris, to a subject particularly dear to the ladies, mesmerism. It was a curious scene when the candles were extinguished and the guests gathered about a bowl of sulphurous water whispering the formulas of Cagliostro.[56] Indeed the cultural interests of the aristocracy were a strange blend of classicism, mysticism, troubadour poetry, and enlightened philosophy. But interest was sufficient to occupy much of the nobleman's time during the winter months. Some of his cultural efforts were lasting, others were not; but none of them constituted a threat to his pocket book.

The academies held regular meetings. The chairs of the patrons of the *Académie des Jeux Floraux* were occupied by councilors of Parlement and well known lawyers. The Academy had lost much of the spontaneity of the thirteenth century. Instead of troubadours gathering in an orchard to appeal to

[54] *Ibid.*, p. 5.
[55] A. D., E-642.
[56] Castéras, *op. cit.*, pp. 5-9.

the poets of the province, a member of Parlement, such as President Daguin, would deliver a pompous and pretentious address that often included more politics than poetry.[57] Nevertheless, pastoral sonnets were still composed, and prizes awarded. Councilor Montégut not only occupied a chair of honor, but wrote a number of bucolic verses. He also evinced an interest in archeology and even met Voltaire and Fontenelle once at Paris.[58] The Marquis d'Escouloubre and the Marquis d'Aquila spent years translating Occitan manuscripts for the Academy. The Revolution interrupted their work, but in 1809 they presented their translation and were named patrons. A later report of the Academy alludes to Escouloubre's translation forming eleven notebooks of 837 pages as revealing " a profound knowledge of the Occitan language and a talent for writing." The Marquis d'Aquila's translation filled 20 notebooks of fine writing, and one can appreciate his comment that he was " twenty times on the point of abandoning this arid work." [59] The significant fact is not the doubtful academic value of this work, but the determination and discipline of these gentlemen to carry it through to the end.

Other noblemen chose the easier course of patronizing intellectual life. Riquet de Bonrepos, his cousin Riquet de Caraman, and the President Niquet, each contributed between 500 and 1,000 livres to the Académie des Sciences, Inscriptions et Belles Lettres for the construction of the Observatory, and provided a salle de réunion for the Académie des Jeux Floraux.[60] The papers of the Marquis de Gardouch contain a printed " Essai de mathématiques " by M. Puymaurin de Brassac of the Collège Esquille, dedicated to M. François de Bertier-Pinsaguel in 1763.[61] Apparently, both Gardouch and Bertier were patrons of young students.

Members of the robe nobility were particularly prolific as authors of legal treaties. The President Cambolas edited his

[57] Ibid., pp. 10-14.

[58] Ibid., pp. 61-62. M. de Montégut was a dogged defender of Parlementary rights and family discipline. He sent his profligate son to the " Bastille of Languedoc" by means of a lettre de cachet. Ibid., p. 33.

[59] G. Arnoult, Monumens de la littérature romane depuis le XIVe siècle (Toulouse, 1841), I, Introduction.

[60] Ibid. " Bienfaiteurs de l'Académie jusqu'à la Révolution."

[61] A. D., Gardouch—1010.

Discours notables sur diverses questions de Droit, jugés par plusieurs arrêts du Parlement de Toulouse (1735); Councilor Castellan wrote *Arrêts remarquables du Parlement de Toulouse* (1766); Councilor Cantalause wrote *Historiques sur les Parlements*; and Noble François de Boutaric wrote *Traité des droits seigneuriaux et matières féodales* (1751), a massive textbook of feudal law and seigniorial rights.[62] This was the golden age of the lawyer and specialist on seigniorial rights.

The Marquis d'Orbesson left the magistry to give himself entirely to art, letters, and science. He belonged to all three of the important academies of Toulouse and presented five bound volumes of academic essays, published under the titles of *Mélanges historiques, antiques, de physiques, de littérature et de poésie* (1760), and *Variétés littéraires pour servir de suite aux Mélanges* (1779). Orbesson had a versatility that combined an interest in archeology, botany, and geology with an interest in the works of Horace, Vergil, and Catullus, and a variety of songs and fables.[63] Similarly, Councilor de Lamote produced numerous works in prose and verse, among others two tragedies, *Turnus* and *Andromaque*, a translation of Horace, and a *Miroir magique*.[64] Both Orbesson and Lamote, it should be added, were better known to their colleagues and contemporaries than to posterity.

The library of the Toulousan aristocrat was further evidence of his intellectual bent. That of the Comte de MacCarthy acquired a European reputation. The count amassed 825 precious first editions printed on vellum and a superb collection of manuscripts decorated with fine miniatures.[65] The library of Baron Ledesme contained 2,838 volumes, well organized in the most beautiful room of the château at Saint Elix. The baron's papers give a complete inventory of his collection. The volumes include the works of Ovid, Homer, Cicero, and Vergil; the memoires of all the famous French ministers and generals, from Richelieu to Maréchal de Saxe; treatises on "*Libertés politiques*," royal taxes, seigniorial rights, and the hunting code; histories of England, works on English commerce, and Captain

[62] All these books are to be found in the Departmental Archives at Toulouse.
[63] Paul Mesple, *Vieux Hôtels de Toulouse* (Toulouse, 1948), pp. 167-68.
[64] Castéras, *op. cit.*, p. 23.
[65] Mesple, *op. cit.*, p. 163.

Cook's voyages; and the complete works of Fénélon, Fontenelle, Bayle, Turgot, Montesquieu, Diderot, Beaumarchais, Voltaire, and Rousseau.[66]

To be sure, these libraries belonged to two of the most prominent noblemen of Toulouse. Comte MacCarthy lived in what many connoisseurs of architecture call the most beautiful townhouse in Toulouse. The château of the Baron de Saint Elix was the habitual autumn meeting place of the administrative and military nobility of the province. Nevertheless, there is evidence that even the more modest gentlemen possessed libraries which helped them occupy many long winter evenings. Of narrow scope, and containing few *Encyclopédistes*, the library of Noble d'Espinasse at Balma contained a few hundred volumes, including the Memoires of Cardinal de Retz, Marshals Villars and Turenne; the works of Erasmus, Grotius, Racine, and Fénélon; and 28 volumes of the *Mercure de France*.[67] The library of the Marquis Bertier de Pinsaguel was full of seigniorial titles, dossiers of lawsuits, maps, leases, wills, and marriage contracts, but contained relatively little literature.[68] On the other hand, the Marquis de Gardouch refers often to Joinvilles's *Histoire de Saint Louis*, abbé Velly's *Histoire de France* (Paris, 1758), and Cantalause's *Historiques sur les Parlements*. To be sure, he was intensely interested in establishing his fifteenth century noble ancestry, but the long passages from Châteaubriand copied in his account book indicate that other motives were also present.[69]

In general, even the old military families who rarely came to town were not deprived of instruction and distractions of the mind. In the most remote château there was invariably a room filled with old memoires, chronicles, biographies, a few histories, collections of royal ordinances and local customs, military and religious studies, and the inevitable treatise on seigniorial rights. All families had cadet members in either the military or the Church, and many retired to the family château

[66] A. D., E-1778. The first item on the baron's copious list was the "Collection complète des oeuvres de M. de Voltaire, 98 vols."

[67] A. D., C-114. Noble d'Espinasse to Subdelegate, 1788.

[68] A. D., 6-J, 101, 103, 106, 110. The château inventory of 1752 lists every chair, tapestry, napkin, and cask of wine, but no books. However, the château library today (1955) contains a number of eighteenth century works.

[69] A. D., *Gardouch*, 1006, 966.

with their few possessions, usually including relics, arms, and books. Hunting and fishing were not the only pastimes of the *hobereaux*.[70]

VI

The most beautiful townhouse of Toulouse was that of Comte de MacCarthy. It cost 93,000 livres in 1773, and its original builder, Comte d'Espie, had been unable to keep it.[71] The capitation tax rolls show that there were 29 occupants of this *hôtel* in 1790, indicating an exceptionally large household staff. Similarly, the household of President de Caulet numbered 23 individuals.[72] In 1756 the Solicitor General Riquet de Bonrepos employed 25 regular servants and four porters during nine months of the year. His household budget included 5,830 livres for the staff, 13,000 livres for the pantry, 800 livres for the stables, and 1200 livres for livery, or about 2000 livres per month for current expenses.[73] The townhouse on the rue Velane, inhabited successively by the Riquet and Villèle families is impressive even today with its high carriage gate and its charming walled garden.

However, these households were hardly typical of the local nobility. The capitation rolls indicate that the Parlementary quarter contained 102 families in 31 houses, suggesting that most robe families lived in apartments. Only the wealthiest gentlemen had large carriage gates and double courts. The average townhouse was either a Renaissance brick structure with one small court and one hexagonal tower, or a sober eighteenth century rectangular building with a façade of four windows, three floors, and an interior garden. By the end of the Old Regime gardens had become rare, many of them sacrificed to build apartments for the swollen population of

[70] Castéras, *op. cit.*, pp. 50-51. The term "*hobereau*," best translated as "country-bumpkin," is used disparagingly throughout French literature from La Bruyère to Beaumarchais.

[71] The family d'Espie lost its fortune in the Lisbon earthquake of 1754. Espie is one of the rare examples of a Toulousan noble with money probably in overseas commerce. Mesple, *op. cit.*, p. 162.

[72] J. Coppolani, *Toulouse, étude de géographie urbaine* (Toulouse, 1954), p. 88 f.

[73] A. D., 4-J, " Etat de la dépense annuelle pour la maison de M. le Procureur-Général," July 2, 1756. Recall that the Riquet de Bonrepos family had an income of about 100,000 livres in 1750.

the city. The census of 1790 indicated that only very few noble families had entire houses to themselves.[74] Even in the Saint Etienne quarter townhouses as a rule were modest. Marquis d'Escouloubre's winter residence on the rue Saint Jacques was certainly more characteristic of the class. It was worth about 20,000 livres in 1789.[75]

Country houses were equally modest, and there was little new building in the eighteenth century. The oldest noble families, such as Escouloubre, Hautpoul, Gavarret, and Becarie de Pavie, lived in thirteenth century châteaux, while some of the robe families, such as Dufaur, de Martin, Ledesme-Saint Elix, Rességier, and Lamote lived in sixteenth and seventeenth century dwellings. One is hard put to find a single eighteenth century château in the whole of the Lauragais.[76] This does not mean that the châteaux were not repaired and, in some cases, partly rebuilt in the eighteenth century. About 1750 the Bertier added two new wings to each of their fifteenth century towers. The château of Becarie de Pavie at Fourquevaux underwent a similar remodeling. The brick country-house of Saint-Félix-Maurémont built by Bachelier in the late-sixteenth century was modernized in 1747. The Villèle family built a second château at Mourvilles, probably in the early eighteenth century. Its simplicity was characteristic of the family.[77]

It would be interesting to estimate the cost of this work. On the Marquis de Bertier's private account for 1756, there is an expense of 1,420 livres and a receipt of only 480 livres. In 1751, the grain receipt alone at Pinsaguel was 1640 livres. The discrepancy of over 1,000 livres in revenues and the unusual expense in 1756 may be attributed to the remodeling of the château. This would mean a cost of about 2,000 livres if the work took only one year.[78] The Baron de Saint Elix repainted the interior of his château in 1769 for 575 livres.[79] The Marquis de Gardouch repaired the village church and the parish house

[74] Coppolani, *op. cit.*, p. 88 f.
[75] A. M. G², 42-44. These declarations for the Forced Loan give similar evaluations for the majority of townhouses at Toulouse.
[76] Guillaume du Barri's "*La Folie de Reynery*" and his sisters' "*Purpan*" are the only eighteenth century châteaux I have found in the diocese.
[77] L. Dutil, *La Haute-Garonne et sa région* (Toulouse, 1928), II.
[78] A. D., 6-J, 13, 35.
[79] A. D., E-1777.

for 364 livres and President Cambon spent 91 livres on his park in 1780.[80] Although the evidence is fragmentary, repair costs do not seem to have been high. Labor at 10 sous per day was cheap, and building block was plentiful.

During the winter season the average noble family at Toulouse had three servants, a valet, a chamber maid, and a cook. The Du Barri sisters on the rue de la Pomme had 13 servants, but most families were satisfied with two or three.[81] In general, a chamber maid was paid 60 livres annually, a valet 65 livres, and a male cook 120 livres. In the countryside one might add an extra maid servant for 36 livres or a gardener for 18 livres per year. A nobleman who had hunting privileges and a wood or wasteland would probably hire a gamekeeper at 100 livres. In practice, these wages were badly paid, as indicated by the mass of claims by servants for back wages during the Revolution.[82] Legacies to servants usually consisted of unpaid arrears and one year's wages.[83] The household accounts of the Marquis de Barneval indicate, not only that the seigneur was six months to one year behind in payment of wages, but also that costs of clothing and livery were deducted. In 1777, the Marquis was paying his servants in grain at 18 livres per setier, slightly above the market price at Toulouse.[84] In short, servants received lodging and maintenance and a few livres coin.

Much might be written about the interiors of these châteaux and townhouses. Cambon's movables at Bonrepos were estimated at 5,394 livres in 1792, including Gobelin tapestries, Chinese porcelain, a vast collection of old coins, and furniture

---

[80] *Gardouch*, 1009; A. D., E-642.

[81] According to the capitation rolls for the city of Toulouse in 1790, the average noble family (of 134 listing servants) had 3.08 domestics. Thirty-six of these families with titles of marquis, comte, vicomte, and baron had an average of 4.8 servants while the remaining 98 families (chevaliers, écuyers, and " nobles ") had an average of 2.4 servants. Only two families in the entire group had more than ten servants to staff their townhouses at Toulouse. M. Jean Sentou was kind enough to lend me his complete file of notes on the *Capitation Noble* (A. M., K-Registres de Capitation).

[82] H. Martin, " Les biens du clergé et des émigrés déportés et condamnés, confisqués et vendus sous la Révolution, d'après les Archives de la Haute Garonne," *Revue des Pyrénées*, XXVI (1914), pp. 6-7.

[83] A. D., *Insinuations*, Reg. 34-38.

[84] A. D., E-635, " Livre des domestiques." One of Barneval's footmen had 30 livres deducted from his wages in 1769. The deductions include shoe repairs, 1 livre, 10 sous.

ornamented in gold and bronze filigree.[85] Councilor Gaillard's
château at Frouzins contained a collection of paintings including
Murillo, Mignard, Dumont, and Moreau, most of them copies.[86]
The Marquis de Gardouch had an extensive collection of old
medallions in his townhouse on the rue Bougières.[87] In the
château of Pinsaguel the principal item of value was the household silver. The Marquis de Bertier's "inventory after death"
includes every silver plate and goblet, a total value of 2,393
livres, 11 sous, 9 deniers. Other movables, however, seemed
modest indeed. Part of the inventory reads: [88]

11 pieces of large tapestry	20 livres
5 pairs of Turkish tapestry	70 livres
10 ordinary chairs	3 livres
1 wooden buffet	14 livres
1 wooden cupboard	7 livres
1 table	1 livre, 10 sous
1 table	3 livres
4 muslin curtains	12 livres
4 pairs of sheets	28 livres
2 dozen common napkins	12 livres
10 casks of ordinary wine	48 livres
2 casks of "special wine"	51 livres
kitchen utensils	48 livres

The total value of Bertier's movables, including farm tools,
carriages, and household furnishing at Pinsaguel and Toulouse,
not including the silver, was only 7,624 livres, 12 sous.[89] The
furnishings of the château of Saint Elix, among the most
luxurious of the region, were valued at 17,932 livres.[90] These
evaluations for three of the most prominent noble families of
Toulouse do not suggest excessive expenditure for interior
decoration.

VII

The picture of modest aristocratic living at Toulouse would

[85] H. Martin, *Documents relatifs à la vente des biens nationaux*, (*District de Toulouse*) (Toulouse, 1916-1924), pp. 147-247.
[86] Castéras, *op. cit.*, p. 66.
[87] H. Ramet, *Histoire de Toulouse* (Toulouse, 1939), p. 606.
[88] A. D., 6-J, 110.
[89] *Ibid.*
[90] A. D., E-1810. Cf. *Inventaires après décès* for more evidence on the modest value of the personal property of the Toulousan nobility.

be unblemished were it not for gentlemen like Jean du Barri and Louis Gaspard de Sales. Du Barri was the sort of *bon vivant* who prided himself on the art of spending. Despite a handsome income of 70,000 livres from the Royal Treasury fifteen years after the disgrace of his famous protegée, the count owed 430,000 livres in 1789.[91] His townhouse on the Place Saint Sernin was valued at almost 100,000 livres and was certainly one of the most controversial monuments of the city. Admired by the average Toulousan, it was described by Arthur Young as the height of folly.[92] English prejudice aside, the *Hôtel du Barri* was the reflection of the bizarre imagination of its owner. The façade was simple enough, but the interior was crowded with Aubusson tapistries, Boucher ceilings, Venetian glass, doric columns of red marble, medallions of Roman Emperors, enormous mirrors and gold filigree everywhere. In the bedchamber the statue of a nude woman was placed in such a way as to appear emerging from her bath. The pastoral garden behind was studded with lead shepherdesses, stone peasants, wooden blacksmiths, marble sphinxes and a few flowers. The art gallery included works of Rembrandt, Rubens, Mignard, Boucher, Greuze, and Fragonard, accumulations of Du Barri's checkered career.[93] To the end, the count lost none of his flamboyance. Faced with the guillotine, he spent his last days in a completely furnished prison-cell drinking fine wine and playing cards with the other *gens de qualité*.[94]

M. Louis-Gaspard de Sales, Marquis de Gudanes, could trace his pedigree to the tenth century, and his family domains covered a vast area of forest on the French side of the Pyrenees. Until the eighteenth century, the family insisted on rendering homage with the " goblet of water " to its suzerain, the Comte de Lordat. Among the peasants the story was told that the Marquis went to Versailles on a horse shoed in silver. True or false, the story reflected his love of magnificence. When the Marquis de Levis-Mirepoix arrived at Gudanes near sunset, his

[91] A. M. G² " Dubarry." Du Barri sold his magnificent domain of Isle Jourdain to " Monsieur," the future Louis XVIII for 900,000 livres and purchased *rentes* on the *Hôtel de Ville de Paris*. A. Praviel, *Monsieur Du Barri et sa famille* (Paris, 1932), pp. 116 n., 138.

[92] Young, *op. cit.*, I, p. 109 f.

[93] Praviel, *op. cit.*, pp. 152-155.

[94] *Ibid.*, p. 179 f.

host posted a small army of valets with torches for miles along the road to light the way. His immense track of forest permitted him to hunt on a princely scale and earned him the title of " King of the Pyrenees." Curiously, he never hunted himself, but insisted that his valets, retainers, and peasants organize expeditions to massacre as much fox and fowl as possible.

Gudanes entered Toulousan society by the marriage of his daughter to M. de Mengaud, *président à mortier* at the Parlement. The dowry was 200,000 livres, a very large sum for Toulousan noble society. Established on the rue Ninau, the Marquis's " court " gathered hangers-on at a prodigious rate, including numerous amateur " philosophers." His style of living exceeded his revenues, as the sale of his domains at Montgaillard made clear. Oddly enough the Marquis struck upon using his wood supply for iron-making and in 1761 he persuaded the Royal Treasury to lend him 20,000 livres to develop his mines and forges. For twenty years he escaped an accounting with his creditors, despite the obvious failure of the enterprise. In 1782, Gudanes made a " gift in life " of the entire estate to his son-in-law, and thereby escaped foreclosure. His friendship with the Queen gained him another 200,000 livres from the Royal Treasury, before the Revolution put some limitation to his reckless extravagance.[95]

Toulousan aristocratic society could afford exceptional spendthrifts like Du Barri and Gudanes. In 1750, the average landed estate of 192 arpents (average for 226 noble families) in the diocese produced a revenue of about 3,000 livres.[96] By 1785, the prices of all principal farm products had risen at least 60%, and by 1789 at least 100%.[97] Add supplements to income from judicial offices, *rentes,* and royal pensions, and the average noble income at Toulouse might be modestly fixed at 8,000 livres, (5000 from the land and 3000 from offices and *rentes*).[98] In

[95] Castéras, *op. cit.*, pp. 64-79.
[96] Cf. p. 40 n., and Appendix A.
[97] Cf. pp. 48, 89, 95, and Appendix C.
[98] I say " modestly " fixed at 8,000 livres because the change in landed income is based exclusively on the secular rise of wheat prices (67%) between 1740-47 and 1780-87. It does not include: (1) increased revenue from enlarged domains and from clearings, (2) increased revenue from woodland, meadow, mills, and brick ovens, or (3) " super-profits " from stocks of grain held in times of scarcity. Revenue from the *cens* is also excluded though collection of seigniorial

1789, 8,000 livres was two to three times the revenue of a prosperous merchant, a retired bourgeois, or a successful lawyer at Toulouse. It was a sum at least sixteen times the revenue of a skilled artisan (jeweler, tapistry maker, carpenter), and sixty times the wage of a *maître-valet*, the top of the rural proletariat.[99] In relation to other classes, the nobleman was at the head of the scale of revenues. Moreover, his real income was rising. This was due partly to the fact that prices for the goods he bought did not rise as sharply as those he sold. It was also due to an inexpensive mode of living. Arthur Young made this comment about the gentlemen of the *Midi*:

One must admit that the cost of living is cheap. I have been told about a family whose revenue is estimated at 1,500 louis and whose existence is as comfortable as among Englishmen who have 5000 pounds. To compare the cost of living in different countries is a question of great importance but difficult to analyze. If, as I see it, the English have the advantage over the French in all useful arts and manufactures, England must be the less expensive country. But what we find in France is a *mode of living* that is inexpensive, something completely different.[100]

In other words, the rural French nobleman was willing to sacrifice some of the advantages of a more urbanized society in order to live with a certain *éclat* on his own more rustic terms.

Rustic did not mean poor. A Toulousan nobleman's resources were quite adequate to cut a good figure during the winter season at Toulouse. They were sufficient to maintain comfortable townhouses and country châteaux, staffed with three to five servants, a cabriolet and a sedan-chair in the stable, and substantial collections of silver, linen, tapestry, furniture, and books. A gentleman's pantry was always well provided with lamb, pork, poultry, eggs, cheese, vegetables, white bread, and an occasional cask of Bordeaux wine to supplement the local vintage.

---

dues was more rigorous in the later years of the century. The estimate of 8,000 livres is, therefore, a minimum figure.

[99] J. Sentou, " Impôts et citoyens actifs à Toulouse au début de la Révolution," *Annales du Midi* (1948), pp. 159-179. A recent study by M. Georges Marinière for the *Diplôme d'études supérieures* at the University of Toulouse (1958) concludes that the cloth merchants of the city had an average income of only 3000 livres in 1789.

[100] Young, *op. cit.*, I, p. 106. Young's italics.

Aristocratic living in the Lauragais could not hope to achieve the *éclat* of Chambord or the *Faubourg Saint Germain*. However, there were compensations. The provincial theatre, the *salon*, and the academy in winter, the village fête, the outdoor pleasures, and the family reunion in summer made existence more than bearable. The Toulousan gentleman might well agree with Talleyrand that only those who had lived in the last years of the Old Regime understood the true meaning of the " *douceur de vivre*." More important, this mode of living was maintained by adherence to the so-called bourgeois virtues of thrift, discipline, and strict management of the family fortune.

APPENDIX A

ESTIMATES OF ESTATE INCOMES

Thanks to comparatively complete tax rolls for the *vingtième* of 1750, a reliable picture of the area, administration, and revenues of the noble estate in the diocese of Toulouse can be produced. It should be emphasized that the *vingtième* represented the first successful effort, albeit of brief duration, to levy a direct tax of 5% on the landed income of the Second Estate. Moreover, contrary to all precedent, the controller-general, Machault, was able to substitute a new tax administration under the Royal Intendant for the traditional fiscal administration of the Provincial Estates. Given the aristocratic complexion of the Estates, and its bitter opposition to the *vingtième*, only new fiscal personnel, insulated against local and class influence, could assure the successful collection of the new tax. Thus, although the new tax officials were not completely free of local interests, the tax rolls were drawn up in a relatively complete and objective fashion, at least for the first four years of the operation of the tax.[1]

The documents used here and extensively throughout this study are of two kinds: " Declarations of the Communities " and " Declarations of the Nobility " for the first *vingtième* of 1750. The former are declarations of landed income by all social groups in 183 (out of 214) communities in the diocese, and the latter are declarations of landed income of the nobility only. The declarations of the nobility give the total area of the domain and its division into grainland, fallow, woodland, meadow, vines, and wasteland, as well as the claims to seigniorial dues and rents from estate utilities (mills, forges, ovens). Each declaration presents a detailed description of the administration of the land, including provision of seed, payment of the harvest hands, division of grain with sharecroppers, and deductions for wages of *maîtres-valets*, salaries of stewards, taxes and special repairs. Each tax statement concludes with

---

[1] A. Renaudet, *Etudes sur l'histoire intérieure de la France de 1715 à 1789; La finance, " Les cours de Sorbonne"* (Paris, 1946), pp. 40-58; 67. Cf. M. Marion, *Les impôts directs en France, principalement au XVIIIᵉ siècle* (Paris, 1910).

178

an estimate of the gross income and net income based on the market price of grain and other produce sold from the domain.[2]

These details of domain management and farm production can be checked, not only by general works on the agriculture of the Lauragais before the Revolution, but also by contemporary royal administrative correspondence and private papers.[3] Most important in the latter category are the Subdelegate's reports to the Intendant on all phases of agriculture, the private papers of noble families such as Escouloubre, Bertier de Pinsaguel, Villèle, Varagne-Gardouch, Fourquevaux, and Ledesme, and, above all, the agricultural treatise of Picot de Lapeyrouse.[4]

In general, the division of the domain, the crop courses, deductions of seed, harvesting costs, portions of sharecroppers and wages of *maîtres-valets* and stewards, as reported in the tax declarations, appear to be reliable. But the noble declarations contain one cardinal error, making the revenue estimates, as they stand, almost completely valueless. In almost every case, the noble proprietor bases his income on an average wheat yield of three to one on seed or only three setiers per arpent (5.7 bushels per acre). Average wheat yields were actually five to one of the seed, or 9.5 bushels per acre.[5]

It is possible, however, to present a reasonably accurate income picture of the noble estate in 1750 by reworking the declarations on the basis of a five to one wheat yield, as well as by re-evaluating the revenues of the woodlands, meadows, and vines. Calculating by the arpent of wheatland (1.39 acres) and substituting the new yields within the original framework of costs and deductions, one proceeds by the following method:

[2] A. D. C-1331-1346; C-1312-1330.

[3] The indispensable general works are: Théron de Montaugé, *L'agriculture et les classes rurales dans le pays toulousain depuis le milieu du XVIIIᵉ siècle* (Paris, 1869); P. Viguier, *Du colonage partiaire dans le Lauragais* (Paris, 1911); J. R. de Fortanier, *Les droits seigneuriaux dans la sénéchaussée de Lauraguais 1553-1789* (Toulouse, 1932); L. Dutil, *L'état économique du Languedoc à la fin de l'Ancien Régime* (Paris, 1911).

[4] The administrative correspondence and the private papers are cited throughout the study. Cf. Chapters II, III, IV and the Bibliography. The work of Picot de Lapeyrouse, *The Agriculture of a District in the South of France* (London, 1819), contains every detail of estate activity. Moreover, Picot writes that the agricultural methods of his estate are practiced throughout the region of Toulouse.

[5] A. D., C-120 Subdelegate to Intendant, September 15, 1786; A. D., E-1777 " *Mémoire sur les rendements, 1772* "; Picot, *op. cit.*, p. 46.

Setiers

5.0	yield per arpent of wheat	
— 1.0	deduction of seed for the following year	
4.0		
— 0.5	deduction of harvest costs $\frac{1}{10}$ of the yield	
3.5	before portions to sharecroppers, or wages to *maîtres-valets*.	

The average price for wheat on the Toulouse market for the decade of 1750-1760 was 10 livres per setier. Thus, wheatland was worth (10 x 3.5) or 35 livres revenue per arpent before deductions for wages and portions for the sharecroppers. Where sharecropping was practiced, equal division of the harvest between sharecropper and proprietor was the old custom, although, as the century progressed, the noble landlord received more than half. Therefore, a revenue of ($^{35}\!/_2$) or 18 livres per arpent of wheatland worked by sharecropping was a *minimum* for the proprietor.

Maize can be calculated in the same manner, noting, however, that it yielded ten to one on the seed.[6] Hence,

10	yield per arpent of maize.
— 1	deduction of seed for the following year
9	
— 1	harvest costs of $\frac{1}{10}$th the harvest
8	before portions to sharecroppers or wages to *maîtres-valets*.

Maize sold at 5 livres per setier for the decade 1750-1760 and was almost always divided equally with either the sharecropper or the *maître-valet*. Thus, $\left(\dfrac{5 \times 8}{2}\right)$ means a revenue from land in maize of 20 livres per arpent.

Woodland produced about 20 *pagelles* (25 cubic meters) per arpent when cut every twelve years, common practice in the diocese. In 1750 wood sold at about 4 livres per *pagelle*. Thus, an arpent of wood was worth $\dfrac{4 \times 20}{12}$ or 6 livres, 14 sous annually.

Transport and cutting costs reduced this to about 6 livres per arpent. The tax officials made the same estimate for good woodland.[7]

[6] For maize yields in the *Midi*, see D. Faucher, *Géographie agraire, types de culture* (Paris, 1949), p. 64 f.

[7] A. D. C-105. This is an estimate of the Subdelegate for the diocese. The

Meadow produced about 30 *quintaux* (3307.5 lbs.) of hay per arpent in a common year and most of the harvest was sold. Assuming that 20 *quintaux* were sold per arpent at the current price in 1750 of 1 livre per *quintal*, meadow would yield 20 livres per arpent. Again, the tax officials also appraised the return on good meadowland at 20 livres per arpent.[8]

Vines produced about four *barriques* (casks of about 150 litres each) per arpent and the cask sold at 12 livres in 1750. Thus the gross revenue was 4 x 12 or 48 livres per arpent. If the vines were worked by sharecroppers, the return for the land-lord would be a minimum of one-half or 24 livres. If they were worked by wage-labor (usually 30 days labor per arpent at 10 sous maximum per day), costs would be 15 livres, leaving a net revenue of 33 livres per arpent.[9]

In summary, then, each noble declaration may be revised for domain incomes on the basis of the following revenues per arpent:

Wheat:	36#	(wage-labor)	Maize:	20#
	18#	(sharecropping)		
			Wood:	6#
Vines:	33#	(wage-labor)		
	24#	(sharecropping)	Meadow:	20#

The revenues from the mills, forges, and ovens and from the seigniorial dues are usually supported by titles and contracts and can be accepted as declared. All of the revenues in kind are calculated at 10 livres per setier of wheat and 5 livres per setier of maize.

Since the *vingtième* was a tax on net income, deductions were permissible. However, despite the opportunity to exaggerate costs, deductions were not excessive. Annual wages for *maîtres-valets* were fixed by custom at 8 to 10 setiers of grain (half wheat and half maize), plus 12 livres coin, or a maximum value of 87 livres in 1750. The term, "wage" does not include the deductions made in kind at the moment of the harvest and already calculated in the revenues per arpent. It is curious that

Marquis de Bertier sold wood at 6 livres the *pagelle* in 1755. A.D. 6-J, 40. Montaugé, *op. cit.*, p. 24 claims that 4 livres was the price in 1754. Cf. Chapter IV on sales of wood.

  [8] A.D. C-109. This is an estimate of the Subdelegate for the diocese. Cf. Chapter III on sales of hay.

  [9] Picot, *op. cit.*, p. 65. Cf. Chapter III, Part IV.

ordinary estate repairs are not entered as a deduction, nor is any provision made for the depreciation of capital. No doubt the annual expenditure for building repair, tools, and livestock was very small and most of it borne by the sharecroppers.[10] Very little drainage was necessary in the Lauragais. Similarly, steward's salaries are seldom listed on the noble tax declarations, suggesting that stewards (*régisseurs*) were little more than household servants or clerks receiving maintenance. When they are listed, salaries range between 200 and 300 livres annually. The direct taxes, including the *vingtième, taille,* and *capitation,* are accepted as reported by the noble proprietor, although the system of royal indemnities often reduced taxes as much as 50% in a bad crop year.[11]

In all of the calculations above, an effort has been made to weigh the margin of error in the direction of an underestimation of revenues, while accepting the expenditures as declared by the noble proprietor. Table A indicates how this method of revision has been employed to rework the tax declarations of a group of noble families in the diocese of Toulouse. Table B is a summary of estate revenues produced by this method.

I have selected twenty noble families from those tax declarations for which there is sufficient data to make detailed calculations. The twenty selected were among the most prominent families in the diocese. Many of them are used as examples throughout the study, and their genealogies appear in Villain. This is a biased sample; the area of the average estate in this group is 403 arpents (560.2 acres), or about twice the average for the 226 estates (192.4 arpents).[12] The twenty estates examined for revenues may not be " typical " in a strict statistical sense, but they are illustrative of the incomes of a modest size country estate in the Lauragais. Moreover, I have selected only those estates which were administered directly (i. e., by *maîtres-valets* or sharecroppers), another characteristic of the 226 estates. Finally, I am more concerned here with the composition or distribution of sources of income than with the exact annual

---

[10] Cf. Chapter IV on livestock and brick making.

[11] Cf. Chapter I on the system of indemnities (*cas fortuit*).

[12] Cf. pp. 36, 38, 40 n. Note that the average holding for the older nobility of robe and sword (95 families) was 305.2 arpents or 424.2 acres, or about three-quarters of the average estate in this selected group.

TABLE A

A Sample Calculation of Landed Income:
The Estate of Marquis d'Escouloubre in 1750

Farms by Community		Wheat	Maize	Fallow	Total of Grain	Wood	Meadow	Vines	Wasteland
1. Vieillevigne 3 farms worked by maîtres-valets	arp.	70	24	66	160	14	15	5	0
		x 35	x 20	x 0	—	x 6	x 20	x 33	—
Revenues:		2450#	480#	0#	2930#	84#	300#	165#	0
2. Saint-Rome 1 farm worked by maître-valet	arp.	17	10	19	46	0	7	0	5
		x 35	x 20	0	—	6	20	33	—
Revenues:		595#	200#	0	795#	0	140#	0	0
3. Gardouch 2 farms worked by sharecroppers	arp.	40	18	42	100	25	6	0	30
		x 18	x 20	0	—	6	20	24	0
Revenues:		720#	350#	0	1080#	150#	120#	0	0
4. Montesquieu 1 farm worked by sharecroppers	arp.	20	7	17	44	13	0	5	60
		x 18	x 20	0	—	6	20	24	0
Revenues:		360#	140#	0	500#	78#	0	120#	0
Total Areas: (535 arpents)		147	59	144	350	52	28	10	95
Total Revenues: (6,462#)		4,125#	1,180#	0	5,305#	312#	560#	285#	0

revenues. There is no reason to believe that the smaller estate, managed in the same manner, would produce appreciably different results. The twenty estates I have analyzed differ little one from another in the composition of their income, as indicated in the second table.

The above estimates of estate revenues have a false appearance of precision. They are no more than approximations based on a common year's yield of grain and other farm produce. Verification is difficult because of the incompleteness of private estate accounts. However, in two cases where grain receipts do exist, the approximations above are not appreciably different. The Bertier de Pinsaguel papers, for example, contain the grain receipts for the farms at Pinsaguel in 1751. The Marquis re-

TABLE A (2)

1. Total income from seven farms		6,462#
2. Income from *cens* and seigniorial dues (30 setiers of wheat)		300#
3. Income from one mill and one forge (22 setiers of wheat)		220#
Gross Revenue:		6,982#
Expenses: 1. Wages of 5 maîtres-valets	360#	
2. Taxes: Taille	240# ⎤	
Capitation	136# ⎬ 585#	
Vingtième	209# ⎦	
		− 945#
Net Revenue:		6,037#

ceived 131 setiers of wheat of which 100 were sold. By employing the method described above, one arrives at 140 setiers of which 70 were sold, under the assumption that the sharecropper received the other 70 setiers. Bertier's private account indicates that he received 1640 livres for his grain in that year; by my own interpolation, he received 1520 livres. In 1755 the grain receipts of the Marquis d'Escouloubre's seven farms totalled 605 setiers of grain or a value of 6050 livres. My own calculations give an income of 5305 livres from the same grain lands. In both cases the actual receipts were higher than my own estimates. The margin of error in the case of the Marquis de Bertier is small. In the Escouloubre case, the 20% margin

TABLE B

COMPOSITION OF REVENUES OF TWENTY NOBLE ESTATES

Family	Income from Grain	Income from Wood, Vines, Meadow	Cens	Rents from Mills, Ovens, Forges	Gross Revenue	Wages	Taxes	Net Revenue
1. Escouloubre (535 arpents)	5,305#	1,157#	300#	220#	6,982#	360#	585#	6,037#
% of Gross Revenue	76%	17%	4%	3%		5%	8%	
2. Espie-Gaure (296 arpents)	1,840#	996#	–	210#	3,046#		103#	2,938#
% of Gross Revenue	60%	33%		7%			3%	
3. Rabaudy (258 arpents)	3,824#	1,056#	263#	50#	5,193#	216#	1,068#	3,909#
% of Gross Revenue	73%	20%	6%	1%		4%	20%	
4. Varagne-Gardouch (374 arpents)	2,376#	2,256#	229#	680#	5,541#	–	442#	5,099#
% of Gross Revenue	43%	40%	4%	12%			8%	
5. Avessens (362 arpents)	2,214#	956#	80#	–	3,250#	–	873#	2,377#
% of Gross Revenue	68%	29%	2%				27%	
6. Rolland (483 arpents)	8,575#	1,753#	240#	125#	10,693#	1,008#	1,081#	8,604#
% of Gross Revenue	80%	16%	2%	1%		9%	10%	
7. Cassagneau (369 arpents)	2,590#	1,600#	1,886#	362#	6,438#	400#	624#	5,414#
% of Gross Revenue	40%	25%	29%	6%		6%	9%	
8. Martin (257 arpents)	1,676#	550#	568#	–	2,794#	144#ʼ	32#ʼ	2,618#
% of Gross Revenue	60%	20%	20%			5%	3%	

Family	Income from Grain	Income from Wood, Vines, Meadow	Cens	Rents from Mills, Ovens, Forges	Gross Revenue	Wages	Taxes	Net Revenue
9. Dupuy-Montesquieu (766 arpents)	6,037#	2,374#	300#	210#	8,921#	72#	1,539#	7,310#
% of Gross Revenue	67%	27%	3%	2%		1%	17%	
10. Grammont-Lanta (400 arpents)	2,740#	1,408#	823#	200#	5,171#	–	1,410#	3,761#
% of Gross Revenue	53%	27%	16%	4%			27%	
11. Pavie-Becarie (194 arpents)	2,279#	1,099#	780#	675#	4,833#	450#	729#	3,654#
% of Gross Revenue	47%	23%	16%	14%		9%	15%	
12. Gavarret (493 arpents)	4,291#	1,500#	297#	326#	6,414#	168#	1,105#	5,141#
% of Gross Revenue	67%	23%	5%	5%		2%	17%	
13. Cantalouse (476 arpents)	4,640#	1,236#	238#	150#	6,264#	864#	1,000#	4,400#
% of Gross Revenue	74%	19%	4%	3%		14%	16%	
14. Hautpoul (352 arpents)	3,065#	529#	54#	530#	4,178#	648#	665#	2,865#
% of Gross Revenue	73%	13%	1%	13%		15%	15%	
15. Boutaric (535 arpents)	3,727#	2,634#	159#	416#	6,936#	–	727#	6,209#
% of Gross Revenue	53%	38%	2%	7%			11%	
16. Assézat (462 arpents)	3,930#	1,382#	291#	70#	5,673#	200#	790#	4,683#
% of Gross Revenue	70%	25%	4%	1%		3%	14%	
17. Saint Felix-Mauremont (189 arpents)	1,957#	931#	933#	225#	4,046#	216#	333#.	3,497#
% of Gross Revenue	48%	23%	23%	5%		5%	8%	

Family	Income from Grain	Income from Wood, Vines, Meadow	Cens	Rents from Mills, Ovens, Forges	Gross Revenue	Wages	Taxes	Net Revenue
18. Bertier-Pinsaguel (467 arpents)	3,719#	1,976#	1,282#	1,160#	8,137#	–	1,095#	7,042#
% of Gross Revenue	46%	24%	16%	14%			13%	
19. Ossun (531 arpents)	4,746#	1,697#	240#	200#	6,883#	520#	2,081#	4,282#
% of Gross Revenue	69%	25%	4%	3%		7%	31%	
20. d'Amieu-Montbrun (276 arpents)	2,020#	1,594#	75#	–	3,689#	–	386#	3,303#
% of Gross Revenue	55%	43%	2%				10%	
Average of 20 Estates (403 arpents)	3,577#	1,434#	452#	285#	5,748#	262#	836#	4,650#
Percentage of Gross Revenue	62%	25%	8%	5%		5%	15%	

* Estates 11 and 17 may be considered "typical" in the statistical sense since they come close to the "average estate" of 192.4 arpents (267.4 acres).

of error can be attributed to the higher than average yields on the Marquis's domain in the richest part of the diocese.[13]

The real value of reworking the *vingtième* declarations becomes most apparent when we realize to what extent gentlemen like Bertier and Escouloubre undervalued their income for tax purposes. Bertier declared a net income of 1,060 livres for the domain of Pinsaguel while his private accounts reveal an income in grain alone of 1,640 livres in the same year.[14] Escouloubre declared a net revenue of 1,902 livres for his seven farms while his grain alone produced 6,050 livres in 1755 by his own account.[15]

[13] A. D. 6-J, 35; A. D. E-1712.
[14] A. D. C-1342 (Pinsaguel).
[15] A. D. C-1336 (Gardouch), C-1340 (Montesquieu), C-1345 (Saint-Rome), C-1346 (Vieillevigne).

APPENDIX B

STATE OF THE HARVESTS
(A. D. C-119, 120)

The following table gives the estimates of the Subdelegate of the annual harvests of grain, forage, wine, and silk-worm cocoons from 1764 to 1789:

Years	Wheat (set.) (2.64 bu.)	Maize (set.)	Hay (carts)	Wine (barriques) (150 litres)	Cocoons (quintaux) (107 lbs.)
1764	400,000	—	40,000		300
1765	280,000	118,000	48,000	45,000	350
1766	272,000	—	45,000	—	200
1767	410,000	—	32,000	—	250
1768	170,000	—	40,000	—	300
1769	328,000	—	66,000	—	300
1770	244,000	—	44,000	—	322
1771	203,000	—	33,000	—	250
1772	330,000	67,500	48,000	120,000	250
1773	430,000	68,200	48,000	75,000	250
1774	330,000	68,200	60,000	100,000	250
1775	412,000	122,000	24,000	133,000	187
1776	267,000	97,200	60,000	133,000	230
1777	232,000	75,000	60,000	33,000	171
1778	360,000	—	60,000	—	220
1779	495,000	120,000	36,000	—	400
1780	264,000	—	45,000	—	150
1781	110,000	86,250	7,000	99,750	" ruined by rain "
1782	220,000	—	56,000	—	200
1783	330,000	120,000	45,000	74,813	" no object of trade "
1784	288,000	66,667	11,000	74,813	" no supply "
1785	330,000	25,000	9,000	—	" unknown "
1786	220,000	—	22,000	—	" peu con- siderable "
1787	330,000	60,000	45,000	—	" not usual crop " (frost)
1788	110,000	50,000	22,000	37,399	" unknown "

The Subdelegate observed that in a " common year " (an average for ten consecutive years) the diocese produced 330,000 setiers of wheat, 100,000 setiers of maize, 45,000 cartloads of hay, 75,000 casks of wine, and 250 *quintaux* (27,562.5 lbs.)

of cocoons for the silk industry. Needless to add, these estimates were approximate.

The extreme variation in the harvests caused prices to vary as much as 50% in a few months. The years 1781 and 1788 were disastrous crop years for wheat and maize, and 1785 was a crisis year for cattle forage. Seasonal price variation was a phenomenon separate from the long-run increase in grain prices.

APPENDIX C

SOME PRICES OF FARM PRODUCE AT TOULOUSE

Produce	Unit of Measure	Price in Livres at Toulouse			
		1750–55	1770–75	1780–85	1789
Wheat	setier (2.64 bu.)	10	15	16	20
Maize	setier (2.64 bu.)	5	8	10	13
Wood	pagelle (1.25 cub. meters)	3	4	7	10
Hay	quintal (110.25 lbs.)	1	–	2	–
Wine	*barrique* (180 litres)	12	24	–	36
	(47.6 gals.)				

The prices for wheat and maize are based on Viala, *op. cit.*, pp. 110-118. The prices for wood are taken from Montaugé, *op. cit.*, p. 24 and A. D., C-105. The prices of wine and hay are taken from Barthès "Les Heures perdues" (Lemouzèle

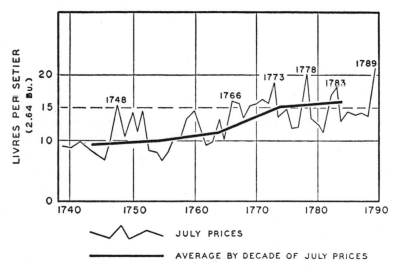

The Price of Wheat at Toulouse, 1739-1789

Average Price Per Decade:		
1739-1748— 9 livres,	4	sous
1749-1758—10	0	
1759-1768—12	4	
1769-1778—15	6	
1779-1789—16	0	

191

edition, 1914) and from the private accounts of Cambon-Riquet (A. D. E-642).

The *setier de Toulouse* is equivalent to .96 hectolitres or 2.64 bushels.

The above table is based on July prices taken from the official registers of the four principal grain markets at Toulouse. These prices are listed in L. Viala, *La question des grains et leur commerce à Toulouse au dix-huitième siècle* (1715-1789), (Toulouse, 1909), pp. 110-18.

APPENDIX D

SAMPLE DOCUMENTS

(1) *A Sharecropping Contract* (*Bail à demy fruits*)
(Register 18105, p. 361. August 1, 1779)

In the year one thousand seven hundred and seventy nine, the first day of August in the afternoon, at Villefranche de Lauragais was present before us, royal notary of the said town, Jaques Maurel, living at Seyres, agent of high and powerful seigneur Marquis d'Hautpoul, administrator of the said land of Seyres, who, by his free will, has leased and hereby leases for work and cultivation at half fruits to Pierre Reynes and Mathieu Reynes, father and son, *laboureurs*, living at the farm of Gérie, consulat of Reneville, both present and accepting jointly (*l'un pour l'autre et l'un d'eux seul pour le tout*) without division or discrimination, unless expressly renounced: the farm called la Grave and the lands in dependence, situated in the consulat of Seyres, diocese of Toulouse, with the exception of one meadow situated in the jurisdiction of Lagarde, which was attached to the said farm, and which the said Maurel expressly reserves as not being part of the present lease. This present lease is established for the time and term of one year, beginning the first of November of this year, during which time the said lessees will act on the said lands as good husbandmen (*bons ménagers et bons pères de famille*). The said lease is also established on the following conditions:

1) The said lessees will furnish all kinds of seed, and the yield will be divided to the *sol* and the *pugnère*, after the said Maurel will have taken twenty setiers of wheat from the harvest, which the said lessees will give to him in advance. The remaining wheat will be divided as it is said. The portion of the said Maurel is to be delivered after cutting and flailing, as well as all the other kinds of grain which will be brought to the château of Seyres without costs for the said Maurel.

2) As the cultivated land is in "three fields" (*trois labours*), the lessees will be held to maintain it in this state, without being authorized to alter the system or to interchange its order, under punishment of being held responsible for all major damages and interests. The land will be cultivated in such a way that one part will be planted in wheat, the second part will be in fallow (*guéret pur*), and the third will be planted with maize, beans, or other vegetables and grains, and if they do not want to plant it entirely, they will notify the said Maurel, so that he can lease the land which they do not want to some other party whom he chooses. In this case, they will not have any right to this portion.

193

3) As the lessees are not permitted to plant anything on the fallow, in case they do, they will not receive any portion of this harvest, unless the said Maurel gives them his permission.

4) All kinds of livestock and sheep will be held in common, and all profits and losses will be shared equally.

5) They will have charge of the hay and straw, and in case there is a shortage of these forages, they will have to buy half of it themselves.

6) They will dig the ditches, cut the brush, and will make drains for the water, in short, do everything necessary on the said lands; they will have charge of the vines which they will work and prune at the proper time and season, and their fruits will be shared as well as the vine-branches; they will furnish the carts, harnesses, plows, iron-tools and other instruments necessary for cultivation, without the said Maurel being held to furnish anything; yet, if there is some tree on the said land which is convenient for repairing work tools, it will be furnished by the said Maurel.

7) They will pay as rent: Thirty six chickens on St. John the Baptist's Day, thirty six capons on All Saint's Day, thirty six chickens on Christmas; the said fowl and six hundred eggs during the course of the year.

8) They alone will buy the young pigs, which will be later divided and of which the said Maurel will have the choice; they will raise geese and ducks and turkeys which will also be divided by the choice of the said Maurel, and in case that he does not wish any of this fowl, they will be held to give six fat geese to the said Maurel, to be delivered on the first of December, and in this case only and not otherwise the said Maurel will pay them the sum of six livres for the said six geese, fat or not.

9) The said lessees will be held to make the plows which are ordered by the said Maurel, and they will have to pay the order to the black-smith themselves. Comprised in the lease is a vineyard which is north of the farm and of a surface of about two arpents.

The parties declare that the said fruits do not exceed the value of two hundred and fifty livres, and in order to observe the above stipulations, the parties pledge their possessions to Justice: The said Maurel those of the said Seigneur Marquis d'Hautpoul and the said Reynes theirs, present and future.

Made and sealed in our study in the presence of the Sirs Jean Paul Pujol and Louis Antoine Majoret, practitioners living in this town, signing below as witnesses. The parties declare not to know how to sign.

Signed: Pujol fils, Majoret, Pujol.

Notice that a natural meadow is reserved for Hautpoul's agent, that he takes 20 setiers of wheat before any division takes place, and that his share is transported to the château without cost. Notice also that the three field system is absolutely obligatory (wheat, maize, fallow), and that the sharecroppers must pay half the cost of any extra forage that is needed. All drainage and upkeep must be done by the sharecroppers; they must furnish all the tools and pay the blacksmith for any repairs. They must pay a substantial rent in fowl and pigs. An estimate of the value of the harvest is made to prevent " errors " in the division of the fruits. Finally, notice that the sharecroppers cannot write. Since the rent in fowl is 36 pairs, the farm is about 75 arpents. If the land was worked in three equal fields or " labors," the seigneur received three-fourths of the net harvest of wheat.

In the Lauragais a farm of 75 arpents had about 20% of its surface in meadow and wood. Hence, about 60 arpents were cultivable. If the " three labors " were equal (20 arpents wheat, 20 arpents fallow, 20 arpents maize), customary practice at Seyres in 1750, the yield of wheat at 5 setiers per arpent would be 100 setiers. Following Article I of the contract above, one can calculate as follows:

```
   100  setiers yield of wheat
 —  20  setiers " taken in advance " by the seigneur
    80
 —  10  setiers cost of cutting and flailing
    70  setiers
 —  35  setiers " half-fruits " to the seigneur
    35
 —  20  setiers seed furnished by the lessees
    15  setiers net for the lessees
```

Hence, the Marquis d'Hautpoul would receive a total of 55 setiers of wheat and the lessees 15 setiers. A family of five would require about 20 setiers of wheat per year for minimum subsistence.

(2) *A Printed Form of a Royal Stay (Sauf-Conduit)*

New Stay of ...., beginning ....,
" In the Name of the King."

His Majesty, wishing M. .... to continue his
affairs by this means, grants him a new stay (*sauf-conduit*) for his
person during .... from this day on, during
which time His Majesty prohibits all his creditors to exercise any
constraint over him.

Dated and signed

" Louis."

The Royal Stays were issued by the Intendant on recom-
mendation of the Subdelegate. They had a time-limit of six
months to two years and could be renewed.

(3) *A Contract of Marriage*
(A. D., Contrats de mariage séparés, 11803, March 24, 1722)

This is not a sample document but a summary of the articles of a
marriage contract.

Prospective Husband: M. François-Denis de Pavie de Becarie, Marquis
de *Fourquevaux* (military nobility)

Prospective Wife: Dlle Henriette de *Catellan* (daughter of a councilor
of Parlement)

Attending:

For Groom:

1. Dame Marie de Prohenques de Fourquevaux, widow, mother
   of the prospective husband.
2. M. de Pavie de Fourquevaux, brother of the prospective
   husband.

For Bride:

1. Dame Marie de Boisset de Catellan, widow, mother of the
   prospective wife.
2. M. Jean-Baptiste de Catellan, Former Canon of the Church
   of Toulouse, great uncle.
3. Dlles. Jeanne et Françoise de Catellan, aunts.
4. M. Jean-Louis de Catellan, Councilor of the King at the
   Parlement of Toulouse, brother.
5. M. Aimable de Catellan, Canon of the Church of Toulouse,
   brother.

Articles of Marriage:

1. The marriage will be celebrated according to the rites and usages of the Roman Catholic and Apostolic Church.

2. Dame de Catellan, mother, promises to "gild" (*dorer*) the bride, that is, provide her trousseau.

3. For the charges of the marriage, Dame de Catellan constitutes *8000* livres for the amount of the paternal portion regulated between the future wife and her brother, Seigneur de Catellan. The future wife renounces all claims to a paternal portion. Seigneur de Catellan pays 2000 livres at present to the prospective husband. The remaining 6000 livres will be paid by the brother of the bride as follows:

> 4000 livres in three months
> 2000 livres in two years at 4% (*denier vingt-cinq*) (to be paid in coin, not in any kind of paper)

4. Dame de Catellan, mother, constitutes 4000 livres, payable by the Seigneur de Catellan, brother, on the same conditions as above (in two years at 4%).

The future wife renounces all claims to a maternal portion, unless the number of Catellan children diminishes before the death of her mother, Dame de Catellan.

5. M. Jean-Baptiste de Catellan, canon, great uncle of the bride, makes a donation to his grand niece of *2500* livres to be paid as follows:

> 1500 livres already "ceded to the Seigneur de Fourquevaux on M. le Comte de Miran."
> 1000 livres paid after his death without interest.

6. Dlles. de Catellan, aunts of the bride, constitute 8000 livres payable by the Seigneur de Catellan after the death of the aunts.

If the prospective wife dies without children, this donation will be returned to the aunts or to other heirs whom they may designate.

7. M. Aimable de Catellan, canon, brother of the bride, makes a donation of *1000* livres payable after his death and under the above conditions of "right of return."

8. All of these sums *total 23,500 livres*, of which only 12,000 are "dotal." Following the Customs of Toulouse, if the prospective wife dies first, her husband will gain the 12,000 livres. In the contrary case, the prospective wife will gain the 12,000 livres and the "increase" (*augment*) of 6000 livres.

9. Nevertheless, the prospective husband will enjoy the revenues on the entire sum of 23,500 livres.

10. The prospective husband will recognize on all his property all of the sums he will receive and he does recognize the 2000 livres received at present.

11. If the prospective wife dies childless, the prospective husband

will retain 12,000 livres of the sums received. The rest will be restored to the family Catellan.

12. If the prospective husband dies first, the prospective wife will have an apartment in the château of Fourquevaux and 1000 livres during the year of mourning.

13. M. de Fourquevaux, brother of the prospective husband, cedes, remits, and transports all of his property, rights, and claims in his quality as heir or beneficiary of his father, Marquis de Fourquevaux (who died of wounds received at the Battle of Hochstädt in 1704) to his brother in return for a life annuity of 600 livres per year. He can claim no change in this annuity for whatever reason. He also reserves the use of a furnished room in the château of Fourquevaux.

14. "Finally, the prospective married couple has given to one of the male children to be born of this marriage half of all their property, present and future, preferring to elect and name him, . . . but if they fail to name him, they have named and elected the eldest son not engaged in Holy Orders."

> Signed at Toulouse, March 24, 1722
> by the Fourquevaux and Catellan
> families before witnesses.

Notice that of the total dowry of 23,500 livres, only 12,000 livres represented the paternal and maternal portions for which Seigneur de Catellan, eldest brother, was responsible. The rest was payable by an array of relatives, generally after their deaths. Of the 12,000, Catellan paid 8000 (4000 in claims on third parties) by August 15, 1772. (Account on cover of marriage contract)

BIBLIOGRAPHY

A. UNPUBLISHED SOURCES

1. The great majority of documents used for this study are to be found in the Departmental Archives at Toulouse, France. The principal series consulted were:

Series C—Administrative correspondence, tax rolls, (principally for the *vingtième* and *capitation*), the minutes and accounts of the diocesan and provincial assemblies, and the reports of the subdelegate and the communities of the civil diocese of Toulouse on all phases of agriculture.

Series E—Family papers. These include the *livres de raison*, miscellaneous accounts, notes, and correspondence of the noble families, Escouloubre, Varagne-Belesta, Riquet de Caraman, Ledesme-Saint Elix, Becarie de Pavie, Cambon-Riquet and the more fragmentary notes and accounts of the families Barneval, de Blagnac, Chalvet-Rochemonteix, Gavarret, Saint Felix-Colombiers, Caumels, and Sentous-Dumont.

Series 2-J—Papers of the Family Campistron de Maniban

Series 4-J—Papers of the Family Riquet de Bonrepos

Series 6-J—Papers of the Family Bertier de Pinsaguel

Fonds de la Terrasse—Papers of the Family Hautpoul

Series B—Parlementary archives. The *arrêts* of Parlement.

Series G—The Church report on the State of Parishes in 1763.

Notarial Archives (same depot)—These are the registers for all kinds of legal contracts including testaments, contracts of marriage, " gifts in life," contracts of *métayage*, and leases of all types. Unfortunately, this enormous fund of information is still uncatalogued. Contracts involving seigniorial rights were, in many cases, torn from the registers during the Revolution.

II. The Municipal Archives at Toulouse also contain important information on noble families during the Revolution. Most important for this study were the Forced Loans of 1793, (G^2 42-44), and the " *Biens des Emigrés* " (I^2 8).

B. PUBLISHED SOURCES

I. *Memoires and Chronicles:*

E. Lemouzèle, *Toulouse au XVIIIᵉ siècle d'après les " Heures perdues " de Pierre Barthès* (Toulouse, 1914). This is the best one volume edition of the chronicle of Barthès found in manuscript at the *Bibliothèque Municipale.*

F. Pasquier, *Notes ou reflexions d'un bourgeois de Toulouse au début la Révolution d'après des lettres intimes*, (Toulouse, 1917).

Picot, Baron de Lapeyrouse, *The Agriculture of a District in the South of France*, (London, 1819). This work, awarded a prize by the Society of Agriculture at Paris, presents a complete picture of the management of a rural estate in the diocese of Toulouse.

Comte de Villèle, *Mémoires et correspondance*, (Paris, 1888), 5 vol. The first

199

volume concerns Villèle's life at Toulouse before he became minister of Louis XVIII.

Arthur Young, *Voyages en France, 1787, 1788, 1789*, (Paris, 1931), 3 vols.

II. *Contemporary Treatises:*

F. de Boutaric, *Traité des droits seigneuriaux et des matières féodales*, (Toulouse, 1751).

J. P. Brillon, *Dictionnaire des arrêts ou jurisprudence universelle des Parlements de France*, (Paris, 1727), 6 vols.

A. d'Espeisses, *Oeuvres*, (Lyons, 1750), 3 vols.

F. V. de Forbonnais, *Recherches et considérations sur les finances de France depuis 1595 jusqu'à l'année 1721*, (Paris, 1758), 2 vols.

V. Riqueti, Marquis de Mirabeau, *L'ami des hommes ou traité de la population*, (Paris, 1756).

J. Necker, *A Treatise on the Administration of the Finances of France*, (London, 1785).

E. de la Pois de Freminville, *La pratique universelle pour la renovation des terriers et des droits seigneuriaux*, (Paris, 1759), 5 vols.

A. R. Turgot, *Oeuvres*, (E. Daire ed., Paris, 1844).

III. *Genealogies and Catalogues of Noble Families:*

L. de la Roque, *Armorial de la noblesse de Languedoc, Généralité de Montpellier*, (Montpellier, 1860). 2 vols.

———, *Catalogue des gentilshommes de Languedoc (généralité de Toulouse) qui ont pris part ou envoyé leur procuration aux assemblées de la noblesse pour l'élection des députés aux Etats Généraux de 1789, publié d'après les procès-verbaux officiels*, (Paris, 1862).

J. Villain, *La France moderne généalogique (Haute-Garonne et Ariège)*, (Montpellier, 1911). 4 vols.

IV. *Histories of Law:*

J. Brissaud, *A History of French Private Law*, (Boston, 1912).

———, "L'histoire du droit du Midi de la France," *Mémoire de l'Académie des sciences, inscriptions et belles lettres de Toulouse*, Xe série, t III, p. 16.

A. Esmein, *Cours élémentaire de l'histoire du droit français*, (Paris, 1925).

Isambert *et al.*, *Recueil général des anciennes lois françaises depuis l'an 420 jusqu'à la Révolution de 1789*, (Paris, 1822-1828).

E. Jurriand, *Histoire de la novelle 118 dans les pays de droit écrit*, (Paris, 1889).

C. Lefebvre, *Cours de doctorat sur l'histoire du droit français, L'ancien droit des successions*, (Paris, 1912-1918). 2 vols.

———, *Les fortunes anciennes au point de vue juridique*, (Paris, 1912).

E. Roquin, *Traité de droit civil comparé*, (Paris, 1904-1912), Vols. III-VII (Les successions).

V. *Local Histories and Monographs:*

Abbé H. Aragon, *La seigneurie de St.-Léon et Caussidières (1030-1793)*, (Toulouse, 1895).

A. Cazals, *Histoire de la ville et communauté de Montesquieu-sur-Canal*, (Toulouse, 1883).

J. Contrasty, *Histoire de St. Jory, ancienne seigneurie féodale erigée en baronnie par Henri IV*, (Toulouse, 1922).
J. Coppolani, *Toulouse, étude de géographie urbaine*, (Toulouse, 1954).
F. Delauruelle, "La maison élémentaire de la région toulousaine," *Revue géographique des Pyrénées et du Sud-Ouest*, III, (1933), pp. 373-383.
Dom C. Devic et Dom J. Vaissete, *Histoire générale du Languedoc*, (Toulouse, 1872-1893). Volumes XIII, XIV.
L. Dutil, *La Haute-Garonne et sa région*, (Toulouse, 1928). 2 vols.
A. Escudier, *Monographie de Labastide-St. Sernin*, (Toulouse, 1936).
———, *Monographie de Castelnau-Estretefonds*, (Toulouse, 1936).
Abbé G. Morère, *Histoire de St. Félix-Caraman*, (Toulouse, 1899).
G. Ousset, *Clermont-sur-Ariège*, (Toulouse, 1934).
H. Ramet, *Histoire de Toulouse*, (Toulouse, 1939).
P. Wolff, *Histoire de Toulouse*, (Toulouse, 1958).

VI. *Histoires of Institutions:*

F. Astre, *De l'administration publique en Languedoc avant 1789*, (Toulouse, 1874).
A. Chereul, *Dictionnaire des institutions de France*, (Paris, 1874), 2 vols.
M. Dubédat, *Histoire du Parlement de Toulouse*, (Paris, 1885). 2 vols.
J. Godechot, *Les institutions de la France sous la Révolution et l'Empire*, (Paris, 1951).
M. Lapierre, *Le Parlement de Toulouse, son ressort, ses attributions et ses Archives*, (Toulouse, 1869).
E. Lemouzèle, *Essai sur l'administration de la ville de Toulouse à la fin de l'Ancien Régime*, (Paris, 1910).
T. Punctous, *Les états particuliers du diocèse de Toulouse au XVIIIᵉ siècle*, (Toulouse, 1909).
H. Ramet, *Le Capitole et le Parlement de Toulouse*, (Toulouse, 1926).

VII. *Economic and Social Studies of the Region:*

L. Anglade, "Un exemple de réaction nobiliaire dans le Comminges à la veille de la Révolution: Les procès entre la communauté de Villeneuve-de-Rivière et le Seigneur Cetrème," *Annales du Midi*, (1953), pp. 171-180.
E. Appolis, "La question de la vaine pâture en Languedoc au XVIIIᵉ siècle," *Annales historiques de la Révolution francaise*, (1938), pp. 97-132.
P. Boissonade, "La production et le commerce des céréales, des vins et des eaux-de-vie en Languedoc dans la seconde moitié du XVIIIᵉ siècle," *Annales du Midi*, (1905), pp. 329-360.
Vicomte de Bonald, "Nobles et marchands," *Revue historique de Toulouse*, X, (1923), pp. 81-96; XI, (1924), pp. 293-301.
M. Bordes, *D'Etigny et l'administration de l'intendance d'Auch (1751-1767)*, (Paris, 1956), 2 vols.
———, *La fortune d'un bougeois d'Auch au XVIIIᵉ siècle*, (Auch, 1948).
H. Bourderon, "La lutte contre la vie chère dans la généralité de Languedoc au XVIIIᵉ siècle," *Annales du Midi*, (1954), pp. 155-170.
R. Boutruche, *La crise d'une société, seigneurs et paysans du Bordelais pendant la guerre de cent ans*, (Paris, 1947).
P. de Castéras, *La société toulousaine à la fin du XVIIIᵉ siècle*, (Toulouse, 1891).
I. Dutil, *L'etat économique du Languedoc à la fin de l'Ancien Régime, (1750-1789)*, (Paris, 1911).

202 THE NOBILITY OF TOULOUSE IN THE 18TH CENTURY

D. Faucher, "Le maïs en France," *Annales de géographie*, XL, (1931), pp. 113-121.

———, "Polyculture ancienne et assolement biennal dans la France méridionale," *Revue géographique des Pyrénées et du Sud-Ouest*, (1934), pp. 241-255.

———, *Les villes de la région de Toulouse*, (Toulouse, 1942).

D. Faucher, J. Godechot, J. Fourcassié, E. Lambert, *Visages du Languedoc*, (Paris, 1949).

P. Féral, "L'introduction de l'assolement triennal en Gascogne," *Annales du Midi*, (July, 1950), pp. 249-258.

A. Feugère, "Le Capitoul David et les jeux défendus," *Annales du Midi*, (1932), pp. 296-331.

J. R. de Fortanier, *Les droits seigneuriaux dans la sénéchaussée de Lauragais, (1553-1789)*, (Toulouse, 1932).

J. Fourcassié, *Toulouse, trente ans de vie française*, (Paris, 1953).

———, *Villèle*, (Paris, 1954).

G. Jorré, "Le commerce des grains et la minoterie à Toulouse," *Revue géographique des Pyrénées et du Sud-Ouest*, IV, (1933), pp. 30-72.

J. Lebrau, *Ceux du Languedoc*, (Paris, 1946).

H. Martin, "Les biens du clergé et des émigrés déportés et condamnés, confisqués et vendus sous la Révolution, d'après les Archives de la Haute-Garonne," *Revue des Pyrénées*, XXVI, (1914).

———, *Documents relatifs à la vente des biens nationaux, district de Toulouse*, (Toulouse, 1916-1924).

———, "Le papier monnaie sous la Révolution française à Toulouse," *Bulletin de l'Académie de Législation*, III, (1919); IV, (1920).

P. Mesple, *Vieux hôtels de Toulouse*, (Toulouse, 1948).

Théron de Montaugé, *L'agriculture et les classes rurales dans le pays toulousain depuis le milieu du XVIIIᵉ siècle*, (Paris, 1869).

M. Pariset, *Economie rurale, moeurs et usages du Lauragais*, (Paris, 1862).

A. Praviel, *Monsieur du Barri et sa famille*, (Paris, 1932).

G. Richert, "Biens communaux et droits d'usage en Haute-Garonne pendant la Réaction thermidorienne et sous le Directoire," *Annales historiques de la Révolution française*, (1951), pp. 274-288.

Mlle. F. Rocaries, "Un cas de réaction seigneuriale: La communauté et les seigneurs de Montesquieu-Volvestre," (diplôme présenté à la Faculté des Lettres de Toulouse, 1954).

G. Saumade, "Les biens du seigneur à Fabrègues (Languedoc)," *Révolution française*, (1908), pp. 514-529.

J. Sentou, "Faillites et commerce à Toulouse en 1789," *Annales historiques de la Révolution française*, (1953), pp. 1-40.

———, "Impôts et citoyens actifs à Toulouse au début de la Révolution," *Annales du Midi*, (1948), pp. 159-179.

Mme. M. Thoumas-Schapira, "La bourgeoisie toulousaine à la fin du XVIIᵉ siècle," *Annales du Midi*, (1955), pp. 313-329.

L. Viala, *La question des grains et leur commerce à Toulouse au XVIIIᵉ siècle (1715-1789)*, (Toulouse, 1909).

P. Viguier, *Du colonage partiaire dans le Lauragais*, (Paris, 1911).

P. Wolff, *Commerce et marchands de Toulouse, 1350-1450*, (Paris, 1954).

———, "Une famille du XIIIᵉ au XVIᵉ siècle: Les Ysalguier de Toulouse," *Mélanges d'histoire sociale*, (1942), pp. 35-58.

VIII. *General Works on the Social and Economic History of the Ancien Regime:*

Vicomte d'Avenel, *Histoire économique de la proprieté, des salaires, des denrées, et de tous les prix en general 1200 à 1800,* (Paris, 1894). 6 vols.
A. Babeau, *Le village sous l'Ancien Regime,* (Paris, 1879).
E. G. Barber, *The Bourgeoisie in Eighteenth Century France,* (Princeton, 1955).
J. R. Bloch, *L'anoblissement au temps de Francois Ier,* (Paris, 1934).
M. Bloch, *Les caractères originaux de l'histoire rurale française,* (Paris, 1952 et 1956). 2 vols.
———, " La lutte pour l'individualisme agraire dans la France du XVIIIe siècle," *Annales d'histoire économique et sociale,* II, (1930), pp. 329-384; 511-554.
———, " Sur le passé de la noblesse française, quelques jalons de recherche," *Annales d'histoire économique et sociale,* VIII, (1936), pp. 366-378.
A. Bourde, *The Influence of England on the French Agronomes, 1750-1789,* (Cambridge, 1953).
Vicomte Calonne, *La vie agricole dans le Nord,* (Paris, 1920).
H. Carré, *La noblesse de France et l'opinion publique au XVIIIe siècle,* (Paris, 1920).
A. Cobban, " The Parlements of France in the Eighteenth Century, *History,* (Feb.-June, 1950), pp. 64 f.
L. Ducros, *French Society in the Eighteenth Century,* (London, 1926).
J. Egret, " L'aristocratie parlementaire française à la fin de l'Ancien Régime," *Revue historique,* CCIII, (juillet-Sept., 1952), pp. 1-15.
D. Faucher, *Géographie agraire, types de culture,* (Paris, 1949).
———, *Le paysan et la machine,* (Paris, 1954).
O. Festy, *L'Agriculture pendant la Révolution française: Les conditions de production et de récolte des céréales,* (Paris, 1947).
F. Ford, *Robe and Sword: Thè Regrouping of the French Aristocracy after Louis XIV,* (Cambridge, Mass., 1953).
L. Funck-Brentano, *The Ancien Regime,* (New York, 1930).
P. Gaxotte, *Le siècle de Louis XV,* (Paris, 1933).
H. Hauser, " French Economic History, 1500-1750," *Economic History Review,* IV, (1933).
———, *Recherches et documents sur l'histoire des prix en France de 1500 à 1800,* (Paris, 1936).
———, " Reflexions sur l'histoire des banques a l'époque moderne de la fin du XVIe à la fin du XVIIIe siècle," *Annales d'histoire économique et sociale,* I, (1929), pp. 355-371.
H. Heaton, *Histoire économique de l'Europe,* (Paris, 1952), II.
C. E. Labrousse. *Esquisse du mouvement des prix et des revenus en France au XVIIIe siècle,* (Paris, 1932).
———, *La crise de l'économie française à la fin de L'Ancien Régime et au début de la Révolution,* (Paris, 1944).
———, *Origines et aspects économiques et sociaux de la Révolution française, 1774-1791.* (" Les cours de Sorbonne," 1946).
D. S. Landes, " The Statistical Study of French Crises," *The Journal of Economic History,* X (1950), pp. 195-211.
E. Lavisse edition, *Histoire de France depuis les origines jusqu'à la Revolution,* (Paris, 1900-1911), VIII, Part 2; IX.
G. Lefèbvre, " Le mouvement des prix et les origines de la Révolution française," *Annales historiques de la Révolution française,* XIV, (1937).
———, *Les paysans du Nord pendant la Révolution française,* (Lille, 1924).

————, "La place de la Révolution dans l'histoire agraire de la France," *Annales d'histoire économique et sociale*, IV, (1929).

————, "Les recherches relatives à la repartition de la propriété et de l'exploitation foncière à la fin de l'Ancien Régime," *Revue d'histoire moderne*, III, (1928).

————, *Questions agraires au temps de la Terreur*, (Paris, 1954).

J. Letaconnoux, "Les subsistances et le commerce des grains en Bretagne," *Annales de Bretagne*, XX, (1904-1905).

————, "Les transports en France au XVIIIᵉ siècle," *Revue d'histoire moderne et contemporaine*, IX (1908-1909).

P. Leulliot, "Des parlements normands à la noblesse de Belgique et d'Europe," *Annales: Economies, Sociétés, Civilisations*, (1954), pp. 529-535.

H. Levy-Bruhl, "La noblesse de France et le commerce à la fin de l'Ancien Régime," *Revue d'histoire moderne*, VIII, (1933).

J. Loutchisky, *L'état des classes agricoles en France à la veille de la Révolution*, (Paris, 1911).

————, *La propriété paysanne en France à la veille de la Révolution*, (Paris, 1943).

M. Marion, "Etat des classes rurales au XVIIIᵉ siècle dans la généralité de Bordeaux," *Revue des études historiques*, (1902).

————, "Les rôles de vingtième et les statistiques de la propriété territoriale sous l'Ancien Régime," *Revue d'histoire moderne et contemporaine*, XIV, (1914).

————, *Les impôts directs sous l'Ancien Régime*, (Paris, 1914).

M. Neufbourg, "Projet d'une enquête sur la noblesse française," *Annales d'histoire économique et sociale*, VIII, (1936), pp. 243-256.

M. Reinhard, *Histoire de la population mondiale de 1700 à 1948*, (Paris, 1949).

A. Renaudet, *Etudes sur l'histoire intérieure de la France de 1715 à 1789: La finance*, ("Les cours de Sorbonne," 1946).

R. de Roover, *L'évolution de la lettre de change, XIVᵉ-XVIIIᵉ siècles*, (Paris, 1953).

G. Roupnel, *La ville et la campagne au XVIIᵉ siècle*, (Paris, 1922).

P. de Rousiers, *Une famille de hoberaux pendant six siècles*, (Paris, 1933).

P. Sagnac, *La formation de la société française moderne*, (Paris, 1945), II.

H. Sée, *Economic and Social Conditions in France during The Eighteenth Century*, (New York, 1927).

————, *Les classes rurales en Bretagne du XVIᵉ siècle à la Révolution*, (Paris, 1906).

————, *Histoire économique de la France*, (Paris, 1951). 2 vols.

A. Soboul, "The French Rural Community in the 18th and 19th Centuries," *Past and Present*, X, (Nov., 1956), pp. 78-95.

H. Taine, *The Ancient Regime*, (New York, 1931).

A. de Tocqueville, *The Old Regime and The Revolution*, (New York, 1846).

A. P. Usher, *History of the Grain Trade in France, 1400-1710*, (Cambridge, Mass., 1933).

P. de Vaissière, *Gentilshommes-campagnards de l'ancienne France du XVIᵉ au XVIIIᵉ siècle*, (Paris, 1904).

G. Weulersee, *La physiocratie sous les ministères de Turgot et de Necker, 1774-1781*, (Paris, 1950).

D. Zolla, "Les variations du revenu et du prix des terres en France au XVIIᵉ et du XVIIIᵉ siècles," *Annales de l'Ecole libre des sciences politiques*, VIII, (1893); IX, (1894).

IX. *Catalogues and Encyclopedias:*

Bibliographie toulousaine, (Paris, 1823). 2 vols.
P. Caron, *Manuel pratique pour l'étude de la Révolution française,* (Paris, 1947).
La Grande Encyclopédie, (Paris, 1885-1902). 31 vols.
C. Langlois et H. Stein, *Les archives de l'histoire de France,* (Paris, 1893).
Table de comparaison entre les anciennes mesures et les mesures modernes, District de Toulouse et District de Muret, (Toulouse, 1791).

X. *Maps:*

Cartes de Cassini, (Institut géographique national), No. 38-19 G; 39-20 G.

INDEX

Academies: at Toulouse, 21–22; nobles as members of, 166–167
Acapte, 35
Accounting: on estates, 49–50, 51
Agriculture. *See* Estates, Grain
Annuities: for widows, 122; in payment of portions, 126. *See also* *Rentes*
Araire, 41, 45
Arrears of rents, 50–51
Arrêts. See Rulings of Parlement
Artificial meadows: reasons for scarcity of, 42–43; planting of, 61–62; relation to communal rights, 81
Artisans: dependence on nobility, 23, 164; relative income of, 176
Assézat, Councilor d': on local tolls, 72
Assézat family: history of, 24
Augment: as supplement to dowry, 121–122
Authors: nobles as, 167–168

Banalités, 34. *See also* Forges, Mills, Ovens
Banks: absence of, 108
Barthès, Pierre, chronicler: on bread riots, 48; on Parlement, 109; on usury, 109; on new *Capitouls*, 151
Bastard, Jean, Comte d'Estang: lawsuit of, 125
Bertier, Abbé de: financial plight of, 127
Bertier, Catherine de: dowry of, 133-134
Bertier family: history of, 24–25; genealogy of, 142
Bertier, Françoise de: dowry of, 134
Bertier, Madame de Gramont de: claims on husband's estate, 122
Bertier, Marquis de: account books of, 50; use of *retrait féodal* by, 53; marketing grain, 74; meadow of, 83; sale of wood by, 93 n.; settlement of estate by, 141–149; château repairs of, 171; dowries of daughters of, 133–134

Bertin, Controller-General: on vacant pasture, 79–80
Bertrand, Antoine-Francois de: use of *retrait féodal* by, 53
Bills of exchange, 139, 164
Birth control: practiced by nobility, 130
Blagnac, Baron de: Collecting *cens* arrears, 51; loans to peasants by, 51; sharecrop contract of, 56–57; brick ovens of, 95–96
Blatiers, 73–74
Bordier. See Métayer
Borrowing: for portions, 123, 138–140, 147–149; for conspicuous consumption, 140, 161–164. *See also* Debts, Loans
Bourgeoisie: feebleness of, 22–24, 102, 118, 157–158, 176, 176 n.
Brick: production of, 94–97; price of, 95
Building. *See* Construction
Buvette, 105

Cadets, 127–130
Cadillac, Madame de: claims on husband's estate, 122; on marriage of son, 131–132
Cagliostro. *See salons*
Cahiers: protesting seigniorial justice, 30 n.; protesting new roads, 67–68
Cambon, Emmanuel de, President of Parlement, 166
Canal du Midi, 17, 25; as means of grain transport, 31, 69–70; revenues of, 136, 136 n., 138
Capitation: of nobles, 34, 39; as a source, 102, 172, 172 n.
Capitoulat: defined, 20–21; as way to nobility, 23, 125–126
Capitouls: defined, 20; speculating in grain, 75–76; investiture of, 157; on theatre, 158–159
Carriages: rarity of, 159–160
Cassagneau St. Felix, Marquis de: brick oven of, 96
Castelnau-Estretefonds, Marquis de:

206

126; enforcing seigniorial rights, 53
Heiresses: marriage to, 141
Hobereau: in French literature, 129 n., 170 n.
Horses (farm): absence of, 85

Income: from estate of Marquis d'Escouloubre; from twenty estates, 38–40, 178–188; from offices, 104–106; of Marquise of Mirepoix, 110–112; of Baron de Castelnau, 112–113; of Marquis de Gavarret, 113–114; from public securities, 110–116; from constituted *rentes*, 117–119; of Riquet de Bonrepos, 136, 138; of Marquis de Bertier, 149; average in 1789, 175, 175 n.; relative to other social groups, 176; of Comte Du Barri, 114, 174; method of calculation of, 178–188; composition of, 182–187
Intellectual life, 166–170
Intendant: as friend of the nobility, 28; on free trade in grain, 72; on vacant pasture, 78
Interest rate, 108–110
Investments: in land, 54–55; in livestock and tools, 44-45, 85–86; in new crop courses, 61–63; in clearings, 63–65; in offices, 103–106; in public securities, 115 117, in constituted *rentes*, 117–118; in commerce, 118
Irrigation, 63

Labor (agricultural): mode of living, 32–33, 39–40, 44–45; cheapness of, 48–49, 55–58, 100
Labrousse, C.-E.: price historian, 9; on wheat prices, 48 n.
Landholdings: distribution of among social classes, 35–36; distribution of among nobles, 36; of peasants, 37, 37 n.; exchanges of, 54; increase among nobles, 54–55; as revealed in tax rolls, 178. *See also* Estates
Languedoc: administration of, 17. *See also* Estates of Languedoc
Lapeyrouse, Baron de: origins of, 25–26; replacing sharecroppers, 56 n.; using forage crops, 61; meadow of, 83; livestock of, 85; sheep of, 86–

87; exploitation of wood by, 93; use of brick by, 96–97
Lawyers: aspirations of, 23; dependence on nobility, 27–29; relative income of, 176
Legacy: revocation of, 126; of Bishop of Grenoble, 127; added to portion, 131
Levis, Adelaide, Marquise de Mirepoix: financial position of, 110-112
Libraries: of nobles: 168–170
Livestock: bovine, 83–86; ovine, 86–87
Livres de raison. See Accounting
Loans: to peasants, 51–52; legality of, 106–107; among nobles, 117–118; on entailed property, 123–124; for payments of portions, 123, 136–140, 144–149; in form of constituted *rentes*, 124–125, 138–140, 147–148; to young noblemen, 161–165. *See also* Debts, *Rentes*
Lods et ventes (mutation fee), 35
Luchon (watering spa), 146, 157

MacCarthy, Comte de: townhouse of, 170; library of, 168
Machault, Controller-General: originator of the *vingtième*, 178
Maize: adaptability of, 62–63; revenue from, 180; price of, 191. *See also* Grain
Magistrates: number and prestige, 18–19, 102–104; ennoblement of, 23, 24–25, 26; fusion with sword nobility, 26–27; revenues of, 103–106; conservatism of, 103; debts of, 164–165; discipline of, 165; cultural interests of, 166, 167–168
Maître-valet. See Labor
Marketing. *See* Grain
Maniban, Marquis de: sale of domain, 139; pride of office, 165
Marriage: of cadets, 127–130; of daughters, 127–136; prestige value of, 131–132; to heiresses, 141. *See also* Contracts of marriage, Dowries
Meadow: scarcity of, 81–82; concentration of, 82–83; revenue from, 181; price of hay from, 191
Merchants. *See* Bourgeoisie
Métairie: description of, 32–34; build-